D0224917

Settlement, Ceremony and Industry on Mousehold Heath

Published by Pre-Construct Archaeology Limited

Copyright © Pre-Construct Archaeology Limited 2011
All rights reserved. No part of this publication may be reproduced, stored in a retrieval system
or transmitted, in any form or by any means, electronic, mechanical, photocopying, recording
or otherwise, without prior permission of the copyright owner.
ISBN 978-0-9563054-4-2

Edited by Victoria Ridgeway

Typeset by Cate Davies

Index by Sue Vaughan

Printed by Henry Ling Limited, The Dorset Press

Front cover: Reconstruction of charcoal burning and extraction and roasting of ore, by Jake Lunt-Davies

Back cover: Early Bronze Age barbed and tanged arrowhead; Archaeological excavation of ore extraction pits at
Weybourne on the north Norfolk Coast in the mid nineteenth century; Early Neolithic flint core

Settlement, Ceremony and Industry on Mousehold Heath

Excavations at Laurel Farm (Phase II),
Broadland Business Park, Thorpe St Andrew, Norfolk

Barry Bishop and Jennifer Proctor

Pre-Construct Archaeology Limited, Monograph No. 13

PCA Monograph Series

Contributors

Principal authors	Barry Bishop and Jennifer Proctor
Publication manager	Victoria Ridgeway
Academic adviser	Trevor Ashwin
Project manager	Peter Moore
Post-excavation manager	Jonathan Butler
Graphics	Cate Davies
Archaeobotanical analysis	Phil Austin and Louisa Gray, QUEST
Lithics	Barry Bishop
Artefact illustrations	Cate Davies (lithics and small finds), David Hopkins (pottery)
Ironworking	Ian Riddler
Post-Medieval small finds	Märit Gaimster
Prehistoric pottery	Sarah Percival, NAU Archaeology
Reconstruction drawing	Jake Lunt
Roman pottery and small finds	James Gerrard
Saxon pottery	Berni Sudds
Slag and industrial residues	Lynne Keys
Stone identification	Kevin Heyward
French translation	Agnès Shepherd
German translation	Sylvia Butler
Series editor	Victoria Ridgeway

Contents

Figures

X

Tables

Summary

Pre-Construct Archaeology Limited undertook a programme of archaeological investigation ahead of the development of a site at Laurel Farm, Norfolk into an extension to Broadland Business Park. The site is situated *c*. 1km north of the village of Thorpe St Andrew and 5km from the historic core of Norfolk, and covers a total area of *c*. 19 hectares. Following geophysical, fieldwalking and metal detecting surveys an archaeological evaluation investigated nearly 200 trenches. Subsequent excavation concentrated on an area measuring 150m x 130m in the north-west of the site, with targeted trenches elsewhere.

The investigations revealed an extraordinarily long and complex history of occupation and exploitation of the area, which is presented here as a series of chapters relating to each major period of the site's history (Chapters 2–9), with a concluding discussion of the occupation as a whole (Chapter 10).

The oldest artefact recovered was a Lower Palaeolithic handaxe, found by Neolithic people hundreds of thousands of years after its manufacture and carefully buried in a pit. The earliest definite evidence for people actually visiting the site indicates that during the Upper Palaeolithic hunter-gatherer communities used the shelter provided by the roots of an upturned tree, possibly as a temporary camp, and while there manufactured flint blades. The use of tree-throw hollows occurs again in the Early Neolithic when an adjacent pair were used to dispose of quantities of pottery, animal bone and nearly 4,000 pieces of struck flint. Analysis determined that this material had been middened before being carefully gathered up and dumped into the hollows.

A substantial Early Bronze Age ring-ditch, interpreted as the remains of a ploughed-out round barrow, was probably part of a much larger barrow cemetery that continued westwards across the fields now covered by the Dussindale Park housing estate, as depicted on a map of 1589 as the 'Gargytt Hylls'. The first evidence for permanent habitation at Laurel Farm dates from the Middle Iron Age, when a farmstead composed of one or two roundhouses along with several refuse pits, was set within a field system.

No evidence was found for settlement at the site during the Romano-British period, but a substantial quantity of pottery, some with firing defects, was dumped here. This may be associated with a more widespread pottery industry in the area as shown by the kilns at Postwick, some 2.5km away.

By the later Saxon period the area had long been on the edge of a vast area of heathland. Unsuitable for agriculture or habitation, the site saw intense industrial activity involving the preparatory stages of iron production, which radiocarbon dating indicates started around AD 700 and continued into the early Medieval period, around AD 1200. This industrial activity is of considerable significance as little was so far known of the early stages in the ironworking process. Alongside large iron ore quarry pits, there was rare evidence for ore roasting, in the form of pits showing intense burning and containing remnants of charcoal and fragments of burnt ironstone. Numerous charcoal burning pits were also present; charcoal would have been vital in the iron processing industry and was evidently manufactured at Laurel Farm in some quantity. The raw materials required for iron processing were all available close to the site, and the nearby town of Norwich, which was becoming an inland port of some importance by the Late Saxon period, provided an easily accessible and large market for wrought iron.

Following the demise of the iron industry during the thirteenth century, the site reverted to isolated heathland. It was probably only visited by passing shepherds and perhaps others coming to gather its natural resources, which included wood, gravel and clays for brickmaking. Pressures on agricultural production towards the end of the eighteenth century resulted in enclosure and the laying out of fields across this part of the heath. The site remained in agricultural production until its recent redevelopment, the catalyst for the archaeological work that has resulted in this publication.

Acknowledgements

Pre-Construct Archaeology Limited would like to thank Rodney Birch of KBC Asset Management (UK) Ltd for commissioning the project on behalf of Lothbury Property Trust Company Ltd, Marco Latella for further project management and Richard Hughes, IHCM, for monitoring the archaeological investigation and for his help and advice. Thanks also to David Gurney of Norfolk County Council for monitoring the fieldwork and assessment.

Thanks are extended to Peter Moore for project management and Jon Butler for the post-excavation assessment management. The archaeological investigations were supervised by Jude Westmacott who would like to thank Sarah Hoad and Mark Dodd for their roles as Assistant Supervisors, and Strephon Duckering and Richard Archer for their assistance with the machine clearance of the site. Pre-Construct Archaeology Limited would also like to thank all of the field team for their hard work. Thanks also to Cheryl Blundy for the on-site photography and Strephon Duckering for finds photography; Guy Seddon, Nathalie Barrett and Aiden Turner for the surveying and Lisa Lonsdale for technical and logistical support.

The authors would like to thank Victoria Ridgeway for her invaluable help with the publication and Ian Riddler for his significant contribution to our understanding of the iron processing activity carried out at the site. Barry Bishop would like to thank Peter Robins from the Norwich Castle Museum and David Adams of the Norfolk Archaeological Unit for showing him and discussing with him the Upper Palaeolithic flint from Carrow Road. Ian Riddler wishes to thank Elizabeth Shepherd Popescu for all her help and for sharing with him her knowledge of Anglo-Saxon Norwich. The authors and editor are indebted to Trevor Ashwin for providing comments on drafts of this text and for sharing his extensive archaeological knowledge of the area.

We would like to dedicate this volume to the memory of David Hopkins, who worked on illustrations in this and numerous other PCA monographs. David died tragically and unexpectedly on the 25th September 2011. He will be sadly missed by all who knew and worked with him.

Chapter 1

Background to the Project

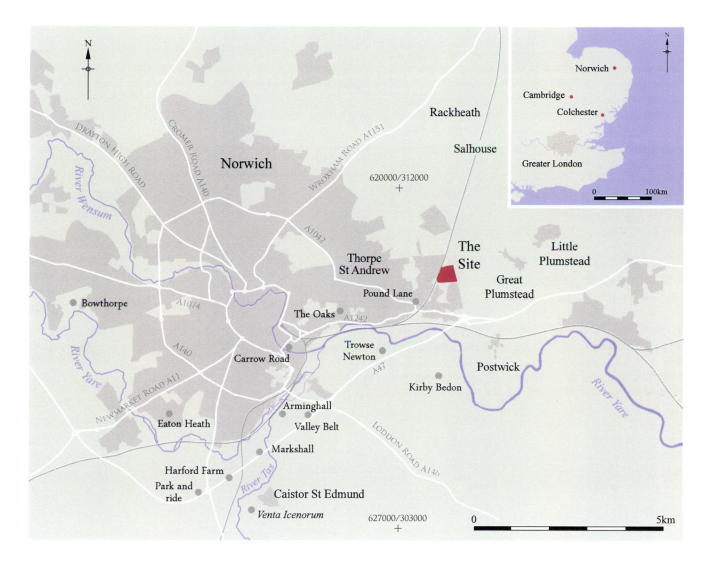

Fig. 1 The site location, shown in relation to Norwich and other sites in the vicinity (scale 1:100 000)

1.1 Site Description and Setting

Archaeological investigations at Laurel Farm have revealed a long and complex history of the occupation and exploitation of the area with archaeological features and artefacts present ranging in date from the Lower Palaeolithic to the Post-Medieval period. This volume describes the results of the investigations and discusses the significance of the findings within a broader regional context of prehistoric and historic development of the area. The city's conurbation now extends eastwards to the western boundary of the site, which lies 5km from the

historic core of Norfolk, *c.* 1km north of the village of Thorpe St Andrew and *c.* 2km west of Great Plumstead, straddling the boundary between the latter two parishes. A phased programme of archaeological investigation was implemented following the submission of a planning application to Broadland District Council, in the Norfolk Borough of Norwich, to redevelop the site as the Phase II extension to Broadland Business Park. The development site is approximately trapezoidal in plan and measures a maximum of 520m east–west by 440m north–south covering a total area of *c.* 19 hectares (Fig. 1). It is centred on National Grid Reference TG 28209 09555 and the Norfolk Historic Environment Record reference number

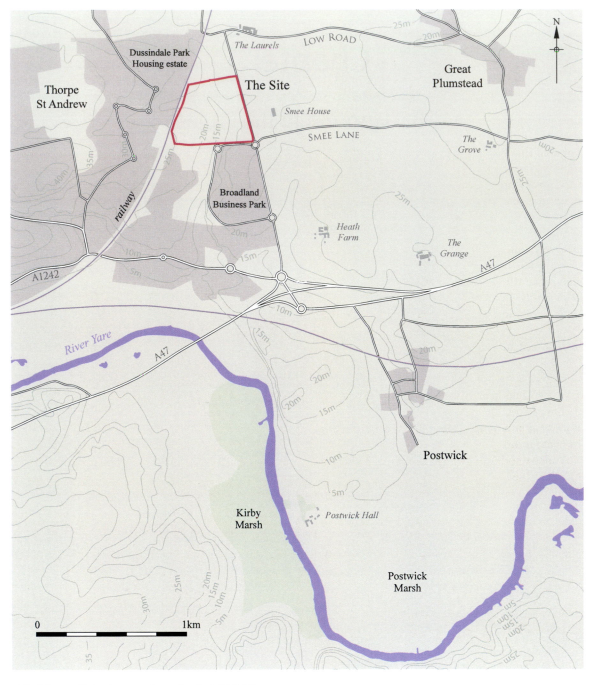

Fig. 2   The Thorpe St Andrew environs (scale 1:25 000)

for the project is HER 44715. It was bounded to the south by the existing Broadland Business Park and grassland, to the west by the Norwich to Cromer railway line and the Dussindale Park Estate, by a ploughed field and council rubbish tip to the north, and to the east by Green Lane South and additional fields (Fig. 2).

The site lies on the north side of the Yare Valley approximately 1.5km to the north of the river and close to the major riverine confluences of the Yare and Wensum and the Yare and Tas, which occur *c.* 5km upstream from the site. Prior to the recent large-scale developments, which have resulted in extensive housing estates and the creation of a business park in the vicinity, Laurel Farm was located within farmland

and, despite the proximity and the views it would have had towards the villages of Thorpe St Andrew and Great Plumstead, not to mention the city of Norwich to the west, it would have seemed a relatively isolated place. The village of Thorpe St Andrew, located by the river, would undoubtedly have provided the main focus for settlement in the parish. Parts of the original village foci can still be seen along the Yarmouth Road and fronting onto the river, but in recent years the expansion of Norwich has resulted in Thorpe St Andrew becoming in effect a suburb. The Laurel Farm site lies on the very eastern edge of the urban expansion and the work described here has resulted from its inevitable incorporation into this conurbation.

Topography

The site lies on the eastern outskirts of Norwich in a dry, minor left bank tributary valley of the River Yare. This is an area of relatively low relief, nowhere rising much above 35m OD (Fig. 2 , Fig. 9). The dry valley heads at this level *c.* 1km to the north-west of the site and it meets with the River Yare to the south of the site at a level of around 4.0m OD. The site is set within a tongue of land that lies on the margins between the predominantly glacial-till covered chalklands to the west and the low-lying, alluvial dominated landscapes of the Broads and coastal areas to the east. It lies on a low plateau towards what was the south-eastern edge of historical Mousehold Heath. Upstream of the site, the river is relatively contained within its valley as it winds through the glacial-till covered chalk. The Yare Valley broadens significantly to the east of its confluence with the River Wensum. The Yare Valley is set within gently undulating countryside although its soft underlying geology is easily eroded, resulting in the presence of a series of steeply cut and predominantly north–south orientated tributary valleys. Traversing the site is a dry valley, Dussindale, which once formed a tributary of the River Yare with its confluence just to the east of the village of Thorpe St Andrew. The importance of this stream in past times may be gauged by the fact that for most of its route it forms the Parish boundary separating Thorpe St Andrew and Great and Little Plumstead, which may date back to the late Anglo-Saxon period, and forms both the modern Civil Parish and the Parliamentary Constituency boundary. This stream appears to be shown as still flowing on Faden's 1797 map (see Fig. 5), though the precise date at which it ceased to flow is not known, and its former course can be traced as a linear depression running north–south down the centre of the site (see Fig. 4). Two smaller former tributaries aligned east–west run along the centre of the site, resulting in four areas of high ground located at the corners of the site. Ground levels fall from *c.* 25m OD at the south-western corner and *c.* 22m OD at the north-western corner, to between 13–14m OD in the base of the dry valley at its lowest point, where it exits the site to the south.

Geology

The underlying bedrock in the area is Cretaceous Upper Chalk and this is overlain by a complex sequence of Quaternary sediments. The British Geological Society have mapped the area (BGS 1991 Quaternary and Pre-Quaternary Geology, 1:50,000 Series Sheet 162 Great Yarmouth) around the site as underlain by sandy clay (till) of the Corton Formation, formerly known as the Norwich Brickearth, which comprise Anglian Glacial outwash sediments, dating to *c.* 450,000–380,000 years before present (Fig. 3). This sequence has been recorded in detail (Postma and Hodgson 1988) at Caistor St Edmund to the south of Norwich where it reaches a thickness of nearly 20m. It comprises, from the base upward, a well-rounded flint shingle of Norwich Crag age, resting

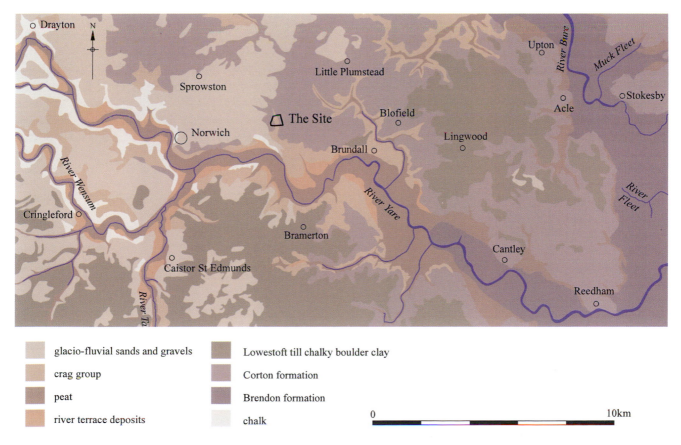

glacio-fluvial sands and gravels   Lowestoft till chalky boulder clay

crag group   Corton formation

peat   Brendon formation

river terrace deposits   chalk

0   10km

Fig. 3   Geology of the Yare Valley in the vicinity of the site (scale 1:160 000)

Fig. 4   Google Earth image of the site prior to the excavations; the courses of the Dussindale and other former streams can be clearly seen traversing the site © 2007 Google; © 2007 Europa Technologies; Image © The GeoInformation Group

directly on the Chalk, succeeded by sands and gravels representing the Wroxham Crag and containing clasts of quartz and quartzite. The Wroxham Crag is overlain by chalky till and chalk-rich sands and gravels of the Middle Pleistocene Anglian glaciation. Elements of this sequence are widely recorded from sites to the north, east and south of Laurel Farm. At the Laurel Farm site, the dry valley has cut through part of this sequence and with the ground level at the site between 12m and 20m OD, the floor of the dry valley and the lower valley side slopes are probably developed entirely in the sands and gravels of the Wroxham Crag with a thin veneer of colluvial material and, on the valley floor, probably sediments of fluvial origin. The upper slopes of the dry valley were formed by the Corton Formation, these deposits being up to 8.20m thick, consisting of silty sands incorporating flint and quartz gravel and, in some places, interbedded with laminated silty clays suggesting glacial pooling (Whitbybird Ltd. 2005, 2). Pebble counts from the archaeological samples showed the clasts within the sand comprised *c*. 80% flint, 5% quartzite, 5% ironstone/conglomerate, 5% hard siliceous red sandstone, 5% chalk/limestone.

Within the dry valley, the upper deposits predominantly consist of colluvium that had accumulated during various periods, and this process of hillwash deposition seems to have continued to occur into recent times. Accumulations of colluvium may in particular relate to episodes of devegetation. Even during the present

excavations, it was noticeable how quickly the loose 'natural' deposits eroded downslope during heavy rain once the topsoil had been removed. The depth of the topsoil encountered at the site varied considerably, being much thicker at the base of the dry valley, with depths of up to 1.30m recorded, than in the higher areas of site where it was often as little as 0.20m thick.

1.2 Archaeological and Historical Background

The River Yare would have been an important transport route for people and goods throughout the prehistoric and historic periods, both by watercraft and, particularly during early periods, via foot along the relatively unwooded valley margins. In historic times it would have allowed access to Norwich and the Norfolk hinterland, as well as downstream to Great Yarmouth, coastal Norfolk and beyond to the rest of Britain and to Europe. As such, the river would have been a prime eastern routeway for people, goods and cultural influences arising from the Continent. The river would also have provided resources such as fish and wildfowl its floodplain and the alluvial dominated Broadlands would have been fertile, rich and very varied, providing a wealth of natural resources, not least verdant seasonal pasturage. The major riverine confluences of the Yare and Wensum and the Yare and Tas would have been of strategic importance during historic periods and were influential in the siting of the Roman regional capital at Caistor St Edmund and the Anglo-Saxon and Medieval town of Norwich. River conditions and levels would have varied considerably in the past, according to fluctuations in sea level and climate; particularly in the Roman period, when deep water would have extended some considerable distance inland in the Yare and Bute Valleys. The area around the confluences appears to have been a major focus for activity during the Holocene period, where a number of nationally important Neolithic and Bronze Age ceremonial monuments have been recorded.

Some of the most significant Lower and Middle Palaeolithic sites dating from the earliest occupation of Britain have been recorded in East Anglia. The three main areas where such evidence is found are the Breckland region of west Suffolk and south Norfolk, the Stour and Gipping Valleys and the Yare and Wensum Valleys (Wymer 1984, 31). The majority of evidence for activity in the region comprises flint artefacts, large quantities of which have been recovered from river gravel deposits during quarrying operations (Austin 1997, 5). Several handaxes from this period have been found in the vicinity of Laurel Farm, listed on the Norfolk HER, and two 'working sites', containing potentially *in-situ* knapping debris, have been identified within the river terrace deposits along the southern margins of the River Yare near Kirby Bedon. During the Upper Palaeolithic period the region was subject to several climatic fluctuations (Wymer 1984, 40). Archaeological evidence for Upper Palaeolithic activity is rare from anywhere in Britain and associated features even rarer; yet of the few sites or artefacts from this period many have been found in East Anglia (Austin 1997, 9). Long blade flintwork assemblages have been discovered at Titchwell, Hockwold-cum-Wilton and Methwold (Austin 1997). A number of contemporary struck flint assemblages have been identified in the Norwich area, and Carrow Road in Norwich is an Upper Palaeolithic site of national importance with *in-situ* flintwork scatters (Adams in prep.). This material appears to form part of a pattern of movement noted along the Yare Valley (Robins and Wymer 2006; Bishop forthcoming a).

Mesolithic sites are much more widely distributed in the region, but again tend to be restricted to surface finds with few sites identified with *in-situ* material (Austin 1997, 9). The Breckland, river channels, the roddons within the Fens and some coastal regions appear to have been widely exploited environments during this period (Austin 1997). The Historic Environment Record (hereafter NHER) records finds of a number of Mesolithic transverse axes, which tend to concentrate along the river margins. Small quantities of microlithic flintwork, associated with burnt plant material dated to the Mesolithic period, were recovered during excavations ahead of the Norwich Southern Bypass (Ashwin and Bates 2000) . In the vicinity of Laurel Farm, a flintworking site which may represent a 'home base', is reported from south of the River Yare at Whitlingham Lane in Trowse Newton

(NHER 13927) and a rare perforated macehead made from quartz was recovered to the north of Laurel Farm near Norwich Road (NHER 8169).

In southern Britain evidence for earlier Neolithic settlement tends to be restricted to pits containing cultural material; domestic buildings are extremely rare (Thomas 1999, 64). Sites characterised by groups of pits containing cultural debris are particularly prevalent in East Anglia, concentrated on lighter soils in coastal regions or lying close to the main river valleys, frequently on relatively elevated positions just above the floodplain (Garrow 2006, 1, 16, 58). Several significant pit sites are known in the region such as at Kilverstone, a short distance south-east of Thetford in the Breckland area, which produced evidence for cereal processing and small-scale woodland clearance (Garrow *et al.* 2006). Similar evidence for intensive pitting has also been identified at Hurst Fen, Mildenhall (Clark *et al.* 1960), at Spong Hill (Healy 1988) and on a lesser scale at Broome Heath near Ditchingham *c.* 18km south-east of Norwich (Wainwright 1972) and Eaton Heath in the south-western part of Norwich (Wainwright 1973). A few Early Neolithic pits were found associated with a possible small circular structure or shelter of Early Neolithic date at Bowthorpe on the western outskirts of Norwich (Percival 2002). Garrow (2006) has outlined the debate about whether such pit sites represent permanent or repeated occupation, concluding that the character, temporality and scale of occupation varied considerably across different places and times and that such sites were re-occupied many times over, with the scale and duration of each episode of occupation varying greatly (Garrow 2006, 59). The large quantities of material at pit sites such as Kilverstone, along with the evidence for cultivation of arable crops, points to the fact that some of these places became the focus for relatively long term settlement, though this would not necessarily need to be permanent (Garrow 2006, 57). Larger collections of struck flints, possibly indicative of more permanent or larger settlement sites, have been recorded close to the River Yare, such as at Postwick, *c.* 1.5km south-east of the site (NHER 22030), and on the south bank at Trowse Newton (NHER 13927). At Little Plumstead Hospital, just over 2km to the east of Laurel Farm, some Early Neolithic activity was attested by stray pottery finds (Trimble 2003) and at Whitlingham Lane, ditches of possible Neolithic or Early Bronze Age date and quantities of worked flint were found (Birks 2001).

Neolithic monuments in the region are broadly located in the same areas as the pit sites, though some examples do occur in areas of higher ground and away from rivers and coastal sites (Garrow 2006, 20). The Yare Valley to the south and south-east of present day Norwich is noted for its rich Neolithic ceremonial landscapes, settlements and evidence for axe manufacturing; numerous Neolithic polished flint and stone axes are known from the area. Cursus monuments with Early Neolithic origins are known in East Anglia, though these are not evenly distributed across the region

(Brown and Murphy 1997, 14) and of the five excavated examples, all lie in Cambridgeshire (Garrow 2006, 143). Aerial photography has identified possible causewayed enclosures including examples in Norfolk at Roughton, Hainford and Buxton, though none has been confirmed by excavation and an alternative interpretation cannot be ruled out (Ashwin 1996a, 46). Crop marks of possible ploughed-out long barrows have been identified in the general area around Laurel Farm such as at Marlingford in the Yare Valley west of Norwich (Ashwin 1996a, 45). In contrast to the pit sites and monuments, Neolithic artefact scatters and stray finds have a very wide distribution across all parts of the region and demonstrate that the landscape as a whole was used for a variety of activities in this period (Garrow 2006, 149).

By the Later Neolithic and Early Bronze Age, the area around the confluences of the Rivers Yare, Tas and Wensum to the south and east of Norwich had become a focus for prehistoric activity, principally of funerary and ceremonial character (Trimble 2006; see Chapter 10.4, Fig. 68). The Arminghall Henge, located at the confluence of the rivers on the southern outskirts of Norwich (Clark 1936a), became the focus for an important group of round barrows, eight of which were excavated in advance of the construction of the Norwich Southern Bypass (Ashwin and Bates 2000), with another possible henge close by at Markshall to the south-east in the fork of the confluence of the Yare and Tas, though this has not been confirmed by excavation (Ashwin and Bates 2000, 231). A cluster of 38 mounds called the "Gargytt Hylls" is shown on a 1589 map of Thorpe St Andrew (see Fig. 69) in the area now covered by Dussindale Park housing estate, adjacent to the western limit of the Laurel Farm site. This seems likely to represent a large barrow cemetery (Lawson *et al.* 1981) although by 1933 no traces of these remained and much of the area has now been developed for residential housing.

In common with the rest of the country, settlements of Late Neolithic/Early Bronze Age date are rare in Norfolk (Brown and Murphy 1997, 14) and are frequently only represented by artefacts found in disturbed or unstratified contexts. In general, ceramic assemblages associated with settlement activity are dominated entirely by Peterborough ware, Grooved ware or Beaker pottery; on present evidence, it seems that the three types of ceramics did overlap but were essentially successive rather than contemporaneous (Ashwin 1996a, 52). An assemblage of Beaker pottery indicative of domestic occupation was found at the Norwich Southern Bypass site at Valley Belt, Trowse (Ashwin and Bates 2000). Similar evidence was also uncovered at the Markshall, Caistor St Edmund site, along with a pit containing Grooved ware pottery (Ashwin and Bates 2000, 194). Settlement activity from this period in the vicinity of Laurel Farm is known at Whitlingham Lane, just south of the River Yare, where ditches and quantities of worked flint have been recorded (Birks 2001). At Little Plumstead Hospital just over 2km to the east of Laurel Farm at the head of a small tributary of the River Yare dense concentrations of features such as

postholes, stakeholes and gullies were found associated with a buried soil (Trimble 2003). These were located along the lower slopes of the valley and are most likely to represent several phases of habitation and associated agricultural enclosures datable to the Late Neolithic or Early Bronze Age.

Evidence for Middle to Late Bronze Age activity in the region is dominated by sites which are funerary in nature such as the disc barrows excavated at the Norwich Southern Bypass site at Harford Farm and Harford Park and Ride (Ashwin and Bates 2000, 133–134; Percival with Trimble in prep.). Cremation deposits within urns from this period are often found inserted into earlier barrows and given the fact that many barrows have been ploughed flat, this may have been a much more widespread practice than appears from the archaeological record (Ashwin 1996a, 54). At The Oaks, Harvey Lane, *c.* 2km to the south-east of Laurel Farm, traces of a Middle Bronze Age settlement of relatively high status have been revealed (Trimble 2006) and the site's position close to river may suggest it had a role in trading or exchange. There were certainly large numbers of bronze objects moving in and out of East Anglia during this period although very little is known of either the communities that organized this or the mechanics and relationships that governed it.

Current evidence suggests that during the Late Bronze Age to Early Iron Age transition and in the Early Iron Age period, settlement in the region clustered on the lighter soils along the river valleys and the Fen edge (Bryant 1997, 23–25). Settlement sites of this period are once again infrequent in Norfolk, though the Breckland area appears to be a focus for occupation (Davies 1996, 67). Adjacent to Laurel Farm, to the west of the Dussindale Park housing estate, pottery, querns and burnt flint, suggestive of Late Bronze Age settlement, were recovered in 1951 and to the east of this, during construction of the housing estate itself, a spread of burnt flint and flintworking waste was identified. By the Middle Iron Age, there is increasing evidence for settlement around the Norwich area. At Park Farm, Silfield, Wymondham, to the south-west of Norwich, an unenclosed domestic settlement has been excavated (Ashwin 1996b). Two extensive Early to Middle Iron sites were also excavated during the Norwich Southern Bypass excavations: a complex of roundhouses and pit groups were revealed at Harford Farm, Caistor St Edmund, and rubbish-filled pits, four-post structures and enclosures were recorded at Valley Belt, Trowse (Ashwin and Bates 2000, 135–137, 189–190).

The Late Iron Age saw significant social and economic developments across south-east England; exchange contacts with Continental Europe brought exotic imports to the county and introduced wheel-thrown pottery and coinage. In Norfolk there is evidence for increased population and a greater number of settlements with habitation spreading onto the heavier Boulder Clay soils and interfluves (Davies 1996, 68). Pollen evidence indicates that extensive deforestation occurred during this period in parts of east Norfolk (Davison 1990). Extensive areas of large multi-period field systems have been identified by the National Mapping Programme (NMP), particularly in Norfolk and Suffolk. Co-axial field systems forming parts of extensively managed landscapes have also now been recognised in parts of the county such as the central Waveney Valley in south Norfolk (Williamson 1987). Generally settlement sites in Norfolk tend to continue to be unenclosed in the Later Iron Age with habitation areas extending over wide areas (Davies 1996, 70), some rectangular ditched enclosures are known from north and west Norfolk (Davies 1996, 77) along with a few large enclosed hillfort sites, situated in the west of the county. These display little evidence for internal occupation suggesting the possibility that they may have been of primarily ritual function (Davies 1996, 73–75; Bryant 1997, 29). A few sites in Norfolk could be classed as *oppida*, though it should be noted that such settlements display much variety in form and function and should not be ascribed to a particular form of social or economic organization (Millett 1990, 21–23). With the exception of the Fison Way area of Thetford, none of these sites have seen extensive excavation (Davies 1996, 78), nevertheless they display several similar characteristics: prolific surface finds including coin moulds, coins and non-Iceni tribal issues, occupation extending over a wide area and they tend to be situated at the confluences of major rivers. Davies (1996, 80) has identified one such possible major settlement at Caistor St Edmund located at the confluence of the Tas and Yare, a precursor to the Roman *civitas* capital.

Six small square ditched enclosures interpreted as Late Iron Age or early Roman funerary or ritual monuments were excavated at the Harford Farm site (Ashwin and Bates 2000). Several enclosures visible as cropmarks are listed on the HER in the near vicinity of Laurel Farm, including a rectilinear enclosure and trackway just beyond the site boundaries to the south and two or more curvilinear enclosures and a trackway located to the west, beyond the railway line.

Many of the settlements established in Norfolk in the Late Iron Age continued to be occupied into the Roman period (Davies 1996, 70). Early military occupation is attested by the presence of a large marching camp situated on a crossing over the River Bure at Horstead, *c.* 8km to the north-west of Laurel Farm. The *civitas* capital of the Iceni, *Venta Icenorum*, was established *c.* AD 70 at Caistor St Edmund (Davies 1996, 88). The location of the capital here, rather than at one of the major sites in the Breckland area that had been a focus of settlement throughout the Iron Age, was presumably a deliberate decision to reduce the political importance of this area (Davies 1996). Roman routes in the region are in general not well mapped. The principal north–south Roman road from Colchester terminated at Caistor St Edmund and an east–west route is known from Water Newton to Brampton, probably continuing eastwards to the coast. The HER describes a postulated north–south road that ran from Thorpe St Andrew riverside to Brampton, possibly continuing southwards beyond the River Yare to *Venta Icenorum* (NHER 7598). An east–west road is postulated

to the south of Laurel Farm, this may be the route taken by the Medieval track of 'Yermouthe Way' which ran east from Kett's Hill across Mousehold Heath (NHER 9690).

At The Oaks, a series of small rectangular enclosures, pits, shallow gullies and an oven, may indicate Romano-British settlement activity (Trimble 2006). Rather intriguingly, in 1862–63 a number of objects were recovered from close to The Oaks (NHER 9628), including large stones, burnt earth, pottery sherds, amphora fragments, copper alloy shield fragments, iron spearheads, Roman coins and a number of human burials thought to date to the Roman or Early Anglo-Saxon period. The pottery appeared to be Late Saxon or early Medieval, and the iron spearheads and an associated shield boss were probably Iron Age in date and thought to belong in a burial context. It is uncertain what all of these high status and multi-period items may represent but they certainly indicate very significant activity in the vicinity. At Pound Lane, less than 1km to the south-west of Laurel Farm, Roman pottery sherds and iron working debris was observed during gravel extraction. Excavations revealed the stokehole of a kiln and a mound of kiln waste including wasters of mid first-century date (Gregory 1979). Significantly, evidence for pottery production has also been identified at Heath Farm in Postwick, *c.* 500m to the south-east of Laurel Farm (Bates 1996; Bates and Lyons 2003).

The HER lists a large quantity of Roman artefacts from the vicinity of Laurel Farm, which probably originated from scattered small rural settlements but the only indications of a more substantial and perhaps higher status building within the area is a mosaic that was reported during the early twentieth century at Kirby Bedon (NHER 9676).

Evidence for late Roman to Early Anglo-Saxon activity is relatively well documented in Norfolk as finds of 'Germanic' material can be used to indicate the presence of cemetery sites and settlements of this period (Going 1997, 41). Little is known of the political structure in the region in the fifth century AD but by the sixth century AD, Norfolk and Suffolk were occupied by the East Angles (Wade 1997, 47) and by AD 750 the East Angles had been subsumed along with other groups into Mercia. The substantial number of Middle Saxon sites known from surface scatters of finds on the Norfolk HER provides evidence for settlement shift and population expansion with the resettlement of the Fen edge (Wade 1997, 48) and by the Late Saxon period the population size and density of occupation had increased further.

The Roman town at Caistor St Edmund seems to have been abandoned by the fifth century AD, when an Anglo-Saxon cremation cemetery was founded beyond the city walls (Myres and Green 1973), but was reoccupied and continued to be so into the eighth century AD (Penn 2000, 101). In Norwich Early Anglo-Saxon activity is indicated by stray artefactual remains from within the city, a cemetery of fifth- to sixth-century AD date at Eade Road (Green and Young 1981, 9), and ditches and pits of Early Saxon and Middle Saxon date at Fishergate

Fig. 5   Extract from Faden's Map of Norfolk, dated 1797, showing the site in relation to Norwich (scale 1:100 000)

(Brown 2005). Street and place name evidence attest to Middle Saxon occupation in Norwich (Atkin and Evans 2002, 236). Settlement had been established on both sides of the River Wensum by the Middle Saxon period and from the early tenth century onwards Norwich was a flourishing and important city; a defensive circuit was constructed on the north side of the Wensum, a number of parish churches were founded and the city became an administrative centre with its own mint, port and market (Atkin and Evans 2002, 237).

Closer to Laurel Farm just to the east of The Oaks, work at allotments in the 1950s recovered a number of inhumations (NHER 9646) and subsequent excavations discovered evidence for Late Saxon occupation, preceding the construction of a masonry church during the Medieval period, which appears to have disturbed the skeletons (Rose and Davison 1988; Batcock 1991). Inhumations, have also been found to the north of The Oaks along with Late Saxon pottery (NHER 9628).

Most villages in the area had been established by the time Domesday Book was compiled. Thorpe, which encompasses the settlements at Thorpe St Andrew, Thorpe End and Thorpe Hamlet, is a common Old Scandinavian name meaning 'outlying farmstead or hamlet' (Mills 1988). Thorpe St Andrew takes its affix from the dedication of the parish church but only acquired this name after 1956. Prior to this it was known as Thorpe-next-Norwich, to distinguish it from other Thorpes in the county and, prior to 1536, as Thorpe Episcopi, due to the Bishop of Norwich owning the manor of Thorpe (Nuthall 2002).

Laurel Farm lies on the edge of what was historically the south-eastern edge of Mousehold Heath, which originally extended from within Norwich's city boundaries and the north-east banks of the River Wensum north-eastwards towards the villages of Rackheath and Salhouse covering around 2,500 hectares or 6,000 acres (Rackham 1986, 299), but is now much reduced in size and only survives *c.* 3km to the west of the site. The sandy nature of the soil in this area, which was of generally low fertility, meant that it was highly susceptible to erosion and soil loss leading to early formation of heathland, probably by the Medieval period. Some areas of heathland may represent former prehistoric woodland which having been cleared for agriculture became open pasture (Penn 2001). There are several Medieval references to the gradual reduction in size of the extensive Thorpe Wood and its replacement by Mousehold Heath due to pressure for grazing land (Rackham 1986, 301); it was likely to have been home to populations of small-holders and sheep farmers and would also have supplied a wide range of foodstuffs, building materials and fuel to both the inhabitants of the heath and for the burgeoning City of Norwich. A Victorian copy of a map from 1624 (Norfolk Records Office Map 1624: MS 457/1) shows the heath pockmarked by numerous brick fields (quarries), kilns (clamps) and gravel pits (see Fig. 73). The area is shown as largely deserted on Faden's Map of 1797 (Fig. 5) with the exception of a few structures marked 'Shepherds ho[uses]'. Also of note on this map is the north–south flowing stream that once ran through the site, a former tributary of the River Yare.

Mousehold Heath was the location of civil unrest on several occasions from the Medieval period right through into the nineteenth century. In 1381, during the Peasants' Revolt, a rebel group led by Geoffrey Lister camped on the Heath before capturing Norwich, though they did not hold the city for long (Whittle 2007). In 1549 Mousehold Heath played a key role in Kett's Rebellion, an uprising in Norfolk led by Robert Kett against the enclosing of land. Rebel forces camped on the Heath and besieged Norwich before being finally defeated by government forces at the Battle of Dussindale. Laurel Farm is located within the northern part of the outline of the battle site shown on the HER, although the precise location of the battle has been the subject of some debate (NHER 21173).

Mousehold Heath survived relatively unaltered until pressures on agricultural production towards the end of the eighteenth century resulted in enclosure of the land. The heath gradually reduced in size over several centuries and the surviving portion, located in the north-east part of Norwich, now covers around 180 acres or 88 hectares (Rackham 1986, 302). The Thorpe St Andrew Enclosure map of 1801 shows that land at the Laurel Farm site was enclosed by this date. The site has been used for agricultural purposes since it was enclosed and at the time of the investigations the area scheduled for redevelopment comprised a large open arable field.

1.3 Methodologies

Planning background

A planning application was submitted to Broadlands District Council, in the Norfolk Borough of Norwich, to redevelop the site as the Phase II extension to Broadlands Business Park. As part of the planning consent, a programme of archaeological investigations was required by Norfolk Landscape Archaeology, on behalf of Broadland District Council. The project was commissioned by Rodney Birch of KBC Asset Management (UK) Ltd on behalf of Lothbury Property Trust Company Ltd and monitored by Richard Hughes, IHCM, on behalf of the client. David Gurney of Norfolk County Council monitored the work on behalf of the local planning authority. The initial investigation comprised a desk top survey of the archaeological potential of the site prepared by the Norfolk Archaeological Unit (Penn 2001), followed by a second desk study prepared by IHCM in 2006 (Hughes 2006). Geophysical, fieldwalking and metal detecting surveys were carried out in May 2006 according to a prepared Written Scheme of Investigation (Moore 2006a) and the results of these used to inform initial proposals for a trial trenching evaluation. It was not possible to position trenches in some parts of the site due to the presence of services; a pylon and overhead electrical cables which crossed the centre of the site in a north-south direction were given a 10m exclusion zone, and a buried gas main which ran across the south-western corner of the site was given a 5m exclusion zone (Fig. 6). The majority of the trenches were located across the high ground to the east and west of the site where a 5%

sampling strategy was proposed. As evaluation progressed individual trenches were expanded as appropriate to enable better definition and interpretation of archaeological features.

Fieldwalking survey

A fieldwalking survey was undertaken at the site between 31st May 2006 and 9th June 2006. A team of archaeologists walked transects at 10m intervals on both east–west and north–south axes and collected, bagged and labelled the finds from every 10m section of grid. The finds were then processed, identified and entered onto a database. The amount of vegetation cover in the field increased significantly during the survey; this resulted in varying degrees of visibility and several squares, mostly concentrated in the north-eastern corner of the site, which could not be walked at all.

Post-Medieval pottery and clay tobacco pipe was found fairly evenly across the site with a slight concentration on the high land towards the south and west and ceramic building material distribution echoed this pattern. Ironworking slag was found distributed quite thinly and fairly evenly across the site with a slight concentration to the south-west. As this material had been spread so much by ploughing it was impossible to target with trench locations. Very little Medieval and Roman pottery was identified (only two sherds of each), and the trial trenching evaluation sought to determine whether this was a consequence of the soil conditions, plough damage, or reflected a genuine scarcity of activity from these periods on the site. The struck flint found during the fieldwalking survey ranged from Early Mesolithic to Late Bronze Age and struck and burnt flints were found in a fairly even distribution across the site, probably as a result of long-term ploughing and any apparent concentrations were thought to be a product of the survey conditions. The results of the fieldwalking survey therefore did not justify any revision to the proposed trench layout.

Geophysics

A Fluxgate Gradiometer geophysical survey was undertaken across the entire site by Pre-Construct Geophysics using the established site grid. The survey, while not greatly effective in the soil conditions present at the site, identified several features and anomalies. These included three pit-like irregularities running in a north-east to south-west line across the centre of the western half of the site, and a larger anomaly at the top of the slope at the north-western corner of the site. Several linear anomalies were also identified on the geophysical survey, which were thought to be either archaeological in origin or related to modern agricultural land use. The position and alignment of the evaluation trenches was altered to allow investigation of all of these possible features. Only one of the six areas noted in the geophysics survey as containing probable ferrous material appeared to correlate with slag found during fieldwalking.

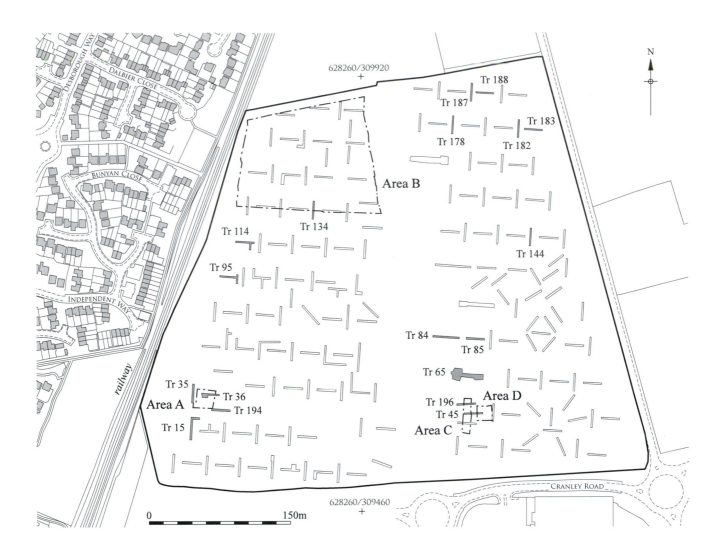

Fig. 6   Areas of archaeological investigation, showing trial trenches excavated during the evaluation process and the four main areas of excavation (A, B, C and D); trenches referred to in the text are shown shaded and labelled (scale 1:4000)
Reproduced by permission of Ordnance Survey on behalf of HMSO © Crown copyright 2011. All rights reserved.
Ordnance Survey number 100020795.

Trial trenching evaluation

In total, 188 evaluation trenches were investigated (Fig. 6), of which twenty were extended to further evaluate, or fully record revealed features, groups of features and further geophysical anomalies, as an immediate mitigation strategy. On the whole, features interpreted as possible ditches in the geophysical survey were identified within the evaluation trenches, but isolated anomalies were not. It was evident that the extreme variability of the natural substratum was the cause of some of the anomalies.

The archaeological evaluation demonstrated that a cluster of ditches, pits and postholes were located in the north-western portion of the development site. This was the area with a concentration of worked flints initially dated to the Bronze Age. The central third of the western side of the development site was found to be relatively empty of recorded features and finds. This area

corresponds with the east–west valley area between the two higher areas to the north and south. The few features that were present in this area consisted mainly of ditches, some of which were interpreted as being contiguous. Some of this activity was Post-Medieval in date and most would seem to be drainage-related given the nature of the topography. The south-western corner of the development site was on high ground and was almost entirely devoid of archaeological features, possibly due to severe plough erosion.

The south-east, central and northern parts of the eastern side of the development site were relatively devoid of archaeological features. Occasional ditches were found but a lack of artefacts from these features made dating problematic. A number of archaeological features were identified in the western side of the south-eastern corner of the site including stratified layers of sand containing unabraded Roman pottery.

Archaeological excavation

The evaluation had revealed the presence of prehistoric, Roman and Saxon activity at the site and four specific areas of archaeological interest were identified where further detailed excavation was to be undertaken (Moore 2006a; 2006b). Area A comprised a 20m² area situated in the south-western corner of the development area. Area B, measured 150m by 130m in plan and was situated in the north-western corner of the development area sloping down to the valley floor to the east and to a smaller tributary to the south. Area C, measuring 37m by 8m, was situated on the floor of the dry valley at the southern end of the development area. Area D, measuring 16m by 16m was situated slightly to the east and upslope (Fig. 6). The excavation was undertaken between 27th July and 31st October 2006.

Topsoil and other undifferentiated soil horizons were removed in successive spits by mechanical excavators under archaeological supervision (Fig. 7). Linear features were sample excavated so that at least 10% by length of each feature was excavated and at least 50% of pits and most other discrete features were excavated. In a few cases, substantial discrete features such as quarry pits, slots were excavated using a mechanical excavator rather than by hand in order to determine the extent of the feature and to record the profile. The archaeology was recorded using the single context recording system (PCA 1999) with individual descriptions of all archaeological strata and features excavated, exposed and entered onto pro-forma recording sheets.

Following the completion of all fieldwork an archaeological assessment report was prepared, detailing the findings from the excavation, assessing its significance, outlining any further work that would be required to achieve that potential and recommending means for the dissemination of that information (Westmacott 2007). Further analysis of the artefactual and palaeoenvironmental material was undertaken as recommended in the assessment report and all of the data from the investigations was then analysed by Barry Bishop.

Archaeological remains encountered at the site were restricted to cut features; centuries of ploughing and erosion at the site had caused horizontal truncation of archaeological features, with this being most severe in areas where the topsoil was relatively thin. As a result, no horizontal stratigraphy, such as surfaces, survived and the upper portions of features had been subject to truncation. The loose nature of the natural sand and gravel sub-stratum at the site meant that upon excavation larger features were prone to collapse, particularly during wet weather (Fig. 8) and it is likely that similar processes may have occurred in antiquity, particularly within larger cut features such as quarry pits which may have been

Fig. 7   General site view, Area B looking north-west, showing excavation in the foreground, with topsoil stripping under archaeological supervision in the background

Fig. 8   Image taken during groundworks at the site showing collapsing edges of a large pit during wet weather

left open for some length of time. The soft, often loose deposits that formed both the underlying strata and the fills of most of the features may also have resulted in a greater degree of intrusiveness of artefactual material than might be witnessed elsewhere, as these sediments are easily disturbed and prone to bioturbation and re-settling. The nature of this soil also resulted in the formation of features through natural processes such as sinkholes and disturbance by roots and animals.

The acidic nature of the sandy soil resulted in very poor bone preservation; only a very small assemblage of faunal remains was recovered from the investigations. Preservation of charcoal recovered from bulk samples was generally good, but plant macrofossils were very scarce with only a small assemblage of plant remains recovered from the later phases of activity at the site. The investigations produced substantial quantities of artefactual remains, including assemblages of struck flint, pottery from several distinct periods, metalwork and slag.

The excavations revealed evidence for activity at the site commencing at least by the Upper Palaeolithic, and continuing, perhaps not continuously but certainly persistently, until the present (Fig. 9). The nature of this activity varied greatly from settlement foci to marginal land to an industrial centre and latterly to an intensified agricultural regime and now a business park. Understanding of much of what was found was limited by the boundaries of the excavation, and the paucity of other investigations in the vicinity, as it was clear that the activities identified extended into the landscape beyond.

The excavated remains can thus only represent localised insights into individual elements that are part of a wider, highly organised landscape of settlement, agriculture and industry.

The site code TSA 06 was assigned to the project in line with internal PCA recording policy. The completed archive comprising written and drawn and artefacts will be deposited with Norwich Museum under the site code 44715 TSA. The Norfolk Historic Environment Record (NHER) reference number for the project is NHER 44715.

1.4 Report Structure

Within this publication the archaeological remains from each main period are described within separate chapters, by phase, with specialist reports and data included. The final chapter discusses the significance of the results of the investigations within a broader regional context.

The archaeological remains from the site have been assigned to nine main phases of activity beginning with geological material and natural features (Phase 1). Anthropogenic remains encountered during the investigations spanned many millennia with the latest activity recorded at the site dating from the Post-Medieval period. Within these main phases of activity, archaeological features have been placed into groups in order to aid description; these groups do not necessarily represent any chronological development within the main periods but simply reflect either groups of similar features or groups within certain areas of the site. Many features did not contain any artefactual or palaeoenvironmental material. An attempt has been made to phase such features when they were evidently of anthropogenic origin and were found in association with datable features and displayed similarities in form and infill to these. In cases where such associations are not evident, features have not been phased and are shown on plan (Fig. 9), but not described within this publication text. Details of all features are contained within the assessment report and site archive.

Due to the considerable chronological span of occupation at the site and the wide variety in the nature of activity between successive phases, the data for each phase is presented in a separate chapter. Each chapter presents a description of the archaeological features from each phase of activity with general and detailed site plans where necessary. The relevant specialist reports are included with each chapter, supported by illustrations, and these include the methodologies used for each class of artefact or ecofact. Where the methodologies are relevant to more than one period, for instance in the case of archaeobotanical analysis, these are presented at the first instance and thereafter cross-referenced. The final chapter considers all of the data and presents a discussion of the site in a wider context.

In this text individual context/feature numbers appear in square brackets [100], registered (small) finds are referenced as <15> and sample numbers appear in curly brackets {6} throughout.

Dating terminology

In recent years there have been laudable attempts to avoid or underemphasize the conventional period nomenclature of Neolithic, Bronze Age, Iron Age etc, with their implications of unflinching boundaries separating batches of social inertia. Nevertheless, the authors here concede that no adequate alternatives are currently available that would be either as familiar to the reader or allow the text to be as easily read. The use of traditional terminology has been recognized as a useful tool, and has been adopted throughout this report as it is widely understood and acts as an aid in structuring the report. Approximate date ranges for the periods used are shown in Fig. 9 with the phases assigned on this site, where identified. This should not be taken to imply that any such distinctions between different periods would have been recognizable to those living through them, or that any meaningful distinction necessarily can be drawn between the end of one period and the beginning of the next.

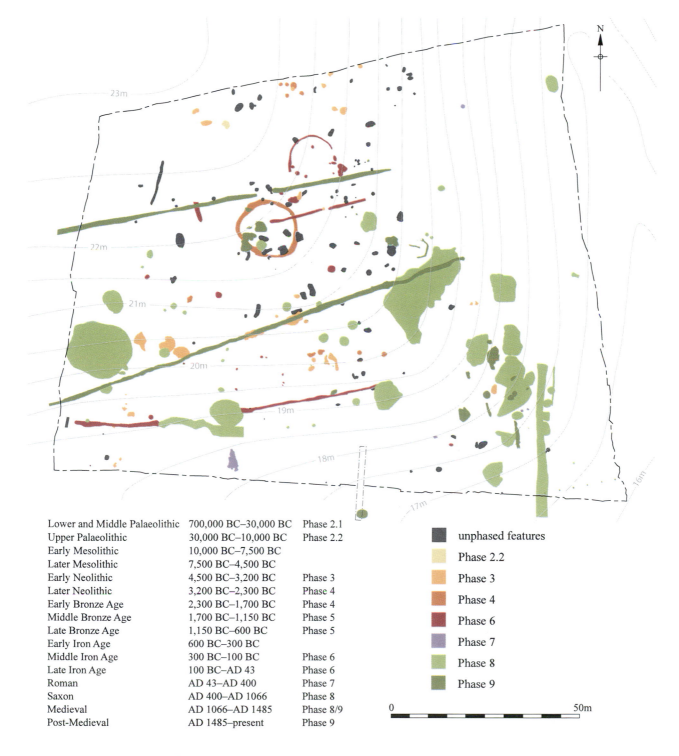

Lower and Middle Palaeolithic	700,000 BC–30,000 BC	Phase 2.1
Upper Palaeolithic	30,000 BC–10,000 BC	Phase 2.2
Early Mesolithic	10,000 BC–7,500 BC	
Later Mesolithic	7,500 BC–4,500 BC	
Early Neolithic	4,500 BC–3,200 BC	Phase 3
Later Neolithic	3,200 BC–2,300 BC	Phase 4
Early Bronze Age	2,300 BC–1,700 BC	Phase 4
Middle Bronze Age	1,700 BC–1,150 BC	Phase 5
Late Bronze Age	1,150 BC–600 BC	Phase 5
Early Iron Age	600 BC–300 BC	
Middle Iron Age	300 BC–100 BC	Phase 6
Late Iron Age	100 BC–AD 43	Phase 6
Roman	AD 43–AD 400	Phase 7
Saxon	AD 400–AD 1066	Phase 8
Medieval	AD 1066–AD 1485	Phase 8/9
Post-Medieval	AD 1485–present	Phase 9

unphased features

Phase 2.2

Phase 3

Phase 4

Phase 6

Phase 7

Phase 8

Phase 9

Fig. 9   Multi-phase plan of all features identified within Area B shown in relation to topography and illustrating the high incidence of undated features (scale 1:1000)

Chapter 2

Phase 1 Natural Deposits and Phase 2 Palaeolithic Activity

2.1 The Natural and Palaeolithic Sequence

Phase 1: Natural deposits and features

Geological deposits

The natural geology of the area is described in detail above (Chapter 1.1). Geoarchaeological assessment identified particular trenches within the development site that illustrated the natural geology (Green and Swindle 2007). Trench 65, located on the western side of the south-western quadrant of the development site, was placed across the north–south aligned Dussindale dry valley. Natural deposits in this area comprised variable gravelly sand passing up into a colluvial sub-soil horizon to a depth of c. 1.0m from the ground surface. Several small palaeochannels, most less than 2m in width, were recorded cutting into the gravelly sand and into one another. Solution pipes (sinkholes) were also recorded to a depth of 5.50m below the ground surface but which evidently extended below this level penetrating the sediments underlying the dry valley floor. These are likely to have developed episodically over a long period of time (>100ka) in the Quaternary and in their present form are not obviously active as sinkholes. A 2m-wide palaeochannel aligned parallel to the valley-side slope was recorded in this area and similar palaeochannels were recorded in several other trenches on the opposite side of the dry valley, also running parallel to the valley slope. On the dry valley floor, the remains of small palaeochannels preserved beneath colluviums probably represent short-lived erosional episodes in the Early Holocene, or possibly attrition associated with land degradation following prehistoric or historic occupation. The evidence of gullying on the east–west valley sides probably relates to the same erosional episodes.

Palaeochannels in Area B

A substantial, irregular natural channel, recorded as [343] and [334] along its western and eastern edges, respectively, aligned approximately north-west to south-east was located in the south-western corner of Area B (Fig. 10). The feature measured over 30m in length by c. 16m wide, continuing beyond the edge of excavation to the south and not fully traced to the north, and was over 1m deep, but not fully excavated. The edges of the feature and interfaces between fills were all very diffuse. The fills of the channel all appeared to have accumulated naturally through erosion and hill wash. A small assemblage of six struck flints of Early Neolithic date were the only finds recovered from the palaeochannel, but whether it had ceased to flow by this date is not known. There is no stream in this area shown on Faden's map of 1797 and the palaeochannel presumably ceased to flow before this date. Palaeochannel [503], which was only revealed in two small slots excavated adjacent to the south-western limit of excavation, appeared to be aligned east-south-east to west-north-west. Its fill [483] produced two Neolithic or Bronze Age struck flints.

A north to south aligned feature was located along the eastern side of Area B on the western valley side of the dry riverbed. Part of the western edge of this feature was recorded as [906] and slots were excavated through the feature to the north, to confirm that this was of natural origin. The maximum recorded depth of the channel in this area was 1.70m but it was not possible to reveal the base of the feature. To the south a T-shaped slot [739] was excavated through the feature to a maximum depth of 1.20m.

The feature was traced for a distance of over 50m in length and although the full extent of this feature was not ascertained, the recorded portion and its alignment suggests that it represents the western edge of the major dry river valley of Dussindale, known to run through the site.

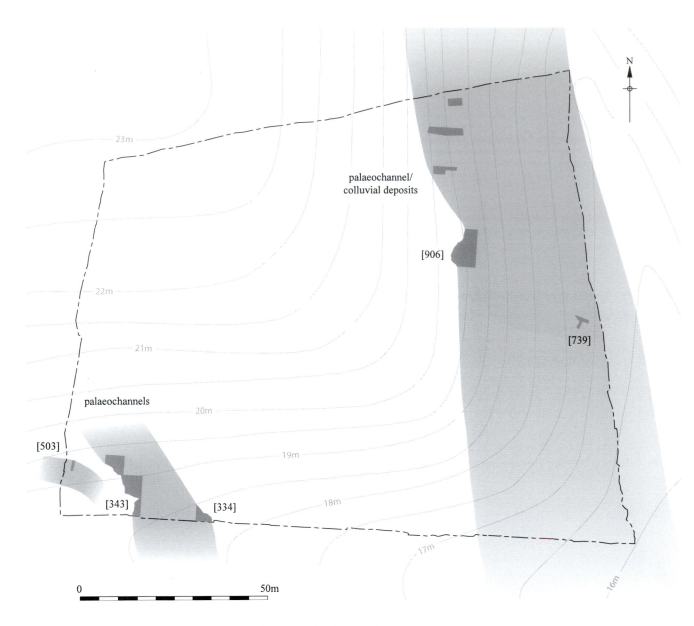

Fig. 10   Phase 1, natural features encountered in Area B (scale 1:1000)

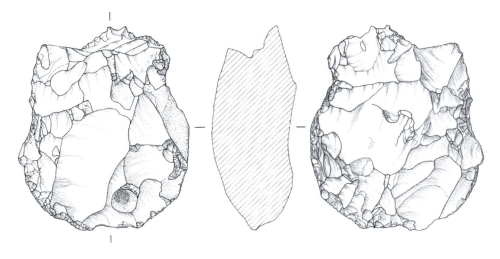

Fig. 11   Lower Palaeolithic handaxe from Neolithic pit [1123] (scale 1:2)

Phase 2: Palaeolithic

The earliest artefactual evidence from Laurel Farm was a Lower Palaeolithic handaxe, recovered from a pit of Neolithic date, with the first certain evidence of activity at the site comprising an assemblage of flintworking waste dated to the Upper Palaeolithic recovered from a tree-throw hollow.

Phase 2.1: Lower Palaeolithic

A single bifacially flaked handaxe of Lower Palaeolithic date was recovered from the fill [1124] of an Early Neolithic pit [1123] (Fig. 11, see Fig. 18). It measured over 110mm in length, its tip having broken off, and was 90mm in width and 43mm thick, weighing 530g. It was probably a pointed or cordiform type but was not particularly regular in shape and one edge remained largely cortical. It had been moderately rolled and had been mineral stained to a mid yellow-brown (ochreous) colour subsequent to its tip breaking off, suggesting it may have spent some time within alluvial gravel deposits. Its recovery from a pit containing predominantly Neolithic struck flint remains somewhat of an enigma and the possibility that it was found and purposefully deposited in the pit should not be excluded.

Phase 2.2: Upper Palaeolithic tree-throw hollow

Evidence for Late Glacial/early Post-glacial activity at the site was provided by an assemblage of 78 pieces of worked flint recovered from an irregular shaped feature [1173] located towards the north-western side of Area B (Fig. 12). This measured 2.20m by 2.00m and up to 0.53m deep and had steeply sloping edges and an undulating base. The form of this feature indicates that it is likely to be a tree-throw hollow – the depression left by the root bowl of an uprooted tree. It contained three fills; the primary fill [1174], which contained the struck flint, consisted of compacted light grey sandy clay with frequent small pebbles and occasional charcoal flecks. The secondary fill was similar to the lower but was brownish in colour and contained no struck flint, whilst the third and latest fill was similar to the middle fill but more silty and friable in texture.

The absence of any flint in the upper fills or in the surrounding topsoil indicates that the flintwork had probably been dumped into the tree-throw hollow rather than being accidentally incorporated into the feature (see Bishop Section 2.2). Tree-throws were often utilized as areas of shelter in the earlier prehistoric periods with some producing evidence for *in-situ* flint knapping (Evans *et al.* 1999; see Chapters 10.1 and 10.2).

A bulk soil sample taken from the lower fill produced three fragments of charcoal twigs identified as oak (*Quercus* sp.). One of these fragments, was submitted for radiocarbon dating and this produced a calibrated age of 19,550 to 18,750 BC (Waikato-22911, see Appendix 1), a date which is clearly problematic (see Chapter 10.1).

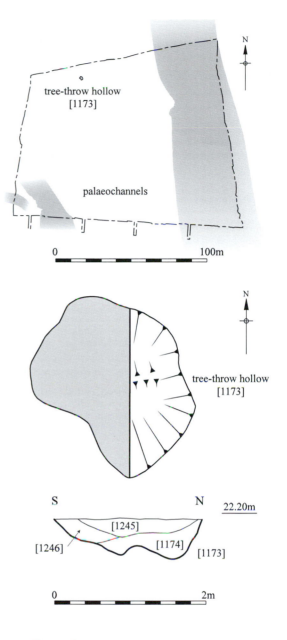

Fig. 12   Plan and section of Upper Palaeolithic tree-throw hollow with inset of Area B showing its location in relation to natural palaeochannels (scales 1:2500 & 1:50)

2.2 Late Glacial/Early Post-Glacial Flint Assemblage

Barry Bishop

An assemblage consisting of 78 struck flints and a single burnt flint fragment weighing 5g was recovered from feature [1173], interpreted as being a tree-throw hollow. The assemblage is technologically homogeneous and distinct from the other flint industries recognised at the site. Although no truly chronologically diagnostic implements were present, several elements within the assemblage are consistent with Late Glacial or early Post-glacial industries and it has therefore been decided to describe the material from this feature separately and in some detail.

The assemblage was all recovered from the lowest fill of tree-throw hollow [1173]; no cultural material was present in the two upper fills nor was any struck flint recovered from the overlying topsoil deposits during machining. The assemblage would therefore appear to be reasonably undisturbed and its condition would indicate that it had been deliberately dumped into the feature, rather than incorporated residually.

Quantification

The assemblage was clearly blade-based with these providing nearly 43% and flakes providing less than 26% (Table 1). Small flakes and flake fragments measuring less than 10mm in maximum dimension contributed almost 27% with two cores, a conchoidally fractured chunk and a flaked hammerstone, completing the assemblage. The small pieces are consistent with core reduction having occurred in the vicinity although too few are present to indicate *in-situ* knapping within the pit. These were nearly all collected from a bulk sample, however, and as the entire contents of the feature were not sieved, they are probably under-represented.

Raw materials

The assemblage was manufactured from thermally fractured, nodular shaped cobbles of flint that are translucent black near the cortex and become mottled grey with depth, the mottling ranging from almost opaque, matt porcelain white through to a semi-translucent creamy grey. The flint has a thin, rough light yellow cortex *c.* 1–2mm thick which is only slightly abraded. The cobbles were evidently large; the largest core measures in excess of 110mm but this is clearly only a small part of the much larger original nodule, which may have been 'quartered' prior to flaking. Occasional proto-thermal faults are visible within the flint, particularly in the cores, but these do not appear to have affected the flaking fracture planes and they may have formed in the cores subsequent to their reduction. The size and condition of the flint nodules is different from the smaller, thermally shattered flint clasts present in the site's geological strata and the raw materials must have been obtained elsewhere. They show no evidence for alluvial abrasion and are most likely to have been obtained from sources close to the parent chalk. The most likely locations are deposits lining sides of the major valleys in the area, where incised rivers have cut into the chalk bedrock, eroding out flint nodules (cf. Adams in prep.) and suitable deposits are likely to have been obtainable within a few kilometres of the site.

Condition

The condition of the assemblage is mostly good with the pieces only exhibiting slight sand-glossing from settling in their burial matrix, although many pieces do display slight edge-nicking, which could have occurred accidentally during manufacture, deposition or excavation. The assemblage was very fragmented, however, with 70% of the flakes and nearly 80% of the blades not being entirely complete. In some cases, particularly with the blades, this breakage may have been deliberate, but overall it suggests the assemblage had received a high degree of post-depositional mechanical damage, such as through trampling. None of the material was recorticated although slight milkiness, indicative of incipient recortication, is present on a few pieces.

The only burnt pieces consisted of a medial segment from a small blade and a distal segment from a blade that measures well in excess of 62mm. This was deposited after fracturing into five pieces, which were recovered separately but could be refitted. They suggest that the flintworking was conducted close to a hearth and this is supported by the presence of a small, unworked burnt flint fragment found within the same fill.

Typology and technology

Core preparation

No true primary flakes are present although five flakes (6% of the assemblage) retained cortex in excess of 50% of their dorsal surface and small patches of cortex were preserved on a third of the flakes and blades. Two crested blades provide further evidence for core preparation. One, a secondary crested blade, was complete and measures 125mm long (Fig. 13.1) whilst the other was broken but still attained 67mm in length (Fig. 13.2). Both involved the removal of cortex and thermal scars.

Type	Blades and blade fragments	Flakes and flake fragments	Flakes and flake fragments <10mm	Cores	Conchoidal chunks	Flaked hammerstone
No.	33	20	21	2	1	1
%	42.3	25.6	26.9	2.6	1.3	1.3

Table 1   Quantification of the lithic assemblage from tree-throw hollow [1173]

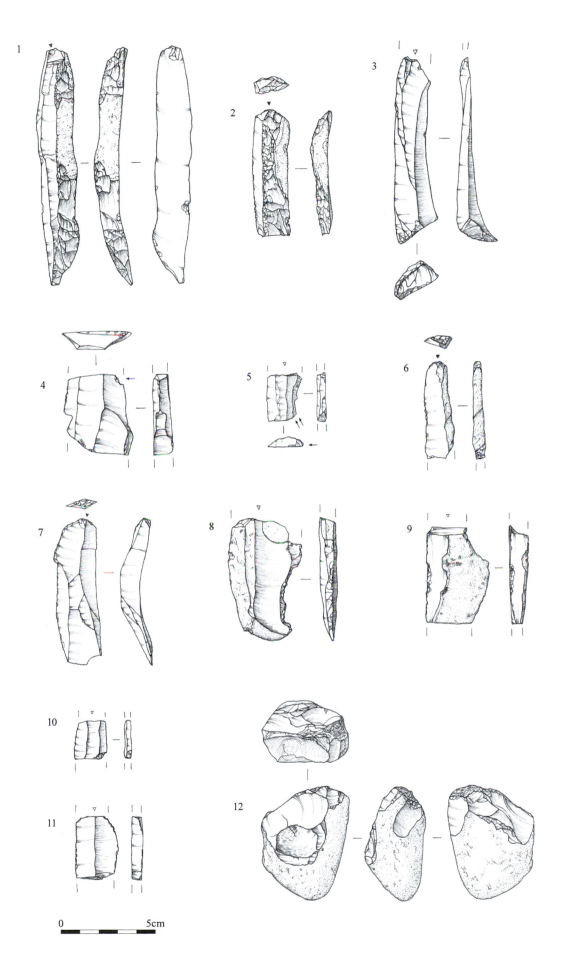

Fig. 13   Late Glacial/early Post-glacial blades and flakes (scale 1:2)

Cores

There were two cores present, abandoned at weights of 263g and 190g but still capable of producing blades in excess of 100mm and 85mm respectively. They had been carefully prepared with the creation of opposed striking platforms operating on the front and sides of the cores, although their backs had only been minimally modified, mostly involving efforts to allow the rejuvenation of the striking platforms. The largest retained both of its opposed platforms (Fig. 14.1), but attempts to rejuvenate the other (Fig. 14.2) by the removal of a plunged flake appears to have resulted in the complete removal of the opposite platform and the creation of a very acute base to the core. This would not have been rectifiable without considerably shortening the core and probably led to its abandonment. Both have markedly acute striking platform/core face angles and two out of the three surviving platforms had been faceted. The productivity of the cores was actively maintained as evidenced by two core rejuvenation flakes. These include an incomplete, but still 99mm long, plunged blade that retains part of the opposed platform on its distal (Fig. 13.3), and a flake that transversely removed part of a striking platform.

The similarities in the colour and patterning of the flint cores with that of the flakes and blades suggest that they were responsible for much of the assemblage, although a few flakes suggest that a further one or two cores that were not present amongst this assemblage may also have contributed.

The high proportion of blades present shows that the production of these was the principle aim of flintworking, with the flakes being dominated by decortication, core-shaping and core maintenance flakes. Due to the small size of the assemblage and the frequent breakages, metrical analysis is not possible, although it is clear that there was an emphasis on producing blades, some in excess of 100mm and several broken pieces suggest that others may have been considerably longer. The majority of the blades are prismatic and were systematically produced, displaying parallel dorsal scars that confirm the use of opposed-platformed blade cores. Of the 24 extant striking platforms on the flakes and blades

Striking Platform Type	No.
Edge-ground	10
Edge-trimmed	4
Facetted	2
Plain	4
Punctiform	2
Shattered	2

Table 2   Striking platform type for the Late Glacial/ early Post-glacial assemblage

only four were unmodified, these all being present on large decortication or core shaping flakes, whilst the others benefited from a variety of platform preparation techniques, particularly grinding the striking platform/ core-face edge (see Table 2).

Demonstrating care and competence in flintworking, two-thirds of the flakes and blades have diffuse bulbs of percussion and three-quarters have feathered distal terminations. Those with pronounced bulbs of percussion and hinged distal terminations were almost exclusively the decortication and core shaping flakes. It appears that the cores were prepared using hard hammers with blade production being accomplished using soft-hammer percussion.

Secondary working and use

Several pieces show evidence of secondary working and utilization. Perhaps the most convincing of these is a medial flake segment, possibly from a large blade, that has been snapped using a small notch and has a narrow burin-like spall removed across the break, initiated from the notch. There are also some utilization traces around the snapped edge, supporting its use as a graving implement (Fig. 13.4). Similarly, a smaller blade segment has what appears to be deliberate burin-like removals taken from the break aligned longitudinally along the segment, as well as smaller flakes removals taken from here and running transversely across the break (Fig. 13.5). It also exhibits traces of wear suggestive of having been used as a graver.

Also showing convincing deliberate retouch is the proximal section of a partially cortical blade that has a short stretch of steep retouch executed from its dorsal arête. The retouch is too incomplete to suggest what its original form was like but it could form a continuation of the 'backing' provided by the cortex (Fig. 13.6). Light spalling along the sharp, opposite margin may indicate a use as a cutting implement.

A relatively short blade has light edge blunting on its side near its distal end, which if not accidental may have helped in holding it (Fig. 13.7). Also convincingly utilized is the distal end of a flake or blade that broke along a fossil inclusion and which has a heavily battered edge and 'cortical backing' (Fig. 13.8). A medial segment of a largely cortical blade or flake has light battering on its sharp edge, suggesting it had been used in a chopping or whittling motion (Fig. 13.9). Also showing evidence of having been utilized is the complete crested blade that has a small area of damage, comparable to that from 'bruised blades', although this is far from extensive (see Fig. 13.1).

As noted above, the blade population was highly fragmented, with six proximal segments, fifteen medial segments and five distal segments being present. A number of the medial blade segments, along with a few other flakes and blades, have light edge damage that would be consistent with usage as cutting implements, although it is often difficult to differentiate this from damage caused accidentally from processes such as

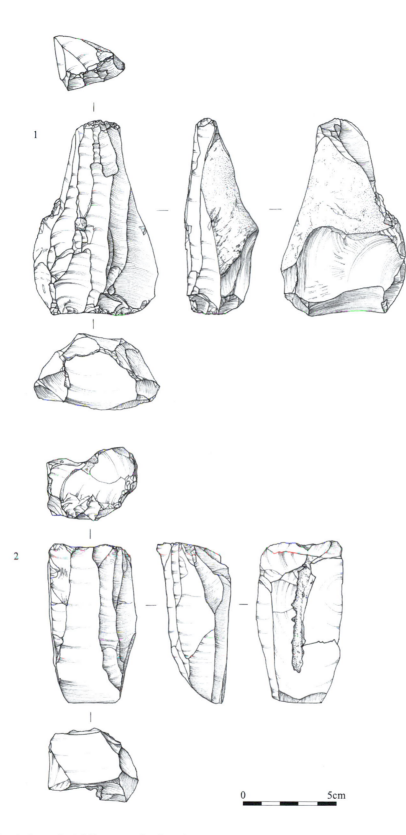

Fig. 14   Late Glacial/early Post-glacial flint cores (scale 1:2)

light trampling. Most of these segments were made by bending the blade and causing it to snap, but others have small impact marks (Hertzian cones) on their dorsal surfaces showing they had been hit sharply (cf. Bergman *et al.* 1986) and others had been made by making small notches on the edges of the blades and using these to initiate and control the location of the break, demonstrating that they had been deliberately snapped (e.g. Fig. 13.10, Fig. 13.11).

The hammerstone weighs 97g and consists of a small globular shaped nodule of translucent mottled grey flint with a thin but unabraded cortex. It has been bifacially flaked at one end, forming a chopper shaped implement but the cutting edge is very worn and battered, suggesting prolonged subsequent use as a hammer and may have been used to abrade the edges of the striking platforms (Fig. 13.12).

Discussion

Elements from all stages in the reduction sequence are present, including decortication flakes, cores, knapping debris, useable and utilized blades and a number of secondarily modified pieces. The lack of primary flakes, along with the general paucity of decortication and core shaping flakes, suggests that the cores may have been previously dressed elsewhere, presumably nearer to the raw material source. In this respect it is interesting that the two crested blades were present, as they are usually removed early in the core preparation stage. It is possible that these long but sturdy blades were brought along for use as implements, and one does have edge damage that, although only light, is consistent with a chopping action and is comparable to 'bruised blades'. The assemblage is heavily dominated by knapping waste

or broken pieces, and it would appear that many of the pieces produced, including useful blades and flakes and any definite retouched pieces, may have been removed for use elsewhere.

There are several technological features of this material that suggests it could belong to within the Late Glacial or early Post-glacial period, dating to *c.* 14700–7700 BC. These include the form of the cores and the use of plunged blades to rejuvenate them, the presence of large crested blades, the size of some of the blades, the types and complexity of the striking platforms, which include edge-ground and punctiform examples, and the probably deliberately snapped blade segments. Notwithstanding the radiocarbon determinations, which would appear to place the assemblage near the Late Glacial Maximum, the lack of specific chronologically diagnostic implements means that the dating of the Laurel Farm material cannot be refined further (but see for example Barton 1991; Barton and Roberts 1996; Barton 1998; Conneller 2009; Cooper 2006; Jacobi 2004 for discussions of technological change and spatial relationships amongst Late Glacial/ early Post-glacial industries).

Chapter 3

Phase 3 Early Neolithic Activity

3.1 The Early Neolithic Archaeological Sequence

There were few indications of a Mesolithic presence at the site, but by the Early Neolithic period there was evidently persistent activity here (Fig. 15). Although archaeological features of this date were only encountered within Area B, quantities of worked flint with Early Neolithic characteristics recovered across the site during fieldwalking and from colluvial deposits indicate that activity from this period was widespread.

A number of tree-throw hollows and pits recorded across Area B were infilled with cultural material. There has been much debate as to the meaning and significance of the artefact-filled pits of this period, but it is widely agreed that they mark out the locations of otherwise ephemeral settlement sites and in East Anglia these pits can be found spread over wide areas, indicating either densely occupied settlements or places to which people repeatedly returned (Garrow 2006). Two of the most notable features of Early Neolithic date at the site were a pair of adjacent tree-throw hollows that contained a considerable quantity of Early Neolithic pottery and worked and burnt flint, and these are considered in some detail below. Along with these was a scattering of other features recorded across Area B, mostly pits or tree-throw hollows, which contained sufficient artefactual evidence to assign an Early Neolithic date to them with reasonable confidence. Scattered amongst these features were a few areas of burning indicative of the locations of hearths or small campfires, which had survived plough-truncation as they were covered by colluvial deposits. A number of palaeochannels and colluvial deposits containing material of this period were also identified, possibly indicating that the area had been de-vegetated, allowing greater water runoff and erosion to occur. Other deposits recorded at the site were variable and probably represent a mix of colluvial deposits, sub-soil remnants and soils preserved within natural channels or hollows. Those discussed here either produced exclusively Early Neolithic artefactual material or had post-Neolithic features cutting through them.

Many other features contained artefacts of Early Neolithic date but, due to the very real problems of residuality, these are only discussed here if there is any further evidence that they may belong to this phase. The features within Area B are described in four main groups, They are grouped spatially for ease of reference and illustration but their grouping has no interpretative or chronological significance.

Group 3.1 Artefact-rich tree-throw hollows

By far the most notable features of Early Neolithic date were two adjacent features [746] and [787] located towards the south-western corner of Area B (Fig. 16 and see Fig. 28). These have been interpreted as hollows caused by the roots of toppled trees, although it is possible that they had subsequently been deliberately modified, before being infilled and sealed with large quantities of dumped artefactual material. A third tree-throw hollow [688] nearby displayed similar characteristics and may have been associated.

The tree-throw hollows comprised substantial irregular oval-shaped areas of disturbed sub-soil with irregular, gently sloping edges and flat bases. Feature [955] measured a maximum of 4.20m by 3.80m and was 0.74m deep whilst [956] was a maximum of 3.30m by 3m and 0.64m deep (Fig. 16). The disturbed sub-soils [973] and [1003] within these features comprised loose sandy silts which did not contain any cultural material. It is suggested that the disturbance to the soil was caused by toppled trees whose roots would have ripped and cast up the soil in which they had grown, the soils subsequently falling and eroding back into the hollows thus created. Within both areas of disturbance were hollows that had not been fully infilled by the up-cast, and it is possible that these may have been slightly modified or enlarged as their edges were rather more regular than usually encountered within naturally-formed tree-throw hollows.

The hollow [746] within tree-throw [955], which measured 4m by 3m and up to 0.30m deep, was an irregular crescent shape in plan with gradually sloping edges at angles of *c.* 20–30° and a steeper sided central hollow at *c.* 70°, its base being slightly concave (Fig. 16). Within tree-throw [956] was a crescent-shaped hollow [787] with gently sloping sides and a concave base, measuring 1.90m by 1.62m and up to 0.41m deep. Regardless of whether or not these hollows had been deliberately modified or enlarged, it was within these

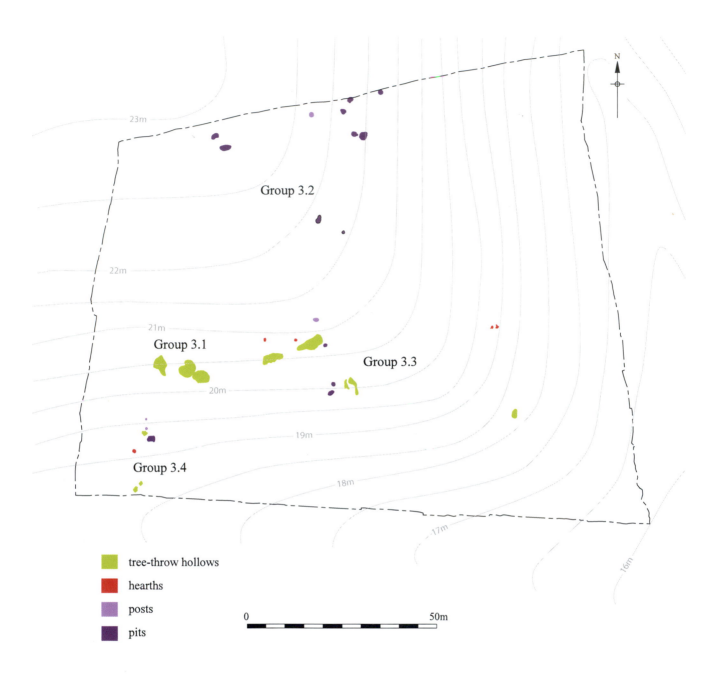

Fig. 15   Phase 3, Early Neolithic features, Area B (scale 1:1000)

features that large quantities of artefactual material had been dumped, conjoining pottery sherds between the two hollows indicating that this process was contemporary. When the hollows had become infilled, dumping continued, resulting in a contiguous midden-like layer [744] up to 100mm thick forming across the features.

The fills of both hollows and the overlying layer were essentially the same, consisting of loose silty sands, although the colour and the quantities of cultural material present varied, both within the hollows and the layer. Consequentially, the deposits were divided into a 0.25m grid and excavated in 50mm thick spits to allow an understanding of the spatial distribution of the material. The overlying layer [744] was divided into two spits, Spits 1 and 2, the fill [745] of the hollow [746] in tree-throw [955] was excavated in three spits, Spits 3, 4 and 5, whilst the fill [786] of the hollow [787] in tree-throw [956] was

excavated in two spits, Spits 6 and 7. The composition of the spits is detailed in Table 3 (see Fig. 28).

The fills of the two hollows were essentially the same as each other and reflect the trends seen in the overlying layer [744]. The colour of the fills darkened with depth, either suggesting that there was more comminuted charcoal and other organic material in the lower depths, or that percolating water had leached the deposits. The former is supported by the decline in other artefactual material that occurred with depth. The darkness of the fills was initially thought to be due to the presence of high quantities of charcoal. However, when sieved, the samples showed that although charcoal fragments were present, it was only in moderate quantities, and much of the colour must have been due to either very small, comminuted, charcoal 'dust' or other dark-coloured humic compounds. This is likely to indicate that, along with the more obvious cultural material deposited, high quantities of organic material such as vegetal material was included. Fragments of charcoal recovered from Spits 2 and 7 were submitted for radiocarbon dating and both produced the same calibrated date range of 3970 to 3790 BC (Waikato-22910 from Maloideae charcoal and Waikato-22912 from oak (*Quercus* sp.) charcoal, see Appendix 1).

Layer [744] contained large quantities of pottery and flintwork, virtually all of which could be dated to the Early Neolithic, although a few intrusive sherds of later pottery, perhaps introduced through ploughing, were recovered from the upper parts of the layer. There was more evidence for burning in the lower spit and it became darker with depth, although as with the earlier deposits, it was not certain whether this was due to higher quantities of charcoal and other organic material within the lower parts or because the upper parts had been more leached of minerals. Spit 1, the uppermost part of layer [744], also contained a broken polished axe, which was found placed in an upright position with its cutting edge facing upwards (Fig. 17). As this was unlikely to have occurred by chance, it appears likely that it had been deliberately placed in such a position, its presence at the top of the deposits and being one of the last items discarded may suggest a role as a closing offering.

A short distance to the west of the two tree-throw hollows was a deposit of material [688] (Fig. 16) extending across an irregular shaped area measuring 5.15m by

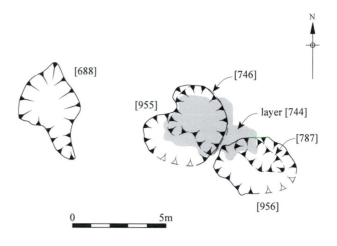

Fig. 16   Phase 3, Group 3.1, Early Neolithic tree-throw hollows, Area B (scale 1:200)

3.40m. Due to time constraints it was only possible to excavate a 1m-wide slot through the centre of this feature; this revealed it to comprise silty sand with a moderate quantity of flint pebbles up to 0.33m thick. A small assemblage of struck flint of Early Neolithic date was recovered from this feature. Although interpretation is not certain, it is possible that this feature may represent another tree-throw which had been used as a shelter or as a hollow in which to deposit midden material.

Layer [744]	Spit	Context	Description
744	1	558	Loose light to mid yellow brown silty sand (10:90) containing frequent struck flint, occasional flint pebbles, pottery, burnt flint and animal bone
744	2	571	Loose mid yellow brown silty sand (10:90) containing frequent struck flint, moderate pottery, occasional flint pebbles, burnt flint and very occasional animal bone
Hollow [746]			
745	3	645	Loose black brown silt sand (10:90) containing frequent struck flint, occasional Early Neolithic pottery (and a single intrusive sherd of Middle Iron Age), flint pebbles, burnt flint, charcoal, burnt clay and burnt daub inclusions
745	4	666	Similar to [645] but darker and with less frequent artefacts
745	5	686	Similar to [666] but very few artefacts
Hollow [787]			
786	6	608	Loose dark brown silt sand (10:90) containing frequent struck flint, pottery, charcoal fragments and flecking, occasional rounded flint pebbles and burnt flint. Very occasional intrusive Late Neolithic/Early Bronze Age pot
786	7	636	Slightly darker in colour and more humic in nature; ranging from dark brown to brown black. This context contained less pottery and occasional animal bone.

Table 3   Description of material recovered from within the Early Neolithic tree-throw hollows

Fig. 17   Broken polished Neolithic axe as found with its cutting edge upwards

Group 3.2 Features in the northern part of Area B

A group of features located adjacent to the central northern limit of excavation in Area B produced material of Early Neolithic date. These comprised two groups of paired pits and a cluster of features that may possibly have formed part of a circular structure. Several other pits, which did not produce any datable material, but were of similar form to those that produced Early Neolithic material were also located in this area (see Fig. 9). It is likely that some of these may have been contemporary and the juxtaposition of artefact rich and sterile pits is a common phenomenon on Neolithic sites.

Pits

Two pits [1243] and [1256], located *c.* 2m apart, were situated towards the north-western edge of Area B (Fig. 18). Feature [1243], which was oval in plan with steeply sloping sides and a stepped and concave base, measured 2.80m by 1.50m and was up to 0.90m deep. Its single fill [1244] comprised yellowish brown silty sand with a moderate quantity of medium flint pebbles and charcoal flecking. A large assemblage of 43 struck flints in sharp condition was recovered from this feature, including

flakes, blades, cores and a serrate. This represented a typical assemblage of Early Neolithic flintworking waste, although the flints did not refit and were often chipped which may indicate that they were residual or redeposited. Feature [1256] was a sub-oval, slightly crescent-shaped feature with very steeply sloping edges and a fairly flat base, which measured 1.70m by 1.10m and was up to 0.38m deep. Its single fill [1255] comprised brownish orange sandy silt with frequent small to medium flint pebbles and shattered fragments and occasional charcoal flecking. An assemblage of 31 struck flints, dominated by blades, in a very sharp condition and of Early Neolithic date, were recovered from the feature and may represent a 'cache' of unretouched but potentially useful implements. Both features are interpreted as Early Neolithic pits or perhaps modified tree-throw hollows, associated with flint knapping activity or the disposal of waste material from a flintworking area nearby.

To the south-east of these was a sub-oval pit [1016], which measured 2.24m by 1.30m and 0.75m deep and produced a sherd of Early Neolithic pottery. Further to the south-east of this was a sub-circular feature [846], either a small pit or posthole, measuring *c.* 0.80m in diameter and 0.21m deep, which produced three sherds of Early Neolithic pottery, including two possible sherds of Peterborough ware and an undecorated plain bowl body sherd.

Possible Structure

Adjacent to the northern limit of excavation was a group of features from which Early Neolithic material was recovered. Feature [1123], a sub-circular pit that measured *c.* 1.90m in diameter and 0.61m deep, had moderately sloping edges that became vertical in the lower two thirds of the cut, and a flat and regular base. Its single fill [1124] comprised mid brown sand with frequent inclusions of small flint pebbles and burnt flint. An assemblage of nineteen Early Neolithic struck flints was recovered from this feature, including flakes, blades, cores and a flake struck from a polished implement. A broken Lower Palaeolithic axe was also recovered from the fill, the only item datable to this period that was found on the site (see Chapter 2.1). This had been moderately rolled and mineral-stained subsequent to its tip being broken, which may suggest that it had spent some time within alluvial gravel deposits. It is possible that it was found and purposefully deposited within this feature during the Early Neolithic period.

To the immediate west was a sub-circular feature [1052], measuring 1.65m by 1.14m and 0.36m deep, with steeply sloping edges and a concave base. Although no artefactual material was recovered, its fill was very similar in composition to that of [1123] and is likely to be contemporary.

To the north-west was a sub-circular pit [1172] measuring 1.46m in diameter and 0.48m deep. It contained three fills, the earliest of which [1171] included a high proportion, around 50%, of flint gravel, pebbles and small cobbles set with a compacted sand and placed around the western side of the cut, rising to nearly the top of the feature. Over this were placed further shattered flint fragments along with a few larger flint nodules, which were also set in very compacted silty sand [1170] and which covered the western side of the cut. Sealing these and filling the pit was a moderately compacted greyish brown silty sand [1169] with occasional small gravels from which 22 struck flints were recovered. Like the assemblage recovered from pit [1256], this material was dominated by blades and may also represent a 'cache' of selected implements.

This feature appears to have been shored up on its steeply sloping western edge with compacted, gravel-rich soil and large flint nodules, probably to prevent the loosely compacted natural sand through which it was cut from slumping into it. The feature was substantial enough to have been used as a shelter, and although no evidence for flint knapping was identified amongst the assemblage, the 'cache' of blades may indicate that it was constructed for such activity and that the occupants either intended to return or that this material was left as an offering.

In close proximity to the north-east of this was a sub-circular feature [1180], which measured 1.37m by 1.35m, continuing northwards beyond the limits of the excavation, and was 0.86m deep. Its eastern edge was very steeply sloping and the west more moderate, the base was

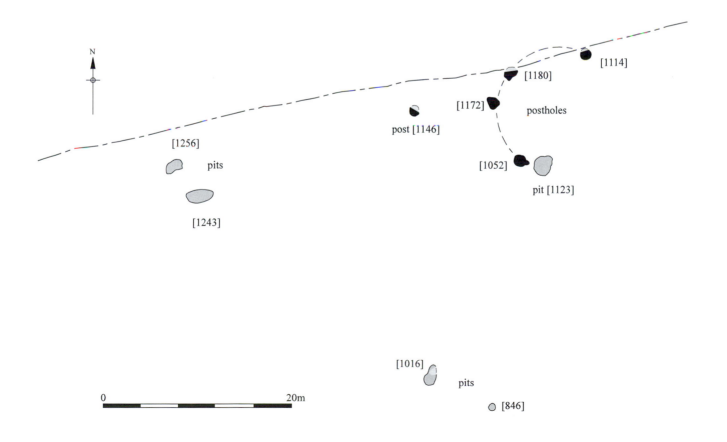

Fig. 18   Phase 3, Group 3.2, Early Neolithic features, Area B (scale 1:400)

flat and it contained two fills. Seven struck flints with Early Neolithic affinities, including blades and a serrated flake, were recovered from the upper fill [1178]. To the east was a similar feature [1114] up to 1.17m across and 0.33m deep and although no artefactual material was recovered from its single fill, the similarity between this and the lower fill of feature [1180] suggests that they were contemporary.

Interpretation of the function of this group of features is uncertain but the possibility that the easternmost group may represent structural elements should be considered. If this were the case, then these would have been substantial post pits forming an arc *c.* 17.5m in diameter, perhaps part of a circular structure such as a very large post-built roundhouse or timber circle. Early Neolithic pottery and lithics recovered as residual material from later features in this area indicate that fairly intensive activity may have occurred in this part of the site during this period. The base of the dry valley lies less than 60m away to the east and this high point may have been a topographically significant spot on top of the valley and in close proximity to the stream.

To the west of this putative structure was a sub-circular feature [1146], *c.* 1.15m in diameter and 0.23m deep, which had steeply sloping edges and a concave base with a deeper depression in the centre of its base, this profile suggesting that it may represent a posthole. Its single sandy silt fill [1145] contained occasional flint pebbles, a single Neolithic to Bronze Age flint flake and two sherds of Early Neolithic pottery. It had been largely truncated by a later Phase 4 feature [1144] and this contained a number of struck flints of similar characteristics to those contained within [1146], from which they may have been derived.

Group 3.3 Features in the central and eastern part of Area B

A colluvial layer [687] (not illustrated), which may have formed in the Early Neolithic, was located towards the centre of Area B. This measured 12m east–west by 10m north–south and was up to 0.28m thick. Pottery retrieved from the layer was dated to the Early Neolithic period, while two fragments of clay tobacco pipe, and Neolithic to Bronze Age flints are believed to be intrusive.

Two irregular shaped features truncated layer [687]. Feature [735] was an irregular sub-linear shape in plan measuring 6.60m by 2.50m and 0.23m deep, with concave sides and an uneven but predominantly concave base (Fig. 19). Its single fill [734], which comprised very loosely compacted mottled brown and yellow sandy silt with occasional small flint and quartzite gravels, produced burnt flint, struck flint broadly characteristic of Early Neolithic industries and a single sherd each of Early Neolithic and Iron Age pottery. A few oyster shells were also noted within this fill. To the south-west was a feature of similar profile [640] on the same alignment which measured 5.50m by 2.0m and up to 0.22m deep.

The fill [639] of this feature comprised mottled orange brown silty sand, also very loose in compaction, which produced two Neolithic flint flakes.

Both of these features have been interpreted as tree-throw hollows of Early Neolithic date, which may have been used as shelters, including during episodes of flint knapping. The oyster shell and Iron Age pottery sherd are interpreted as being intrusive as both features were truncated along their centre by a Post-Medieval ditch and features from several other periods of activity were located in the near vicinity. Although only a few worked flints were recovered from tree-throw hollow [640], sections excavated across the later ditch in this vicinity produced lithic material similar to that recovered from the tree-throw hollows and is considered likely to have originated from these features. Early Neolithic pottery and lithic material was also recovered from other later features in the vicinity of these tree-throw hollows. The largest quantities of struck flint were present in a Phase 8 circular pit [696] immediately north of tree-throw hollow [735], which produced fifteen pieces. The material incorporated within these features indicates the presence of a spread of material representing an episode of occupation in the vicinity of the tree-throw hollows.

Located close by was another pair of irregular, slightly curvilinear features [493] and [537]. These are also interpreted as tree-throw hollows, possibly even created by the same tree (Fig. 19). Feature [493], which measured 5.10m by 1.35m and 0.60m deep, had near vertical to steeply sloping sides and a slightly concave base. Its silty sand fill, which contained very occasional charcoal and burnt flint, produced two pieces of struck flint of Neolithic or Bronze Age date. To the immediate west was feature [537], of similar profile, which measured 2.80m by 1.35m and 0.60m deep. Several fills were recorded within this feature, including one that contained inclusions of burnt flint. Ten struck flints of Early Neolithic date were recovered along with a core of Neolithic or Bronze Age date.

To the east was another feature interpreted as a tree-throw hollow [490]. This measured 2.55m by 1.42m and was 0.32m deep. A small quantity of struck flint, including a blade of Neolithic or Bronze Age date, and burnt flint was recovered from this feature along with a large sherd of Early Neolithic pottery. To the immediate west of tree-throw hollows [493] and [537] was a layer [683] (not illustrated) comprising mid orange brown sand with frequent inclusions of flint pebbles and occasional burnt stones, which had accumulated within a shallow natural depression measuring 3.65m by 3.40m and up to 0.74m deep. The layer itself presumably was the result of the erosion of material from upslope to the north accumulating within the hollow. An assemblage of Early Neolithic struck flint was recovered from this deposit.

The layer was truncated by two pits of similar size which both contained relatively sterile fills. Pit [681] was sub-circular in plan with sloping edges and a concave base, measuring 1.22m by 1.10m and 0.30m deep. Two sherds of pottery dated to the Early Neolithic period were recovered from this pit. Pit [408], oval in plan with vertical to sloping sides and a flat base, measured 2.0m by 1.10m and up to 0.31m deep. An assemblage of fourteen Early Neolithic flints was recovered from this pit; this material appeared to be debris from a single knapping episode and included some refittable pieces (see Bishop, Chapter 3.2). A similar sub-circular pit [773] located to the north measured 1.10m by 0.86m and was 0.36m deep with steeply sloping sides and a flat base. Early Neolithic pottery and five Neolithic to Bronze Age struck flints were recovered from this pit. A short distance to the north of tree-throw hollow [735] was a sub-circular feature [804], which measured 1.66m by 1.10m and 0.43m deep. This had steeply sloping edges and a fairly flat base with a circular depression in the centre. Its sandy silt fill [803] contained burnt flint and an assemblage of eleven struck flints of Early Neolithic date was recovered along with a sherd of Early Neolithic pottery. A single small sherd of Middle Iron Age pottery is considered to be intrusive. The profile of the feature suggests that it may represent a robbed-out post pit, with the remains of the post pipe visible in the base of the feature.

Also in the near vicinity of tree-throw hollows [640] and [735] was a sub-circular feature [690] which had steeply sloping edges and a fairly flat base and measured 0.85m by 0.70m and was 0.18m deep. Its single fill [689] comprised loosely compacted dark greyish black sand with abundant inclusions (20%) of charcoal and ash, very occasional flint pebbles, burnt flint, and burnt animal bone. There was patchy evidence of *in-situ* burning at the base of the cut, which may imply that its original function was a hearth that had later been dug over to dispose of the burnt waste. Fifteen fragments of Early

Neolithic pot and some struck flint were recovered from the pit and a fragment of charcoal submitted for AMS dating returned a 2-sigma calibrated date of 3500–3100 BC (Waikato-22914, see appendix 1). This firmly places this material in the Early to Mid Neolithic, but suggests that it is a little later than the Group 3.1 artefact-rich tree-throws located to the south-west.

Approximately 7m to the west of [690] was an irregular ovoid feature [697] (not illustrated) with steeply sloping edges and a fairly flat base which measured 1.04m by 0.37m and 0.24m deep. Its fill comprised yellowish brown sand, becoming darker with depth, with frequent grey ash, charcoal flecking and fragments, and occasional burnt daub. As with [690] there was also evidence of patches of *in-situ* burning at the base of the cut. The similarity between these two features suggests that this was also a hearth and they are likely to have been of similar date.

Some distance to the east, located towards the eastern edge of Area B, were two very similar small *in-situ* burnt layers situated approximately 0.60m apart. Layer [728], which comprised sand with abundant ash, charcoal flecking and fragments, occasional flint pebbles and struck flint, extended over a sub-circular area measuring 0.94m by 0.58m and 100mm thick. The only datable cultural material recovered from this deposit was a single flint blade of Early Neolithic date. Layer [729], which also comprised sand with abundant ash, charcoal flecking and fragments, occasional burnt daub and flint pebbles, measured 1.10m by 0.95m by 60mm thick. These two features are interpreted as representing areas of *in-situ* burning, probably from small hearths or campfires, later sealed by colluvium.

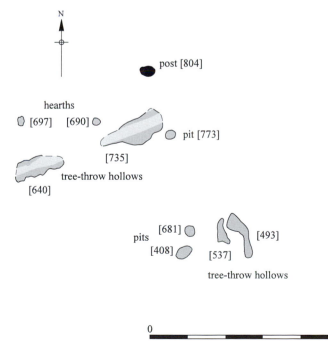

Fig. 19   Phase 3, Group 3.3, Early Neolithic features, Area B (scale 1:400)

Group 3.4 Features in the south-western corner of Area B

In the south-western corner of Area B, a deposit of burnt material [435] lay within the partially infilled palaeochannel [343], described in Chapter 2.1 (Fig. 20). This comprised black sandy silt with very frequent charcoal fragments, identified as oak (*Quercus* sp.), up to 0.10m thick and was recorded across a sub-circular area that measured 0.80m in diameter. The ground surrounding the deposit was scorched, indicating that burning had taken place *in situ* and that this was not dumped from elsewhere, and it appears to represent a hearth or campfire, perhaps positioned within the hollow of the partially infilled palaeochannel to shelter it from the wind. Although no finds were recovered from this feature, it has been phased with the Early Neolithic activity as it was situated within the vicinity of a cluster of features from this period and due to its similarity with the two burnt layers [728] and [729] described in Group 3.3 above. A later ditch [369], which truncated the northern edge of this deposit (see Fig. 39), produced an assemblage of twenty struck flints of Early Neolithic date from its fill [368], comprising flakes, blades and cores, along with a sherd of Early Neolithic pottery.

To the north of hearth [435] was a sub-rectangular pit [418], with near vertical edges and a concave base that measured 2.13m by 1.08m and was up to 0.36m deep. Its single fill [417] produced an assemblage of 48 struck flints comprising mostly small flakes and fragmented pieces, but including a number of small blades and blade-like flakes, likely to be of Early Neolithic date. There were some very similar pieces amongst this material, but no refitting was evident

and certainly a number of different nodules were represented. The struck flint was in good condition and a few pieces were possibly utilized. A possible small tree-throw [389], located to the north-west of pit [418], produced eight struck flints of Early Neolithic date. To the north, a small circular feature [374] produced no artefactual material, but its infill was very similar in composition to the fill of tree-throw [389] suggesting they may have been contemporary. In the vicinity was a small sub-circular feature [358] and in profile this was inclined upon an axis to the east, with the eastern edge steeply sloping and the western undercut, indicating that it may have held a large inclined stake. Its single fill [357] produced an assemblage of nine Neolithic to Early Bronze Age flints.

Located adjacent to the southern limit of excavation was a pair of small irregular features [345] and [347], 1.0m apart, interpreted as tree-throws. Two flint flakes of Early Neolithic date were recovered from [347] and the similarity in fills between both features indicates that they were contemporary.

Group 3.5 Colluvial deposits

Deposits of hill wash material were encountered in patches across Areas B, C and D (not illustrated). These colluvial deposits are likely to have developed and accumulated over extended periods of time. Some layers produced no finds, others contained material dating from the Early Neolithic through to Post-Medieval periods, suggesting that erosion was occurring, if sporadically, from the Early Neolithic onwards. Such processes were observed during the present investigations when the site had been stripped of topsoil and sub-soil.

Early Neolithic material recovered from these deposits comprised a few sherds of body fragments from undecorated bowls along with struck flint and burnt flint. Most notable were a group of deposits located in the south-western corner of Area B. All these layers were partially excavated by hand and then completely removed using a mechanical excavator. The earliest observed, although not fully exposed, was a sandy, clayey silt layer [338]. Overlying this was an extensive sandy silt colluvial layer, recorded as [329] to the west and [337] to the east, containing pottery, burnt and struck flint, and flecks of charcoal. This was overlain by a 0.30m thick silty sand deposit [328], located within a shallow depression, from which six struck flints, including flakes and blades, were recovered all of which were dated to the Early Neolithic period, along with ceramic building material dating from the Medieval or Post-Medieval period. Pottery retrieved from [329] was dated to the Early Neolithic period and this deposit also produced two worked flint flakes, including one Levallois flake, dated to the Neolithic or Bronze Age. The eastern part, deposit [337], contained a larger assemblage of Early Neolithic flints, which appeared to represent the disturbed remains of a knapping episode.

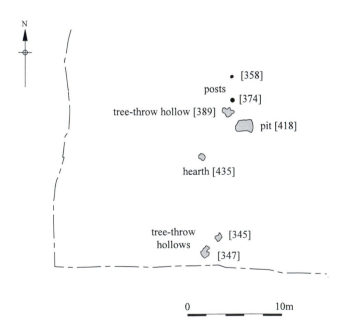

N

posts

• [358]

• [374]

tree-throw hollow [389]

pit [418]

hearth [435]

tree-throw hollows

[345]

[347]

0   10m

Fig. 20   Phase 3, Group 3.4, Early Neolithic features, Area B (scale 1:400)

The cultural material in these layers appears to have been brought down the hill via colluvial action from the area of prehistoric features and flintwork scatter to the north.

A layer of colluvium [1177] was observed extending across the whole of Area D, and this produced a single Early Neolithic blade and an Early Bronze Age barbed and tanged arrowhead (see Fig. 33.4, Fig. 67), along with Roman pottery.

3.2 Early Neolithic Flintwork

Barry Bishop

Worked flint of probable Early Neolithic date forms the largest component of the struck material recovered from Laurel Farm. The most notable assemblage came from the conjoined artefact-rich tree-throws but Early Neolithic struck flint was present in many of the stratified contexts as well as being prolific amongst the material recovered during the fieldwalking project and from topsoil deposits removed during machining. A few stratified features are likely to be contemporary with the flintwork that was found within them, but it is also probable that much of this had been residually deposited into later features and therefore cannot be reliably used to date the features.

It should be noted that much of the struck flint from the remaining features and the unstratified contexts could only be dated very approximately, using technological criteria, to the Mesolithic or Early Neolithic periods. However, a number of chronologically diagnostic implements of Early Neolithic date, such as leaf-shaped arrowheads, laurel leaves and flakes struck from polished implements are present, and conversely there is a complete absence of diagnostic Mesolithic flintwork. This suggests that at least the bulk of this does belong to the Early Neolithic and that no, or only limited, Mesolithic occupation is indicated.

Assemblage from the artefact-rich tree-throw hollows

Assemblage size and composition

The tree-throw features [746] and [787] produced 3,994 pieces of struck flint and almost 6kg of unworked burnt flint fragments. The assemblage is typical of Early Neolithic industries and such a date is confirmed by both the associated pottery and the radiocarbon determinations taken from material within the feature. Fieldwalking was not undertaken in this part of the site but as only three struck flints were recovered from topsoil deposits in the vicinity of the hollows it would appear that they had escaped the worst excesses of ploughing and the assemblage remains reasonably intact.

Context	Decortication flake	Rejuvenation flake	Mis-struck flake	Chips (<20mm)	Flake	Flake fragment	Prismatic blade	Non-prismatic blade	Blade-like flake	Core	Conchoidal chunk	Retouched	Polished flake	No. Burnt struck	Total struck	Hammerstone	Burnt stone (no.)	Burnt stone (wt g)
All																		
no.	236	72	56	833	441	1430	92	286	245	42	155	100	6	1263	3994	5	512	5731
%	5.9	1.8	1.4	20.9	11	35.8	2.3	7.2	6.1	1.1	3.9	2.5	0.2	31.6	100.1			
Excluding Samples																		
no.	224	71	56	283	398	763	85	272	240	42	151	100	6	674	2691	5	390	5201
%	8.3	2.6	2.1	10.5	14.8	28.4	3.2	10.1	8.9	1.6	5.6	3.7	0.2	25	100			
Over 20mm																		
no.	236	72	56	-	441	667	92	286	245	42	155	100	6	-	2398	5		
%	9.8	3.0	2.3	-	18.4	27.8	3.8	11.9	10.2	1.8	6.5	4.2	0.3	-	100			

Table 4   Composition of the lithic assemblage from the Early Neolithic tree-throw hollows

Of the 3,994 pieces of struck flint recovered from the hollows, 833 consist of chips, here defined as flakes less than 20mm in maximum dimension, and a further 667 pieces are unclassifiable flake fragments that also measure less than 20mm. These diminutive pieces comprise almost 40% of the total assemblage. Taken together, these are referred to below as micro-debitage. The arbitrary figure of 20mm was chosen as an analytical dividing point for the micro-debitage as it was thought that the larger and more technologically distinctive pieces are more likely to reflect how lithic materials were perceived and used at the site (cf. Brown 1991).

The bulk of the micro-debitage was recovered from the samples taken from layer [744] and hollow [787], which were sieved using a 2mm mesh. As a consequence, the micro-debitage is dominated by very small pieces that are often less than 5mm in size and would be unlikely to have been recovered by hand. As the samples were not systematically taken, none were taken from hollow [746] for example, the material from these have been excluded from some of the comparative analyses recorded below. Table 4 therefore shows: the complete assemblage from the hollows; the assemblage excluding the material recovered from the samples; and the assemblage excluding pieces measuring less than 20mm in size. In addition to the micro-debitage, the samples contained copious charcoal fragments, small unworked burnt flint fragments and pieces of burnt clay.

Micro-debitage is generated as 'shatter' during knapping and from the fine trimming of cores and retouched pieces. The quantities recorded here certainly indicate that the full spectrum of knapping waste is present but are arguably fewer than might be expected if knapping had occurred *in situ* and directly into the hollows.

The hollows contain material from all stages in the reduction sequence; from primary core working debris to discarded used tools. It is the product of a single technological tradition, characterised by the manufacture of flakes of a variable shape and size but including a high proportion of blades and narrow flakes. The retouched component is varied and of similar proportions to what may be expected from generalised settlement type activities. It has what is often described as a 'domestic' character, in that in addition to flint reduction, a wide range of tools, including light and heavy-duty types, were manufactured, used and discarded together.

Raw materials

The struck assemblage was manufactured from a wide range of raw materials although most commonly used was a translucent black flint containing abundant semi-opaque grey mottling and crystalline and cherty inclusions. Cortex varies from being relatively thick and unweathered to thin and abraded, and many pre-flaking thermal surfaces are present, with thermal flaws continuing throughout the flint. The raw materials used appear to comprise complete nodules as well as relatively large but thermally fractured nodular chunks.

Smaller rolled flint and cherty pebbles were also occasionally used.

Variations in the raw materials suggest that while some could have been easily obtained at or close to the site, sources from further afield may also have been used. The unweathered nodules may have been gathered from deposits located close to the parent chalk, such as from exposures within incised river valleys (see Chapter 2.2). The thermally shattered pieces are likely to have come from derived, glacial till deposits, possibly including those present at the site, although no similar materials were noted during the excavation, and these too may have been brought in from elsewhere. The natural deposits at the site did, however, contain some rolled pebbles similar to those occasionally used for flintworking and these may have been obtained at or close to the site.

Condition

The condition of the assemblage is variable in terms of degrees of chipping, breakage and burning, and this variability is maintained throughout the fills of the hollows. Most pieces are in a sharp condition but significant quantities show some weathering and have slightly abraded or chipped edges. There is also a high degree of breakage amongst the assemblage with around a third of the flakes being broken to some degree. Around a quarter of the struck pieces show evidence of having been exposed to heat, this having occurred after manufacture but prior to incorporation into the hollows.

The variable condition of the struck flint would suggest that it had experienced a complex history between manufacture and final deposition. It would be consistent with limited trampling and sporadic burning, suggesting an interval between it being manufactured and it entering the hollow, but there were no indications that it had been exposed for any great length of time. Instead, it is more consistent with the material having been accumulated elsewhere and subsequently dumped into the hollows after a short period. Many pieces had become slightly discoloured to a brownish colour, possibly through mineral staining or from the high humic conditions noted within the hollow.

Technology and typology

Flakes and blades

Flakes vary in shape and size considerably. There is some evidence that systematic blade production was undertaken due to the presence of prismatic blades with parallel dorsal scars and lateral margins which, excluding the micro-debitage, contribute 3.8% of the overall assemblage. Non-prismatic blades contribute a more substantial 11.9% and blade-like flakes a further 10.2%. There is also evidence for the deliberate manufacture of wider and thicker flakes. This probably reflects the varying needs and goals of the flint knappers and the wide range of tools required. Blades were reserved for certain implements, including the serrates and some of the edge modified flakes, piercers and even arrowheads, but thicker and more sturdy flakes were needed for other implements types, such as the scrapers and other, heavier duty, tools.

Metrical analyses

In order to provide a more complete impression of the flakes and blades, and to allow comparisons between the material from the three main contextual units of the hollow and with contemporary assemblages from other sites, metrical and technological analyses were conducted on a sample of 317 complete and unretouched flakes and blades measuring 15mm or more in length. This entailed taking a randomly selected sub-sample of 150 flakes from Spit 2, layer [744], and all of the complete unretouched flakes and blades from hollows [746] (i.e. Spits 3–5) and [787] (i.e. Spits 6–7), which amounted to 61 and 106 pieces, respectively.

Such approaches have inherent biases as pieces selected for retouch are excluded, although this is mitigated to some extent as it would appear that a wide range of flake shapes and sizes were considered suitable for retouch. More importantly, thinner and narrower pieces are likely to be under-represented as these are more prone to breakage; it has been noted that the assemblage was probably moved on at least one occasion prior to deposition, and some breakage may also have occurred during the excavation process. Conversely, there will be a bias towards primary and decortication flakes, as these tend to be thicker and therefore less likely to break. A number of siret flakes are also included as these are not, strictly speaking, broken but split along natural fracture lines.

Flake size

The sample of complete flakes and blades from the three main contextual units of the hollows were measured according to Saville (1980), and their average size in mm given in Table 5.

Table 5 shows that flakes tend to be relatively small although there is significant variation in size. The flakes from Spit 2, layer [744], and hollow [787] are very similar in size with no meaningful differences apparent. Those from hollow [746] are noticeably larger although it is difficult to ascertain whether this is due to a real technological difference between the material from the three contextual units, or merely a result of statistical abnormalities due to its smaller sample size. It should be borne in mind that the actual shape of these flakes closely matched those from the other contexts in the hollow and a difference in the technological strategies employed (in the sense of Pitts 1978, or Pitts and Jacobi 1979) is unlikely to be a causal factor in explaining the size differences. Some difference may be due to variations in the flake typologies; there are higher proportions of decortication flakes, which tend to be larger, in hollow [746] but, conversely, this feature also produced higher proportions of blades, which tend to be smaller and are certainly thinner. The main cause of the high average flake sizes in this hollow is the near absence of flakes measuring less than 25mm in maximum dimension, although why there are so few remains unclear.

Flake shape

Following the standard analytical methodology of Pitts (1978), the shape distribution of all measured unmodified complete flakes was established by dividing their breadths by lengths, and these were compared to a sample of dated assemblages given by Pitts (1978, 194) (Table 6).

Table 6 confirms the assemblage from the hollows is principally a blade/narrow flake based industry although this is far from exclusive and there is a wide variability in the shape of flakes. This is partly due to the whole knapping sequence being present but also suggests that a range of flake types were needed.

Considerations of the three main contextual units of the assemblage show that Spit 2, layer [744], has relatively fewer blades and flakes but a higher proportions of broad flakes than the hollows. Hollow [746] contained the highest proportions of blades as well as the highest proportions of relatively larger flakes than the other hollow and the layer although again, it is uncertain what this may imply.

	No.	Ave. Length	Ave. Breadth	Ave. Width	Ave. L/B	Ave. B/L
All	317	39.5	27.4	6.9	1.6	0.7
All SD	-	+/-18.2	+/-14.0	+/-4.7	+/-0.7	+/-0.3
Layer [744] Spit 2	150	36.9	26.7	6.9	1.5	0.8
Hollow [746] (Spits 3–5)	61	50.6	33.0	8.1	1.7	0.7
Hollow [787] (Spits 6–7)	106	36.7	25.1	6.4	1.7	0.7

Table 5   Shape and size of the flakes from the Early Neolithic tree-throw hollows

	Very narrow blades	Narrow blades	Blades	Narrow flakes	Flakes	Broad flakes
Pitts 1978, 194						
B/L	<0.2	0.21-0.4	0.41-0.6	0.61-0.8	0.81-1.0	1.0+
Pitts: E. Meso	2	43	27	13	6.5	9
Pitts: L. Meso	0.5	15.5	30.5	22	14.5	17
Pitts: E. Neo	0	11	33	27.5	14.5	13
Pitts: L. Neo	0	4	21.5	29	20	25.5
Pitts: Chalcolithic	0	2.5	15	24	24	35
Pitts: Bronze Age	0	3.5	14.5	23	23	35.5
TSA All %	0	11.4	24.9	31.6	18.9	13.2
TSA Layer [744] (Spit 2) %	0	8.7	20.7	34.0	17.3	19.3
TSA Hollow [746] (Spits 3–5) %	0	13.1	37.7	21.3	19.7	8.2
TSA Hollow [787] (Spits 6–7) %	0	14.1	23.6	34.0	18.9	9.4
Harford Park and Ride E. Neo %	0	2.2	17.6	25.3	30.8	24.2
Kilverstone E. Neo %	1	17	32	23	11	16

Table 6   Flake shape ratios for flakes from the tree-throw hollows, following Pitts (1978) and shown in comparison to data from Kilverstone and Harford Park and Ride

The assemblage from the hollows does compare favourably to the values for the aggregated Early Neolithic assemblages compiled by Pitts, although there are fewer blades and more narrow and normal flakes, suggesting that blade production, although important, was not such a paramount concern as seen elsewhere. It also compares favourably to other Early Neolithic sites in the region where comparable data exists but is not included in Pitts' survey, such as Kilverstone, near Thetford (Beadsmoore 2006, table 10). Again the Laurel Farm material has fewer narrower flakes and blades and higher proportions of broader flakes. As the occupation recorded at Kilverstone dates to slightly later than the hollows at Laurel Farm – it has radiocarbon dates clustering around the middle of the fourth millennium cal BC and is dominated by Mildenhall ware pottery – the metrical data does not in this case support the widely held view that blade manufacture declined during the Early Neolithic. The Laurel Farm assemblage differs markedly from the comparably dated assemblage recorded at the Harford Park and Ride site, near Caistor St Edmund, whose flake shapes are more akin to the values given by Pitts for the Bronze Age. This can be attributed to the prevalence of axe manufacturing at Harford Park and Ride, as this generates large quantities of large and broad flakes (Bishop forthcoming b).

Technological analyses

Striking platform types and widths

Table 7 shows that the majority of flakes from the hollows (79.2%) had either plain or simple edge-trimmed striking platforms with a small minority having more complex types, such as dihedral or facetted forms that are associated with greater core preparation. Cortical striking platforms are also rare, indicating that cores were nearly always prepared to some degree prior to flake production.

A similar pattern is evident from the individual assemblages from the two hollows and the overlying layer, although a few minor variations are apparent. Hollow [746] has perhaps the greatest variation, containing fewer flakes with cortical striking platforms, more with dihedral but none with facetted striking platforms, than seen in the other hollow or the overlying layer. The striking platform widths were also greater in hollow [746], which probably relates to the fact that it also contained proportionally larger flakes.

Notable are the very similar values recorded for shattered striking platforms. These occur most commonly when the blow is aimed very close to the edge of the striking platform in an attempt to produce large but thin flakes. Often the point of percussion is so close to the platform's edge that it disintegrates, although this

Striking Platform Type	Plain	Cortical	Dihedral	Facetted	Slight trimming	Fully trimmed	Shattered	Ave. SP width
All %	25.9	6.6	4.1	3.5	24.0	29.3	6.6	3.5
Layer [744] %	28.0	7.3	4.0	4.7	18.7	30.7	6.7	3.6
Hollow [746] %	24.6	4.9	6.6	0.0	27.9	29.5	6.6	4.2
Hollow [787] %	23.6	6.6	2.8	3.8	29.3	27.4	6.6	3.2

Table 7   Striking platform types and widths for flakes from the Early Neolithic tree-throw hollows

rarely affects the effectiveness of the flake and should not be regarded as necessarily indicating a failed strike. Conversely, it usually indicates an effective control over the blow and is an indication of skilled flake production. As a technological indicator, the similar proportions of flakes with shattered platforms indicate homogeneity in the reduction strategies employed in the three sub-assemblages.

Bulbs of percussion

Table 8 shows that just under half of the flakes have diffuse bulbs of percussion, slightly more than those with pronounced examples, although this relationship is inverted in the case of hollow [746]. The somewhat surprisingly high number of flakes with pronounced bulbs suggests that hard hammer reduction was routinely practiced, at least during the decorticating and shaping of cores, but probably also during the manufacture of useable flakes. This would be perfectly adequate when thick sturdy flakes were required, such as for turning into scrapers. Discrete hemispherical bulbs were mostly encountered in the blades and, considering these variations together, suggest that a number of different approaches were taken to flint reduction, depending on whether sturdy flakes, thinner flakes or blades were required.

Noticeable differences are the much lower proportions of flakes with diffuse bulbs of percussion in hollow [746]. This could indicate less controlled or skilful

knapping, although there were fairly similar numbers of hemispherical bulbs of percussion in both hollows. As these tend to occur during soft-hammer blade production, they would indicate that similar technological strategies were employed.

Distal termination

Table 9 demonstrates that the majority of flakes had feathered distal terminations, which is indicative of a generally high level of competency involved in the reduction process. The hinged terminations were frequently found on larger flakes removed during earlier stages in the reduction sequence where slightly less control is perhaps evident. The overshot flakes are sometimes considered to represent deliberately applied techniques involving the modification of the shape of a core and is often related to the plunged method of core rejuvenation. Many of these, however, were probably mistakes where the force applied was too hard, causing the fracture plain to move through to the back of the core. The number of stepped platforms reflects the thermal flawing of the raw materials.

The proportions of feathered distal terminations remained constant at just over 70% for both hollows and the layer. Again, the greatest divergences from the hollows were within hollow [746] which, at the expense of hinged distal terminations, had slightly higher numbers of overshot and stepped termination types.

Bulb of Percussion Type	Diffuse	Pronounced	Hemispherical
All %	45.7	36.7	18.6
Layer [744] %	47.3	37.3	15.3
Hollow [746] %	36.1	44.3	19.7
Hollow [787] %	49.1	28.3	22.6

Table 8   Bulb of percussion types for flakes from the Early Neolithic tree-throw hollows

Distal	Feathered	Hinged	Overshot	Stepped
All %	71.0	19.9	4.7	4.4
Layer [744] %	71.3	20.7	4.0	4.0
Hollow [746] %	70.5	16.3	6.6	6.6
Hollow [787] %	70.8	20.8	4.7	3.7

Table 9   Distal termination type for flakes from the Early Neolithic tree-throw hollows

Cores

A total of 42 cores were recovered, representing a relatively low 1.1% of the total assemblage and rising to only 1.8% if the micro-debitage is excluded. There were slightly higher proportions of cores from layer [744] than hollow [787] and no cores at all were recovered from hollow [746]. Conchoidally fractured chunks, many of which probably represent fragments of cores that shattered during reduction, contribute a further 3.9% of the overall assemblage or 6.5% if the micro-debitage is excluded. Nevertheless, the relative paucity of complete cores suggests that, although raw materials were being reduced and worked into tools at the site, many still-serviceable cores may have been taken away for use elsewhere.

The complete cores range from 16g to 186g in weight, averaging at 82g. They were very variably reduced and reflect the variety of different approaches that were taken in order to produce the wide range of flake types. Consequently, the shape of the cores also varied considerably; domed, lenticular, wedge-shaped and globular examples were all recorded, but most were irregularly shaped and it is clear that standardisation in core morphology was not an important concern for the knappers.

Generally, core preparation appears rather perfunctory; no truly prismatic or elaborately prepared cores are present. Instead, they tend to have been reduced rather expediently with only minimal pre-shaping of the raw material and with little evidence for attempts to fashion an 'ideal' core shape that would permit a greater degree of subsequent manipulation. Once flake production had commenced, there is only little evidence for the maintenance of striking platforms. Rejuvenation flakes are present but contribute less than 2% of the overall assemblage. They include both true core-tablets and flakes that remove hinge and step fractures on the cores' faces. Striking-platform edges are frequently

trimmed but this usually only extends to removing the most prominent overhangs, and the striking platforms themselves are rarely modified. The few flakes with facetted or dihedral striking platforms were probably removed from keeled cores. The scar morphology of the cores suggested the routine use of both hard and soft hammer percussion, as this is supported by the technological attributes of the flakes themselves (see above), and this appears related to the types of flake required.

The cores were classified according to the scheme devised by Clark *et al.* (1960) (Table 10). This revealed that the most frequent types are those with multiple striking platforms, with all other types represented but in notably lesser proportions. Many of the unclassifiable cores were single-platform types that were discarded due to shattering at an early stage during reduction.

The majority of cores utilize either conveniently sized angular cobbles (e.g. Fig. 21.1, Fig. 21.2, Fig. 21.3) or larger nodules that had been 'quartered' through flaking (e.g. Fig. 21.4, Fig. 21.5, Fig. 21.6, Fig. 21.7). Around half showed some evidence of having produced blades or narrow flakes, although it appears that as the cores became worked down production frequently reverted to making flakes (e.g. Fig. 21.8, Fig. 21.9, Fig. 21.10). Most of the cores were initiated by removing a single flake and using the scar from this to produce useable flakes and blades (e.g. Fig. 21.1, Fig. 21.3). When this failed, further platforms were often created, usually contiguous to the first and using the old core face as the new platform. As many of the cores started off as what may be regarded as large flakes, they were often relatively thin and these are often centripetally worked (e.g. Fig. 21.4, Fig. 21.6, Fig. 21.7, Fig. 21.9), sometimes involving the use of alternate flaking, or keeling (e.g. Fig. 21.5, Fig. 21.8). Others are more randomly worked, with a few flakes taken off of any suitable surface (e.g. Fig. 21.2). The cores present had usually been worked to exhaustion, suggesting that when a good piece was found it was worked down until

Core type (Clark *et al.* 1960)	All No.	All %	Layer [744] (Spit 2) (no.)	Hollow [787] (Spits 6–7) (no.)	Hollow [746] (Spits 3–5) (no.)
Unclassifiable	8	19.0	5	3	0
A1	2	4.7	1	1	0
A2	6	14.3	5	1	0
B1	1	2.4	1	0	0
B3	1	2.4	1	0	0
C	15	35.7	12	3	0
D	1	2.4	0	1	0
E	6	14.3	3	3	0
Minimal	2	4.8	2	0	0
Total	42	100	30	12	0

Table 10   Typology of cores from the Early Neolithic tree-throw hollows

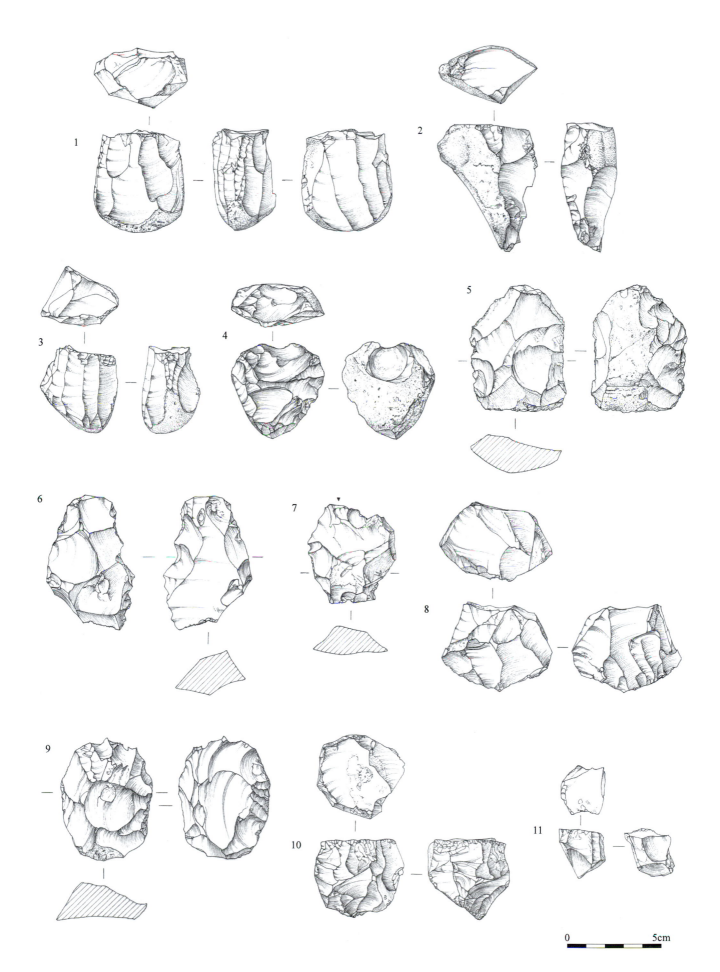

Fig. 21   Early Neolithic cores (scale 1:2)

very small and, even if it shattered, the fragments may have continued to be used (e.g. Fig. 21.11). A few cores have only small flakes removed and these may have been intended as crude denticulated or chopping type core tools, rather than as a means of producing useable flakes (e.g. Fig. 21.6, Fig. 21.7). Some of the cores, particularly the globular shaped examples, have been reused as hammerstones (Fig. 21.10). They complement the five other hammerstones that were recovered, all from layer [744]. Four of these comprise rounded flint cobbles and one was made from quartzite. They varied in weight from 100g to 210g.

The cores from Laurel Farm are broadly comparable with those from other Early Neolithic sites within the region. At Kilverstone and Harford Park and Ride, multi-platformed types were the most common (Beadsmore 2006; Bishop forthcoming b), although at Kilverstone the cores appear to have generally been more extensively reduced prior to discard, possibly reflecting site-specific differences in raw material size, quality or availability. At Broome Heath, single-platformed cores contributed the greatest proportions (Wainwright 1972, 48) and they were also the most common type at Hurst Fen, Mildenhall, but other types were also strongly represented there, particularly two-platformed and keeled types (Clark *et al.* 1960, 216). Nevertheless, similar reduction methods, involving the relatively unsystematic production (at least compared to earlier periods) of a variety of flakes and blades, could be discerned at all of these sites. A similar variety in the degree and the skill to which cores were worked is matched at other contemporary industries, such as at Fordham (Bishop forthcoming a) and the Great Wilbraham enclosure (Edmonds 2006), both in Cambridgeshire, and at Kilverstone. In the latter case it was suggested that these differences may, in part at least, reflect the differing skill levels amongst the knappers (Beadsmore 2006, 70).

Type	No.	% of all Retouched
Axe	1	1
Arrowhead	5	5
Bifacially Worked Flake	3	3
Burin	2	2
Denticulated Flake	1	1
Edge Modified Flakes	42	42
Scraper	13	13
Notched Flake	2	2
Piercer	4	4
Serrate	27	27
Total Retouched Implements	**100**	**100**

Table 11   Quantification of retouched implements from the Early Neolithic tree-throw hollows

Retouched implements

Retouched and heavily edge-worn flakes and blades formed 2.5% of the overall assemblage, which rises to 4.2% if the micro-debitage is excluded (see Table 11). Only the more obvious and heavily edge-worn pieces have been included in this total and it is likely that many more pieces had been utilized but these remain less identifiable. The proportion of retouched implements is comparable, although marginally lower, to that seen at most Early Neolithic settlement sites in the region; 5% was recorded at Kilverstone (Beadsmore 2006, 60), 5–6% at Hurst Fen (Clark *et al.* 1960, 214), 5% at Broome Heath (Wainwright 1972, 66) and 6% at Spong Hill, North Elmham, *c.* 25km north-west of Norwich (Healy 1988, 32: table 14). It is, however, much higher than seen at some 'specialist activity' sites in the region, such as the 1.3% recorded at the axe manufacturing site at Harford Park and Ride (Bishop forthcoming b), the 1.4% recorded at Colney, just west of Norwich (Robins 2004) or the 0.6% present at Fordham, Cambridgeshire (Bishop forthcoming a), the latter both being considered as primary reduction sites where raw materials were initially worked for use elsewhere and which saw little evidence for tool manufacture or use.

The most common retouched types were the simple edge-trimmed and edge-worn flakes and blades, with serrates and scrapers also well represented. In addition, leaf-shaped arrowheads, piercers, notches, a burin and a broken polished flint axe were also present. As well as the axe, a number of flakes are present that had been struck from polished flint implements, probably from axes that had been reflaked or used as a convenient source of raw material. The overall repertoire is typical of Early Neolithic inventories with the only typical implement type absent being the Laurel Leaf point. These are, however, generally relatively rare in Early Neolithic assemblages and an example was recovered at Laurel Farm, from topsoil deposits adjacent to the south-western limit of excavation, in the vicinity of Group 3.4 features. There are also no formally retouched knives present, although many of the edge trimmed flakes may have been used for cutting tasks.

The axe

A polished flint axe was found near the upper surface of the artefact-rich tree-throw hollows, placed in an upright position with its cutting edge facing upwards (see Fig. 17). Unfortunately, it went missing shortly after it had been excavated and is no longer available for examination. Notes taken at the time of excavations indicate that it was incomplete with only approximately half of its cutting end present. It was made of a fine-grained opaque and very slightly mottled light grey flint and the surviving part had fine all-over polish. Its upright position at the top of the fill of the hollows is unlikely to have occurred through chance and it is possible that it was deliberately placed in what was by then a largely infilled hollow, perhaps indicating a closing deposit or some other ceremonial practice.

In addition to the axe, six pieces from polished implements were also recovered from the hollows, these consist of four deliberately struck flakes, one having been burnt after being flaked, and two thermal spalls that had 'popped' off either a polished implement or flakes struck from one. The flakes were most probably struck from polished axes. They were all made from such similar flint that they could easily have come from the same implement, although as none of the flakes refitted, this cannot be confirmed and the flakes and fragments would only form a small proportion of the material created by the reduction of a single implement. They had not been removed from the axe placed at the top of the deposits as this had not been reflaked, but could, conceivably, have come from the reduction of its missing base. The distribution of the polished flakes within the feature was apparently not random, the three burnt pieces were found close together in Spit 7 and two of the flakes were also found close together in Spit 2. The remaining piece was found at some distance to these in Spit 1. Five further flakes struck from polished flint implements were recovered from other contexts at Laurel Farm, including in pit [1124], of probable Early Neolithic date, and from unstratified contexts in the south-western corner of the main excavation area just to the east of the Group 3.4 features, towards the centre of the main excavation area, and from Trench 85 which was located in the south-eastern quadrant of the development site to the north of Area D.

The flint used for all of the polished flakes was similar to that used for the axe. It is comparable to the porcelain-like 'Lincolnshire' flint, and similar types of flint were commonly utilized for axe manufacture in the region during the Neolithic period (Healy 1988, 33). However,

comparable opaque grey flint nodules are found within the glacial tills of the region and were used for making axes at Harford Park and Ride, *c.* 8km upstream in the Yare Valley (Bishop forthcoming b). Although a few possible biface thinning flakes were found within the hollow and in other contexts at Laurel Farm, there was no evidence to suggest that axes had been manufactured here in any quantity.

Arrowheads

Five certain arrowheads were identified; these are all relatively small and narrow (all Green (1980) types 3B or 3C). Two have invasive thinning retouch (Fig. 22.1, Fig. 22.2) and three have retouch that is mainly confined to the margins of the flake (e.g. Fig. 22.3 and Fig. 22.4).

A few other flakes are also leaf-shaped with marginal retouch and, although recorded here as edge-trimmed flakes or piercers, could conceivably also have been used as arrowheads (e.g. Fig. 22.5, Fig. 22.6). They are similar to the marginally retouched arrowheads recorded by Clark at Hurst Fen (Clark *et al.* 1960). Such identification relies purely on the shape of the blank, however, as the retouch is minimal, non-invasive and indistinguishable from other edge trimmed flakes that would have been unsuitable as projectile points.

The arrowheads were recovered from two locations within the hollows; three were found close together in hollow [787] and the other two from adjacent squares in hollow [746]. There is little evidence for the actual manufacture of arrowheads at the site; a few bifacially retouched flakes may have represented abandoned arrowhead blanks but few pressure-thinning flakes were identified amongst the flakes, even the smaller ones recovered from the samples.

Bifacially worked flakes

Three flakes are present that have bifacial working along parts of their edges but which cannot be easily placed within standard tool typologies. All are made on thick flakes, one has a steeply and partially bifacially retouched distal end that appeared to have removed a substantial part of the flake, along with inverse retouch around its bulbar end (Fig. 23.1). Another consisted of a distal flake fragment that has been bifacially worked along the break (Fig. 23.2). The third consisted of a flake that has been bifacially trimmed around one of its edges, forming a rectangular wedge-shaped tool (Fig. 23.3). It is uncertain what these implements may represent; they could have been used as wedges or may even represent abandoned attempts at manufacturing arrowheads.

Burins

Two burins were recovered. These implements are most commonly associated with Mesolithic or earlier industries but continued to be made in small numbers into the Neolithic, as amply demonstrated by an example made on a polished flake from Hurst Fen (Clark *et al.* 1960, 224). One of the examples here was made on a thin, thermally

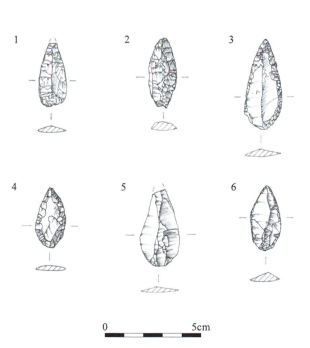

0   5cm

Fig. 22   Early Neolithic leaf-shaped arrowheads and flakes (scale 1:2)

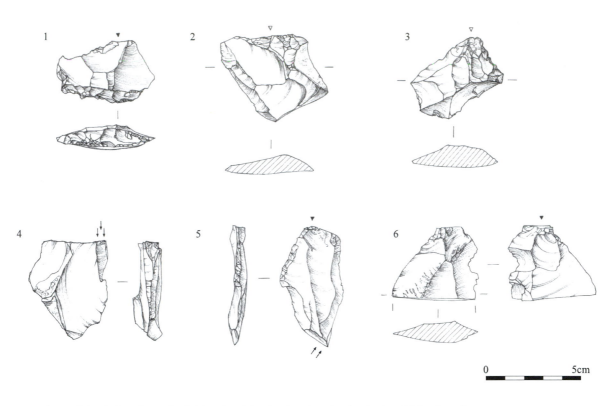

Fig. 23   Early Neolithic bifacially worked flakes (1–3), burins (4–5) and a denticulate (6) (scale 1:2)

shattered piece of flint that had been flaked on one side and has had several burin spalls removed along one of its edges (Fig. 23.4). It appears to have been re-sharpened and its working edge is worn. The other was made by removing one or two burin spalls longitudinally from the hinged distal end of a flake (Fig. 23.5). Its right lateral margin had been crudely blunted near its bulbar end, which may have been done to aid holding or hafting of the implement.

Denticulate

The only tool that may be considered as a denticulated implement is a thick bulbar flake fragment with crude deep notching along its right ventral side (Fig. 23.6).

Edge-modified flakes and blades

The simple edge-modified implements are the most numerous retouched category with 42 examples identified. Nevertheless, they represent a disparate group and include flakes and blades of variable shapes and sizes that can only associated by the presence of light retouch along their edges (see Fig. 24). In some cases, the modification clearly consists of very fine retouching, effectively lightly blunting the piece. With some, however, it is not clear whether the modification was deliberately executed or consists of micro-chipping formed through utilizing the flake (e.g. Tringham *et al.* 1974).

The extent of modification is variable although it nearly always focuses on the longer, lateral, edges of the flakes. It ranges from being limited to short lengths of the edge to encompassing most of the perimeter of the flake, and from being straight, convex or concave to sinuous.

It appears that retouching may have arisen from

disparate needs. In some cases the flakes may have been used for cutting, with parts of the edges deliberately blunted to aid handling. In others, it is likely that the retouch formed a cutting edge and many have cortex along the opposite edge, which could also have facilitated handling. Some of the implements could pass for minimally worked versions of formal tool types, such as lightly retouched scrapers. Others may have represented formal tools that were abandoned early in the manufacturing process, whilst some may represent worn-down serrates. They were probably used in a variety of ways and on many different materials but, despite the great variability in the size and shape of the blanks and in the nature of the modification, most were likely to have been used as cutting, sawing or scraping tools. Two leaf-shaped examples may represent minimally modified arrowheads (see Fig. 22.5, Fig. 22.6).

Scrapers

Thirteen examples of scrapers were recovered. These all consist of convex end-scrapers although their morphology and the nature of their retouch are variable. They also vary in size and include large sturdy flakes (Fig. 25.1, Fig. 25.2) and in one case, a reused core fragment (Fig. 25.3), although most were made using relatively thin flakes (Fig. 25.4), many of which are also narrow (e.g. Fig. 25.5, Fig. 25.6, Fig. 25.7, Fig. 25.8). Several of the scrapers survive only as burnt fragments, although none of these refit and, again, demonstrate that only a proportion of the waste was deposited in the tree-throw hollows.

Retouch on the scrapers varies from sporadic and

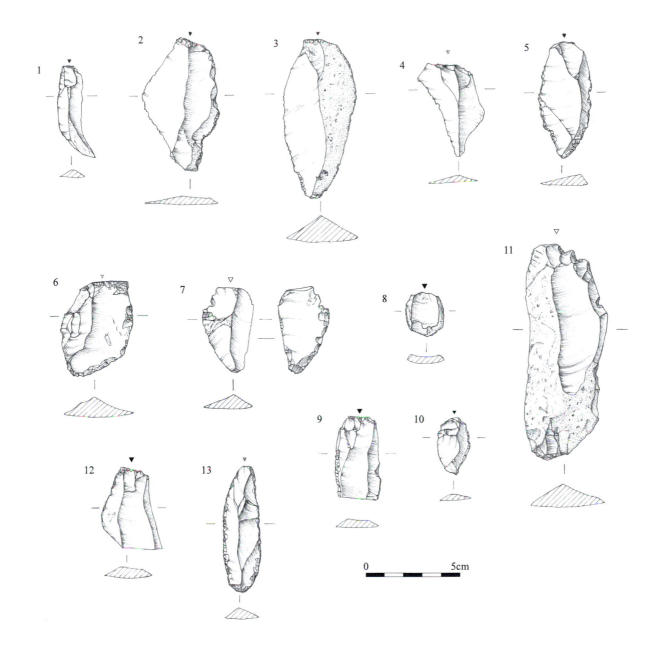

Fig. 24   Early Neolithic edge-modified flakes and blades (scale 1:2)

uneven to very fine, and from very steep to relatively shallow. Several show evidence of resharpening and a few have slightly smoothed working edges. One of the larger scrapers has its bulbar end heavily modified with bifacial retouch, which may have been intended as a tang to aid hafting (Fig. 25.2).

Notched flakes

Two notches were identified, both made on large flakes. One has a small notch cut into its ventral side (Fig. 26.1). The other has two notches forming a blunt spur-like point, one made by heavy retouch and the other by minimally modifying an earlier flake scar (Fig. 26.2). Interestingly, this also has an area of battering, caused by the flake being repeatedly hammered, opposite the lower notch.

Piercers

Four piercers were identified, consisting of two very different types. The first, represented by a single example, was made on either a chunk or a thick flake, which had been extensively, if somewhat crudely, flaked into a heavy-duty piercer with a thick, blunt tip (Fig. 26.3). The other three all consisted of fine, systematically produced blades that had competent but minimal retouch accentuating convergent ends. One had been worked on its distal end (Fig. 26.4) and two had modified bulbar ends (Fig. 26.5, Fig. 26.6). The latter two had bi-directional retouch, suggesting they were used as awls, and all three have further retouch blunting their lateral edges, presumably to aid handling.

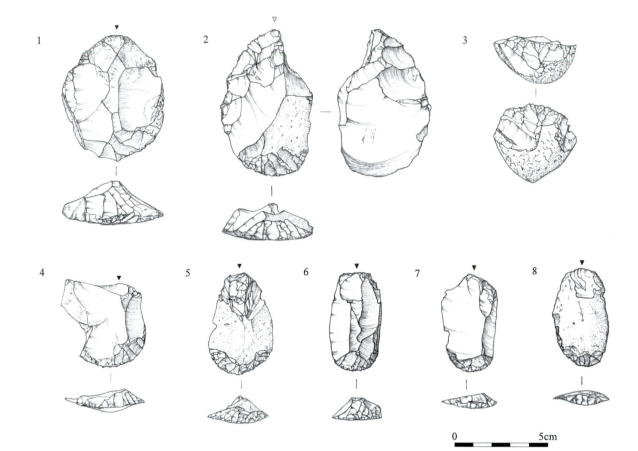

Fig. 25   Early Neolithic scrapers (scale 1:2)

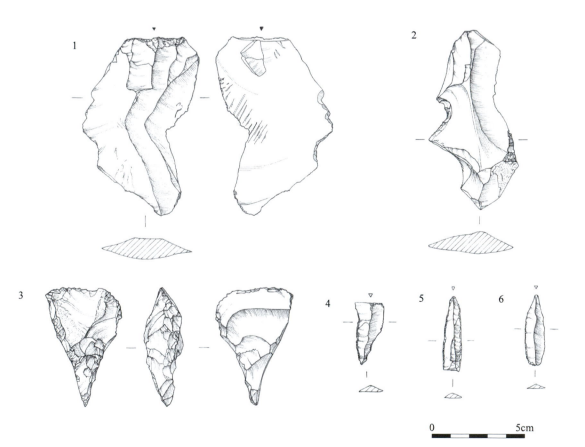

Fig. 26   Early Neolithic notched flakes (1–2) and piercers (3–6)

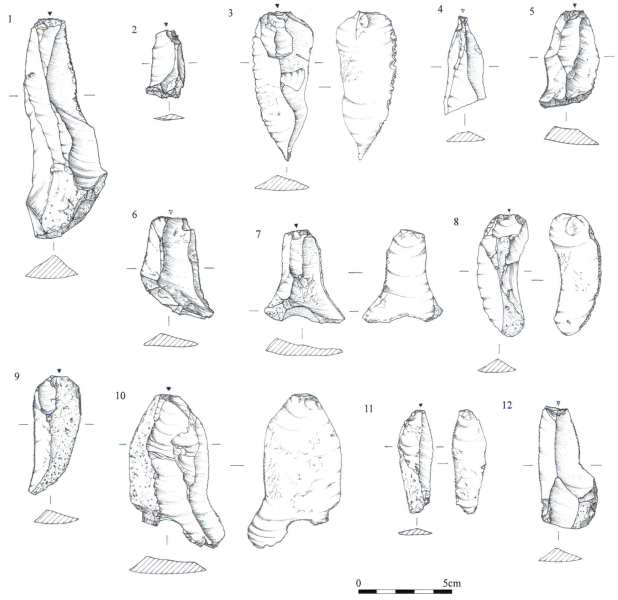

Fig. 27   Early Neolithic serrates (scale 1:2)

Serrates

Twenty-seven serrated flakes and blades were identified. As with the scrapers and edge-modified implements, these also vary considerably in size, shape and in the degree that they were modified. The majority, however, were made on blades with a further quarter on blade-like flakes, the rest either using flakes or are unclassifiable due to fragmentation. The sizes of the blanks varied considerably; the largest blank measured 116mm long (Fig. 27.1) with the smallest complete example being only 34mm long (Fig. 27.2).

The serrations vary in their execution, from clearly defined and regularly spaced to rather splintered and somewhat irregularly notched and unevenly spaced. Some were very fine and others had deep and pronounced serrations. The number of serrations ranges from six (Fig. 27.3) to sixteen per cm (Fig. 27.4, Fig. 27.5). They tend to be rather sporadically undertaken, often only part of

edge of the flake has been modified and, in many cases, unmodified gaps remain along the serrated edge.

The majority exhibit only minor wear along the serrations with only one example showing more extensive wear, suggesting that they had been used over a variety of durations but that most had been discarded before the end of their useful life had been reached. Only three show any evidence of 'sickle gloss', the distinctive bright polishing caused by processing silica-rich plants, but in all three cases this is light and does not extend beyond the teeth. Most had been serrated along only one side, with a slight preference for the right margins to be used, and only two had been serrated along both margins.

Probably the most important factor determining the location of serrations is the morphology of the blanks. In many cases the blanks have one relatively sharp lateral margin that was serrated, with the opposed margin being either naturally blunt (e.g. Fig. 27.1, Fig. 27.6, Fig. 27.7) or blunted through retouching (e.g. Fig. 27.2, Fig. 27.5, Fig. 27.8). These are often wedge-shaped, so providing a steep, and therefore blunt, opposed margin and many have fortuitous dorsal scars that would enable the implement to be held firmly, safely and comfortably. Just over half retain some cortex and of these, two-thirds have cortex on the opposed margin, suggesting they may have been hand held (e.g. Fig. 27.9, Fig. 27.10, Fig. 27.11). The others have cortical distal ends, which often splay out slightly, forming the widest part of the flake, which may also have aided handling (e.g. Fig. 27.1, Fig. 27.2, Fig. 27.6, Fig. 27.7). Concern for safe or at least effective holding of the implements is evidently important, Fig. 27.12, for example, has an area of blunting and a flake scar that would make an ideal 'thumb hold' near its bulbar end. Beyond this, there appeared to be an overall lack of concern with standardization or symmetry, no attempts were made at altering the morphology of the flakes through retouching beyond light blunting, and there was little evidence to suggest that they were intended to be hafted. Overall, there was a feeling of a rather casual approach to producing the implements, with utility, rather than aesthetic concerns, in mind.

Serrates can be found in Mesolithic to Early Bronze Age contexts but they are probably most common within Early Neolithic assemblages. The precise type and range of the activities in which they were employed remains obscure, although they have traditionally been regarded as composite sickles, essential elements in the Neolithic tool-kit and linked to harvesting silica-rich plants, particularly cereals. Experimental work involving micro-wear analysis suggests that serrated blades could have been used in cutting or sawing soft plant material, such as bracken or green wood (Levi-Sala 1992) and other micro-wear experiments have tended to confirm an association with plant processing (Avery 1982, 38; Grace 1992; Bradley 1993; Donahue 2002). Although cereal harvesting remains a possibility, the processing of other and perhaps varied plant resources is equally possible and the paucity of 'sickle-gloss' on these specimens combined with their varied morphology may even suggest that they were used on many different materials, from green plant material to harder substances, such as wood or bone.

Burnt flint

Unworked stone fragments weighing just under 6kg were also recovered from the artefact-rich tree-throw hollows. These consist predominantly of flint, which accounts for perhaps 90%, with occasional burnt fragments of a variety of quartz and other stone types present. It is variably burnt, ranging from lightly reddened to heavily burnt pieces that had completely changed to a grey/white colour and become fire-crazed, typical of burnt stone that has been incidentally generated during hearth use. It was variably distributed throughout the hollow, being concentrated in the top of hollow [787] and the base of layer [744], but there are no indications of any *in-situ* burning and it is most likely to have been dumped.

Distribution

The tree-throw hollows

The struck flint from the hollows is technologically homogeneous but there is some variability in its distribution throughout the fills. Hollow [787] contained the highest quantities of struck flint, at just under 2,000 pieces and this is only slightly higher than that from layer [744], but hollow [746] contained only just over 100 pieces. The densest concentrations of material occur not in the bases of the hollows but near the interface of hollow [746] and the overlying layer. No artefactual material was present in the earliest fills of the hollows [973] and [1003] and very little in the lowest parts of the hollows. It appears that the hollows may have started to infill, probably naturally, before the artefact-rich deposits began to be dumped in. The distribution of the material, both flintwork and pottery, suggests it might have dumped in from the western side and formed a mound within the hollows (Fig. 28).

Table 12 gives the breakdown for various classes of struck flint recorded from each of the spits excavated through the hollows and includes only hand-recovered material in order to retain some consistency. It demonstrates the differences apparent in the typological make-up of the assemblages from the hollows and the layer. Hollow [746], for example, contained higher proportions of blades (23%) than either layer [744] (12%) or hollow [787] (14.5%). Notably, however, the proportions of the technologically related blade-like flakes were more comparable between the three main features, though slightly lower in hollow [746], therefore despite the wide variations in the proportions of blades present, the predominant technological strategies employed for all three assemblages remained blade-based. Other notable differences include a much higher incidence of trimming flakes in layer [744] (twice that noted in hollow [787] and nearly six-times greater than hollow [746]). Conversely, hollow [746] produced nearly twice as many useable flakes than either the layer or the other hollow but contained no cores. The proportions of retouched pieces are similar in layer [744] and hollow [746] respectively, but higher in hollow [787]. However, the range of retouched types present was more notable. No arrowheads were present in layer [744] whilst notches and burins were only present in hollow [787] and polished flakes only in layer [744] and hollow [787]. The retouched inventory for hollow [746] was limited to arrowheads, piercers and serrate, but hollow [787] had a much wider range of implement types. All of the hammerstones, including cores reused, were recovered from layer [744]. Hollow [746] also contained proportionally larger flakes than the other contexts although those from layer [744] tended to be broader. The proportions of worked burnt flints are also variable, hollows [746] and [787] held comparable proportions (28.2% and 29.5% respectively) but both of these are higher than the 22.6% recorded for layer [744].

There is also some evidence for the occasional clustering of lithic material within the deposits. The arrowheads, for example, were found close together in two clusters and the unworked burnt flint concentrated around the interface between the layer [744] and the fill of hollow [787]. Nevertheless, there is little evidence that the clustering or differences in composition of the material represents purposeful arrangement or structuring of the deposits. Many of these differences may be attributed to inherent statistical variations, particularly as hollow [746] contained a much smaller assemblage than either the layer or the other hollow. However, the differences do suggest that although the overall assemblage from the hollows originated from basically similar technological methods and cultural objectives, variations within the deposits do exist and these may reflect temporal adjustments to knapping strategies linked to the changing requirements for different types of flakes and tools. Perhaps the most likely explanation for the variability observed within the fills is that the deposits originated from a primary source of material accumulated over a period of time, each episode of deposition reflecting slightly different flintworking practices according to the immediate needs and requirements of the knappers. Although the material had been considerably disturbed through redeposition, the clusters of implements and occasional short refittable sequences suggest that vestiges of these individual episodes of flintworking were preserved to a limited degree.

Context and spit	Decortication flake	Rejuvenation flake (Core Tablet)	Rejuvenation flake (Longitudinal)	Rejuvenation flake (Transverse)	Mis-hit flake	Trimming flake (<20mm)	Flake	Flake fragment	Systematically produced blade	Blade	Blade-like flake	Core	Conchoidal chunk	Retouched	Polished flake	Total struck	Burnt struck flint	Hammerstone	Burnt stone (no)	Burnt stone (wt g)
Layer [744]/[588]																				
Spit 1 No.	71	4	11	7	13	76	97	141	28	57	66	21	34	24	1	651	107	0	45	620
Spit 1 %	*10.9*	*0.6*	*1.7*	*1.1*	*2.0*	*11.7*	*14.9*	*21.7*	*4.3*	*8.8*	*10.1*	*3.2*	*5.2*	*3.7*	*0.2*	*(100.1)*	*16.4*			
Layer [744]/ [571]																				
Spit 2 No.	85	8	17	14	21	151	138	344	22	100	86	10	45	33	2	1076	284	5	136	2057
Spit 2 %	*7.9*	*0.7*	*1.6*	*1.3*	*2.0*	*14.0*	*12.8*	*32.0*	*2.0*	*9.3*	*8.0*	*0.9*	*4.2*	*3.1*	*0.2*	*100*	*26.4*			
Hollow [787]/[608]																				
Spit 6 No.	43	4	4	1	16	53	102	199	25	77	56	9	52	28	0	669	191	0	123	1195
Spit 6 %	*6.4*	*0.6*	*0.6*	*0.1*	*2.4*	*7.9*	*15.2*	*29.7*	*3.7*	*11.5*	*8.4*	*1.3*	*7.8*	*4.2*	*0*	*(99.8)*	*28.6*			
Hollow [787]/ [636]																				
Spit 7 No.	14	0	0	0	5	1	26	61	4	17	22	2	12	11	3	178	59	0	55	911
Spit 7 %	*7.9*	*0*	*0*	*0*	*2.8*	*0.6*	*14.6*	*34.3*	*2.2*	*9.6*	*12.4*	*1.1*	*6.7*	*6.2*	*1.7*	*(100.1)*	*33.1*			
Hollow [746]/ [645]																				
Spit 3 No.	6	1	0	0	1	1	22	14	3	13	8	0	4	2	0	75	21	0	20	257
Spit 3 %	*8.0*	*1.3*	*0*	*0*	*1.3*	*1.3*	*29.3*	*18.7*	*4.0*	*17.6*	*10.7*	*0*	*5.3*	*2.7*	*0*	*(100.3)*	*28.0*			
Hollow [746]/ [666]																				
Spit 4 No.	5	0	0	0	0	1	11	4	2	6	2	0	3	1	0	35	10	0	10	140
Spit 4 %	*14.3*	*0*	*0*	*0*	*0*	*2.9*	*31.4*	*11.4*	*5.7*	*17.1*	*5.7*	*0*	*8.6*	*2.9*	*0*	*100*	*28.6*			
Hollow [746]/ [686]																				
Spit 5 No.	0	0	0	0	0	0	2	0	1	2	0	0	1	1	0	7	2	0	1	19
Spit 5 %	*0*	*0*	*0*	*0*	*0*	*0*	*28.6*	*0*	*14.3*	*28.6*	*0*	*0*	*14.3*	*14.3*	*0*	*(100.1)*	*28.6*			
Total No.	224	17	32	22	56	283	398	763	85	272	240	42	151	100	6	2691	674	5	390	5201
Total %	*8.3*	*0.6*	*1.2*	*0.8*	*2.1*	*10.5*	*14.8*	*28.4*	*3.2*	*10.1*	*8.9*	*1.6*	*5.6*	*2.7*	*0.2*	*100*	*25.0*			

Table 12   Typological composition of the lithic material from the spits within the Early Neolithic tree-throw hollows

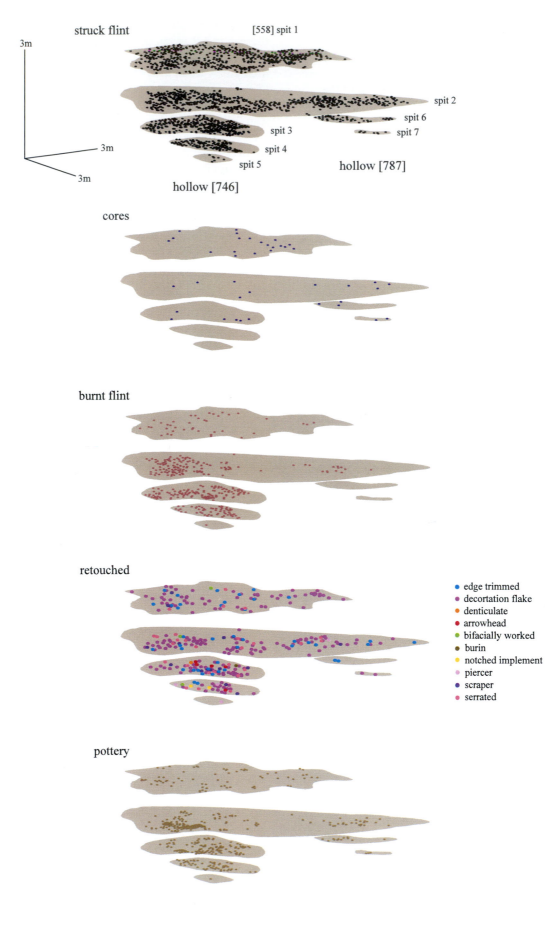

struck flint

[558] spit 1

spit 2

spit 6

spit 7

spit 3

spit 4

spit 5

hollow [787]

hollow [746]

cores

burnt flint

retouched

- edge trimmed
- decortation flake
- denticulate
- arrowhead
- bifacially worked
- burin
- notched implement
- piercer
- scraper
- serrated

pottery

Fig. 28   Diagrammatic representation of spatial distribution of struck flint and pottery within the Early Neolithic tree-throw hollows

Other features

Many of the remaining features at Laurel Farm contained struck flint that had technological or typological characteristics consistent with Early Neolithic industries. Frequently, however, such pieces were present in only small quantities and often in a chipped or abraded condition suggesting that, in many instances, the struck flint may have been residually introduced, and the features dated to much later. This may include some of the chronologically diagnostic pieces identified, such as the leaf-shaped arrowhead recovered from fill [370] of Phase 6 Iron Age pit [371] (see Chapter 6.1) or the axe fragment recovered from fill [872] of ring-ditch [790].

Fig. 29　A selection of Early Neolithic blades and broken blades from pit [1172]

A few features have larger assemblages that are in a less weathered condition, and the dating of these may be in closer accordance with the flintwork they contained. These include a tree-throw hollow [86] in Trench 114 (not illustrated, located south of the south-western corner of Area B) that produced fifteen struck flints, including a minimally worked core and two scrapers. In the main area of excavation, the struck flint assemblages of two features are of interest. Pit [1172], adjacent to the northern limit of excavation in Area B, contained 22 struck flints of which ten are blades and a further three blade-like flakes (Fig. 29). Similarly, pit [1256], located adjacent to north-western limit of excavation, contained 31 struck pieces of which fifteen are blades and another three blade-like flakes (Fig. 30). Neither contained any cores or retouched implements but their assemblages are dominated by perfectly useable blade segments and appear to represent a 'cache' of potentially useful implements. Other features with significant Early Neolithic assemblages include pit [408] in the central part of Area B which contained fourteen pieces, including blades, blade-like flakes and a scraper. This assemblage appears to consist of debris from a single knapping episode and included some refittable flakes. Other potentially Early Neolithic features include pit [418] in the south-western corner of Area B, which contained a substantial assemblage of 48 pieces, including blades and blade-like flakes, and pit [1243] in the north-western corner, which produced an assemblage of 46 pieces, including a narrow flake core and a serrated blade. Both of these assemblages are dominated by knapping waste and perhaps reflect individual or a short series of knapping events.

Scattered evidence

Although it was not analysed in detail, it is apparent that a significant portion of the struck flint recovered during fieldwalking is also consistent with an Early Neolithic date, although undoubtedly mixed with material spanning the Later Neolithic and Bronze Age. Around a fifth of the cores recovered had clearly produced blades, although recovered blades only contributed 4%. This rather low figure is probably at least partly attributable to the fragility of blades, however, as narrow flakes, also predominantly of Early Neolithic derivation, contribute a further 18%. No notable concentrations of lithic material were identified from the fieldwalked assemblage, but it does suggest that activity during this period, although episodic, was more extensive than indicated by the certain features of this date. It is uncertain, however, whether this material derives from ploughed-out or otherwise truncated sub-soil features or was discarded onto the surface.

A similar pattern is notable amongst the struck flint recovered from topsoil contexts during the archaeological interventions. This, again, was not examined in detail but it is evident that pieces with Early Neolithic characteristics form a significant proportion

0   5cm

Fig. 30   A selection of Early Neolithic blades and broken blades from pit [1256]

of the assemblage. No striking concentrations are apparent, but minor concentrations occur in the south-western portion of the main excavation area in the vicinity of Group 3.4 and towards the centre of the main excavation area, these areas producing 85 and 27 pieces, respectively. The north-eastern corner of the development site also produced relatively high quantities of predominantly Early Neolithic struck flint which were recovered during the machining of Trenches 178, 182, 183, 187 and 188.

There are many later features that contained occasional pieces of Early Neolithic flintwork, often of a rather chipped and abraded condition and this probably relates to the general low-density surface spread of Early Neolithic material. Later features with more significant collections of Early Neolithic flintwork include Post-Medieval ditch [583], which contained a notched flake and a scraper. The ditch truncated Early Neolithic tree-throw hollows [640] and [735], presumably the source of this material. Anglo-Saxon pit [696], also located in the central part of Area B in the near vicinity of these two tree-throw hollows, produced a further fifteen struck flints including a burin and, along with the densities of

struck flint present in the topsoil in this area, further confirms this location as a focus of Early Neolithic flintworking. Ditch [369] in the south-western corner of Area B produced an assemblage of 20 pieces suggesting that this too had truncated an Early Neolithic feature or scatter.

The colluvial layers also contained flintwork of predominantly Early Neolithic characteristics, notably layer [337], located in the south-western corner of Area B, which contained 23 struck pieces including a high proportion of blades but which predominantly consists of knapping waste and may represent a possible *in-situ* knapping episode.

3.3 Early Neolithic Pottery

Sarah Percival

The Early Neolithic pottery assemblage, which comprised 565 sherds weighing 4,512g, was analysed in accordance with the Guidelines for analysis and publication laid down by the Prehistoric Ceramic Research Group (PCRG 1992; 1997). The total assemblage was studied and a full catalogue was prepared, this is included in the site archive. The sherds were examined using a binocular microscope (x10 magnification) and were divided into fabric groups defined on the basis of inclusion types present. Fabric codes were prefixed by a letter code representing the principal inclusion (F representing flint, G grog and Q quartz). Vessel form was recorded; R representing rim sherds, B base sherds, D decorated sherds and U undecorated body sherds. The sherds were counted and weighed to the nearest whole gram. Decoration and abrasion were noted.

The Early Neolithic pottery was recovered from 27 features, principally from deposits [744], [745] and [787] within tree-throw hollows [746] and [787] which produced 90% of the assemblage (4,450g). The assemblage represents the remains of a minimum of 30 vessels, mostly undecorated carinated bowls. The sherds are small and fragmentary, each representing a very small percentage of the complete vessel. One sherd of possible Peterborough ware with impressed decoration was also found. Radiocarbon dates associated with the pottery from deposits within the tree-throw hollows suggest a date of around 3970–3790 BC (Waikato-22910 and 22912; see Appendix 1) corresponding with the 'early or developing' phase of Neolithic ceramics (Cleal 2004, 181).

Fabric

Seven fabrics were identified. The majority of the sherds are of flint-tempered fabrics, which contain varying proportions and sizes of sub-angular or angular white to grey flint pieces (Table 13). Flint-tempered sherds represent 95.1% of the assemblage (4,254g). The flinty fabrics are divided by inclusion size although, as Healy notes of the Early Neolithic pottery from Spong Hill, the coarser and finer fabrics 'appear to form a continuum'

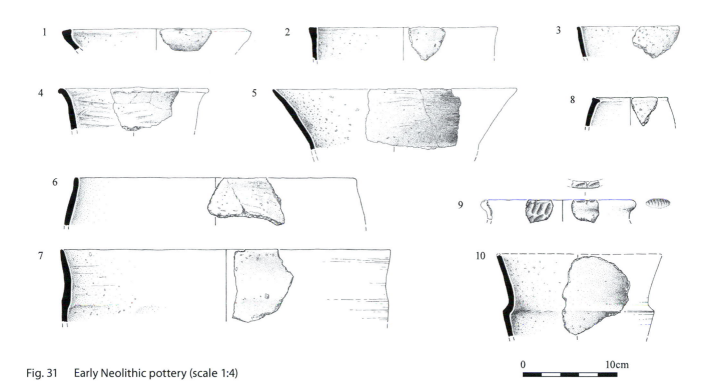

Fig. 31   Early Neolithic pottery (scale 1:4)

0   10cm

(Healy 1988, 64). Small quantities of sandy and grog-tempered fabrics were also found, sandy fabrics making up 3.8% of the assemblage (169g) and grog-tempered sherds 1.1% (48g). No fabrics with shelly inclusions or organic voids were identified. The sherds are hard and well-fired some with smoothed or burnished surfaces and range in colour from dark brown/orange to buff/orange.

The predominance of flint tempering compares well with Early Neolithic assemblages from much of East Anglia and south-eastern England (Healy 1988, 71). At Harford Park and Ride, around 98% of the Early Neolithic pottery

recovered from preserved soils layers and pits is made of flint-tempered fabrics (Percival with Trimble in prep.) and at the John Innes Institute, Colney, west of Norwich a large midden-like pottery and flint accumulation again produced approximately 98% flint-tempered sherds (Percival 2004). Flint fabrics are also dominant within other Early Neolithic assemblages from northern East Anglia such as Broome Heath (Wainwright 1972, 23), and Spong Hill, (Healy 1988, fig. 54). The small quantities of additional fabrics are a feature of Earlier Neolithic assemblages, modest amounts of sandy fabrics are also found within the assemblage from

Fabric	Description	Quantity	% quantity	Weight (g)	% weight
F	Undiagnostic flint-rich fabric	9	1.6%	4	0.1%
F1	Moderate to sparse, fine, sub-angular, flint. No flint protrudes onto the surface	49	8.6%	415	9.2%
F2	Moderate, fine to medium, sub-angular, flint	358	63.4%	2553	56.6%
F3	Abundant, medium to course, sub-angular, flint. Flint protrudes from exterior surface	48	8.5%	319	7.1%
F4	Moderate to sparse, medium, angular, flint. Occasional organic inclusions. Flint protrudes onto the surface	77	13.6%	835	18.5%
F5	Abundant, fine, sub-angular, flint. Speckled	10	1.8%	165	3.6%
G1	Moderate to sparse, medium to fine, sub-angular, grog. Moderate quartz-sand	4	0.7%	55	1.2%
Q1	Common rounded quartz sand grains	10	1.8%	166	3.7%
Total		**565**	**100%**	**4512**	**100%**

Table 13   Quantity and weight of Early Neolithic pottery by fabric

Harford Park and Ride (Percival with Trimble in prep.) and Spong Hill (0.4%; Healy 1988, fig. 54), although not at Colney (Percival 2004). The grog-tempered sherds are more unusual, but were found at Colney, where they represent less than 1% of the assemblage (*ibid.*). Cleal (1995, fig. 16.2) concluded that grog is not found within Earlier Neolithic assemblages from southern Britain, perhaps suggesting that the examples from Laurel Farm and Colney may represent later Neolithic intrusive material.

Form

The assemblage includes rim sherds from a minimum of 30 vessels. The rim forms have been classified following the typology devised for Hurst Fen (Longworth 1960, 228), Windmill Hill (Smith 1965), and Spong Hill (Healy 1988, fig. 57).

Simple rims dominate making up 53.3% of the total number of classifiable rims. A number of other rim types are also present including folded, rolled, externally-thickened and T-shaped forms (Table 14). The highly fragmentary nature of the sherds prohibits reconstruction of many vessels, but it is clear that the assemblage contains several vessel forms. Both thick- and thin-walled body sherds are present indicating a mix of fine and coarse forms. Open or neutral vessels with long necks (Fig. 31.3, Fig. 31.4, Fig. 31.5) above either sharp angular (Fig. 31.10) or thickened angular shoulders are present in small numbers (ten examples) suggesting that many of the vessels were less carinated and perhaps bag shaped (Fig. 31.6, Fig. 31.7, Fig. 31.8). Burnishing survives on the exterior of five sherds and 73 sherds have smoothed surfaces. Burnishing, especially to the upper parts of the vessel, might be expected to have been more frequent, however the low number of burnished sherds may reflect the high fragmentation and significant abrasion exhibited within the assemblage. The low ratio of burnished sherds may reflect the poor preservation of the assemblage.

The assemblage does not appear to be of the shouldered bowls typified by the assemblage from Broome Heath (Wainwright 1972; Cleal 2004, fig. 4) which tend to have curved necks, high carinated shoulders and rolled or folded rims, and were dated by Herne as latest Early or Middle Neolithic (Herne 1988, 16). Neither are the majority of the bowls of the classic carinated form found at Hanging Grimston, N. Yorks which have long necks and angular shoulders but tend to have folded or rolled rims (Herne 1988, 15). The vessels from Laurel Farm may instead be of Cleal's 'straight-necked carinated' form which have long necks with simple rims. No cups or small bowls were identified, although the small sherd size meant rim diameter was not measurable. The lack of rolled or folded rims is of note and contrasts with the assemblages from both Harford Park and Ride (Percival with Trimble in prep.) and Colney (Percival 2004).

Three flint-tempered sherds, including two rim sherds from a vessel with an in-turned flat-ended rim, are decorated with cord-impressed maggots on the exterior of the body and exterior and interior of the rim (Fig. 31.9). These sherds may be of Peterborough ware, a regional variant of Neolithic impressed ware which post dates the undecorated carinated bowl being in use from around the second half of the third millennium to *c.* 1700 BC (Gibson and Woods 1990, 220). Peterborough ware is fairly rare in Norfolk and, although found mostly in 'domestic' pits its context of use is poorly understood. The sherds were recovered from pit [846] and as surface finds overlying Iron Age pit [850].

Deposition

Early Neolithic pottery was principally recovered from tree-throw hollows [746] and [787]; these deposits contained over 90% of the total Earlier Neolithic assemblage (Table 15). The Early Neolithic assemblage has an average sherd weight of just less than 8g the same

Rim type	Quantity	Weight (g)	Number of vessels	% vessels	Illustrated
T-shaped	2	16	2	6.7	1
Simple rounded	13	264	10	33.3	2
Simple upright	4	126	3	10.0	3
Folded	3	12	3	10.0	4
Externally thickened	3	17	2	6.7	6, 9
Simple pointed	3	134	3	10.0	8
Rolled	5	44	5	16.6	11
Flat	2	9	2	6.7	
Total	**35**	**622**	**30**	**100**	

Table 14   Quantity and weight of Early Neolithic rim sherds by type

as that for the sherds from the flint scatter layers. Larger sherds were recovered as single examples from within tree-throw hollows [490] and [735]. The remaining Early Neolithic pottery, which was residual within a variety of later features, is small and abraded with a mean sherd weight (MSW) of 3g or less. The distribution of the pottery mirrors that of the Early Neolithic flint, although no contemporary pottery was collected during fieldwalking perhaps because the sherds did not survive well in the topsoil.

The assemblage from the flint scatter filling the tree-throw hollows is characterised by a mix of medium to small abraded sherds. A little less than 10% of the assemblage has been burnt post-breakage. No complete vessels were found and most of the vessels identified are represented by a very small number of sherds and this, along with the presence of post-breakage burning, suggests that the sherds were deposited in the soils at different stages in their post-use histories (Garrow 2006, 52). The MSW of 8g for these sherds is comparatively large, being double that of the sherds found within a colluvial soil from Harford Park and Ride (Percival with Trimble in prep.) and larger than those from a midden-like accumulation from Colney, which had an MSW of only 3g. The pottery does not show the same degree of post-discard attrition noted within the assemblages from

Phase/Group	Feature type	Cut	Quantity	Weight (g)	% weight	MSW
Early Neolithic features						
3	Tree-throw (evaluation trench 114)	86	2	7	0.2	3.5g
3.1	Layer 744 over hollows	746/787	286	2326	51.4	8.1g
3.1	Layer 745 over hollow	746	28	431	9.6	15.3g
3.1	Fill 786 of hollow	787	174	1293	28.7	7.4g
3.2	Pit	1016	1	24	0.5	24g
3.2	Pit/posthole	846	3	9	0.2	3g
3.3	Pit	681	2	3	0.1	1.5g
3.3	Colluvial layer	687	1	7	0.2	7g
3.3	Pit/hearth	690	15	165	3.7	11g
3.3	Tree-throw	735	1	10	0.2	10g
3.3	Pit	773	5	16	0.4	3.2g
3.3	Posthole	804	1	2	0.0	2g
3.4	Pit	418	1	2	0.0	2g
3.4	Tree-throw	490	1	17	0.4	17g
3.5	Colluvial layers	329	3	5	0.1	1.6g
Later features with residual material						
6	Posthole	1005	4	52	1.2	13g
6	Pit (surface find)	850	1	40	0.9	40g
6	Posthole	874	1	3	0.1	3g
6	Posthole	1146	2	11	0.2	5.5g
6	Pit	1059	3	5	0.1	1.6g
6	Ditch	854	1	6	0.1	6g
6	Ditch	369	1	2	0.0	2g
7	Colluvial layers	488	2	4	0.1	2g
10	Pit	583	3	10	0.2	3.3g
	Topsoil	1	16	53	1.2	3.3g
Total			**565**	**4512**	**100**	**7.9g**

Table 15   Quantity, weight, average sherd weight and percentage of total Early Neolithic ceramic assemblage by feature

Colney and Harford Park and Ride, perhaps suggesting that the sherds found at Laurel Farm had remained relatively undisturbed since deposition.

Pit [690] contained fourteen sherds weighing 153g. The undecorated body sherds have a MSW of 10g. Pit [1016] contained a single large sherd weighing 24g with a roughened or textured surface and pit [773] contained five sherds weighing 16g. The generally larger sherd size noted within the pit assemblages resembles that seen at both Colney and Harford Park and Ride suggesting that the pit deposits had been subject to a lesser degree of attrition than the material within the two artefact-rich tree-throw hollows and had perhaps spent less time in pre-pit contexts before deposition. The pottery within the pits appears to be of similar origin to that preserved within the flint scatter, being again composed of sherds from multiple incomplete vessels.

The sherds from within the tree-throw hollows were slightly larger than average for the site and contained no rims or distinctive body sherds. The deposition of pottery within Earlier Neolithic tree-throw hollows is well-attested (Evans *et al.* 1999), perhaps linking pottery deposition with episodes of tree clearance.

Discussion

The dating of the Early Neolithic ceramic assemblage from Laurel Farm is problematic. The presence of small quantities of Peterborough ware within the assemblage indicates that at least some of the contexts belong to the 'high' or developed Neolithic *c.* 3650–3350 BC (Cleal 2004, 181). The small number of rims from other Neolithic and later features are all rolled or thickened. Gibson has argued that a mix of 'developed' rim forms suggests a later date, post-dating 3600 BC (Gibson 2002). This suggested date broadly agrees with the radiocarbon determination from pit [690], which produced flint-tempered body sherds associated with a calibrated radiocarbon date of 3500–3100 BC (Waikato-22914; see Appendix 1). Rolled rims of classic carinated bowl form are found within the main Early Neolithic assemblage from the tree-throw hollows; however this assemblage is mostly composed of simple flat, rounded and pointed rim forms. The bulk of the assemblage from the tree-throw hollow deposits [744], [745] and [786] may therefore be of slightly earlier date than the material from pit [690], perhaps belonging to Cleal's 'early or developing' phase around 3850–3650 BC. This date ties in well with the calibrated radiocarbon dates of 3970–3790 BC obtained from oak charcoal from Spit 7 within tree-throw hollow [787] and from Spit 2 taken from the layer [744] overlying both the tree-throw hollows (Waikato-22912; Waikato-22910; see Appendix 1). This date is very similar to a radiocarbon determination from Harford Park and Ride where material associated with Earlier Neolithic pottery from a tree-throw hollow gave a calibrated date of *c.* 3940–3650 BC (Waikato-17710; Percival with Trimble in prep.).

The depositional practices identified at Laurel Farm are significantly different from those found on many Earlier Neolithic sites in Norfolk. Almost none of the pottery was recovered from pits, in contrast to many contemporary sites from the region pits are the most productive feature type found (cf. Spong Hill, Healy 1988). Garrow, in his study of Earlier Neolithic pits sites in East Anglia, notes the variation in pit numbers between sites and suggests that there may be a relationship between the number of pits present and the length of occupation at the site (Garrow 2006, 57). Healy has suggested that particularly pit-intensive sites such as Broome Heath may be monumental, with the site being repeatedly revisited for episodes of pit digging (F. Healy, pers. comm.), a point also discussed by Ashwin (2001). The fills of the pits are composed of fragmentary assemblages of multiple vessels, with small numbers of sherds representing each vessel. They also often contain other find types frequently combined in a dark charcoal-rich soil, perhaps composed of curated occupation debris. Further evidence for curation is suggested by the presence of rejoining fresh and burnt sherds within many assemblages, indicating that sherds from the same vessel may have different post-breakage histories prior to deposition. Although pits are rare at Laurel Farm, the composition of the assemblage from deposits within the tree-throw hollows is highly reminiscent of the pottery found in pits at other sites, perhaps suggesting that both assemblage types derived from similar sources of curated material.

The origin of the deposits at Laurel Farm is uncertain, but it seems to include curated material of domestic derivation. Accumulations of artefacts within a soil spread or layer were found not only at Laurel Farm, but also at Colney (Whitmore 2004) and Harford Park and Ride (Percival with Trimble in prep.). At all three sites the sherds were highly fragmentary and of mixed size and condition, including some burnt examples. However, at both Harford Park and Ride and Colney the sherds were much smaller than those found at Laurel Farm. This suggests that the material within the tree-throw hollows at Laurel Farm may have been less subject to attrition than the deposits found at either Colney, where extensive animal trampling took place, or Harford Park and Ride, where the material had accumulated from being washed down a slope.

The Earlier Neolithic assemblage from Colney comprised 865 sherds weighing 2,776g and that from Harford Park and Ride 365 sherds weighing 1,232g. The contemporary assemblages from Harford Park and Ride and Colney are fairly homogeneous, consisting mostly of shouldered bowl forms with rolled or folded rims with a smaller number of other rim forms, including simple and externally thickened types. By contrast, the assemblage from Laurel Farm is mainly composed of straight-necked carinated forms with smaller numbers of rolled, folded and other forms. It is unclear if these differences are chronological, as perhaps suggested by the radiocarbon determinations, or cultural, possibly representing different groups of people depositing pottery distinct to their social group (Healy 1995, 174).

3.4 Analysis of Early Neolithic Archaeobotanical Remains

Phil Austin and Louisa Gray

General methodology for archaeobotanical analysis

The following presents the methodology adopted for all the archaeobotanical analyses at Laurel Farm. A total of 85 bulk soil samples were taken from features of all periods during the investigations in order to recover environmental evidence and from these, 39 samples were selected for processing during the initial assessment phase. After processing by PCA, these were transferred to ArchaeoScape, Royal Holloway College, Egham, University of London, for sub-sampling and assessment. Following the initial phase of work, a total of 48 samples were selected for processing and/or further analysis.

Charcoal analysis was undertaken to recover information concerning the contemporary local vegetation, to determine if this had been altered in some way by human activity and to identify how woodland resources and timber were exploited. Information relating to taphonomic processes that may have affected both the formation of the charcoal, its deposition and its survival was also sought. The range and relative abundance of tree and shrub taxa present in each phase was used to identify differences or significant changes in the local vegetation and the manner of wood exploitation. Charred and uncharred seeds present in the samples were also analysed to give further information on the former vegetation cover and the economy and diet of the inhabitants.

Following the charcoal assessment (Poole *et al.* 2007) remaining material from samples recommended for further analysis were processed by flotation, prepared and examined following standard procedures as described in Hather (2000). In keeping with Keepax's (1988) recommendation, 100 fragments from each sample were picked at random for examination, when appropriate. Where less than 100 fragments were present, 100% of the sample was examined. In instances where it was clear from initial examination that a sample was dominated by a single taxon, specifically - *Quercus*, the least '*Quercus*-like' fragments were preferentially selected for detailed examination. By these means, it is believed that the full range of taxa represented in each sample/context, and for the assemblage as a whole, would be determined as completely as is feasible. Only fragments >2mm, preferentially >4mm, were subject to detailed analysis. Below this size category, anatomical features are too incomplete, especially in transverse section, to enable positive identification.

Qualitative analysis included recording of growth ring characteristics, specifically ring curvature and relative widths, and features indicative of relative maturity, such as tyloses in vessels. In addition, the presence/absence of pith, innermost/outermost wood or bark were also recorded. Possible biological degradation, as indicated by the presence of fungal mycelium in vessels and insect galleries/bore-holes, was recorded when present. The extent of thermal degradation was evaluated by attributing each fragment (somewhat subjectively) a value from 1-3 according to the quality of preservation of anatomical features with an additional category used for fragments that appeared 'vitrified' or partly so. Although 'vitrification' of wood charcoal is not fully understood, exposure to very high temperatures is generally agreed to be one of the most influential factors. Fragments, even of the same taxon, within the same sample can exhibit variation in the degrees of thermal degradation exhibited. Such variation has also been observed to occur within individual fragments (P. Austin, pers. obs.).

On its own, presence/absence analysis provides little information regarding the apparent abundance or scarcity of individual taxa within samples, either over time or for an assemblage as a whole. To allow some measure of relative abundance absolute fragment count and weight for each taxon in each sample were recorded. Neither fragment counts or weight are reliable indicators on their own, not least because a small quantity of large fragments may weigh more than a large quantity of small fragments of the same taxon. Similarly, where more than one fragment of a taxon is present in a sample it is not known how many individual pieces of wood the fragments derived from. However, taken into consideration together fragment count and weight do provide some insight into taxon abundance. Given the problematic nature of attempting to draw meaningful conclusions from quantification of charcoal remains, no attempt was made to subject the values recorded to any form of statistical analysis. Wood anatomical atlases by Schweingruber (1990) and Greguss (1954) were consulted as aids to identification when necessary. Nomenclature follows Stace (1997).

Waterlogged and charred seeds were examined under a stereo microscope with magnifications of between 10 and 40 times and identified as closely as their quality of preservation allowed. Charred remains were counted and uncharred remains were given estimated levels of identifications were made using modern reference material and manuals (such as Beijerinck, 1947; Charles 1984; Tomlinson 1985; Hillman *et al.* 1996; Jacomet 2006; Cappers *et al.* 2006). Nomenclature and habitat information was taken from Stace (1997). Scientific names have been given once in brackets and the common name given thereafter. The term 'seed' refers to seeds, nutlets and achenes. All of the plant macrofossils were analysed using 'habitat and usage' classifications devised by Glynis Jones, Vanessa Straker and Anne Davis in their survey of early Medieval plant use in London (Jones *et al.* 1990).

Early Neolithic archaeobotanical evidence

Fragments of charcoal were recovered from five bulk soil samples taken from the two artefact-rich hollows and three taxa were identified amongst this assemblage: oak (*Quercus* sp.), ash (*Fraxinus excelsior*) and hawthorn type, Maloideae (Appendix 2). This was the only period at the site in which ash was represented. The recurrent presence of narrow rings in oak and ash fragments suggests that these taxa were possibly growing in closed woodland. The Maloideae, probably hawthorn, may have been present as a component of the under-storey of oak-ash woodland.

Whilst it is tempting to conclude that oak may have been the only good firewood available, the presence of ash suggests otherwise; wood from this large tree makes particularly good firewood, with burning properties different from, but on a par with, oak; ash will burn 'green'. The Maloideae is a small tree/shrub taxa that also produces good fuel wood. It is perhaps significant that charcoal from these alternative good fuel sources were not better represented and could reflect the fact that they were not available in any great quantity, that they were reserved for other uses or that they were not considered appropriate for use as fuel.

Chapter 4

Phase 4 Late Neolithic to Early Bronze Age Activity

4.1 The Late Neolithic to Early Bronze Age Sequence

The most notable feature that produced artefactual material of Late Neolithic to Early Bronze date was a ring-ditch located towards the central part of Area B which bore similarities to hengiform enclosures; ritual areas that are dated to the Later Neolithic, and round barrows, the burial mounds of the Early Bronze Age. Few associated features could be confidently identified and the ring-ditch itself provided only a small collection of mostly undiagnostic struck flints, although one example consisted of a worked fragment from a flaked axe. The presence of a few pits within Area B containing both Later Neolithic and Early Bronze Age pottery as well as some diagnostic flint artefacts testifies to continued activity at the site, although the quantity of artefactual material present suggests that this was considerably less intense than that seen for the Early Neolithic.

Possible Early Bronze Age barrow

Ring-ditch [790] was located towards the central part of Area B, situated on the brow of the north-western area of higher ground, as defined by the stream valleys that crossed the development site, and at a level of 21.65m OD. Although approximately circular, it had flattened southern and western sides and may be more accurately described as a recumbent 'D' shape in plan (Fig. 32). It measured 16.50m east–west by 15.50m north–south and, due to the effects of ploughing and erosion, the surviving remnants of the base of the ditch were rather irregular-shaped and varied from between 0.60m to 1.70m wide and survived to a maximum depth of 0.82m. Ten slots were excavated through the feature, comprising around 20% of the total, revealing a variable profile generally with very steep to near vertical sides and a sharply concave base. The number of fills present also varied within the excavated sections, although just over half had single fills. All of the material within the ditch appeared to be naturally accumulated silts and sands with a few lower fills of windblown sand. This presumably represents material that had accumulated rapidly in the base of the ditch and the slower-accumulating upper fills had been lost to truncation. Unfortunately the ring-ditch produced

very little dating evidence, the finds totalled nine struck flints, and inclusions of other cultural debris such as charcoal or burnt flint were entirely absent. Assemblages of worked flint were recovered from fills [848], [872] and [972]; these varied in date from the Early Neolithic to the Bronze Age. Amongst the assemblage was an axe of Early Neolithic date, perhaps deliberately deposited within the feature as with the Lower Palaeolithic axe deposited within the Early Neolithic pit, discussed in Chapters 2.1 and 3.1, above. A fragment of Sarsen stone was also recovered from fill [1066] of the ditch, though this was not worked. This stone could have originated from the surrounding Tertiary sediments or could be an erratic that was brought into this region by the Anglian Glaciation (see Hayward, Chapter 4.4).

Much of the interior of the ring-ditch had been truncated by large, amorphous features that are interpreted as tree clearance hollows (Fig. 9). Many of these were demonstrably later in date than the ring-ditch as they truncated the feature, one example produced a radiocarbon date in the Anglo-Saxon period, and another produced Post-Medieval pot. No contemporary internal features were identified, however, the degree of plough-truncation at the site was severe so that all traces of such features could have been destroyed. This poor degree of survival means that certain interpretation of the feature is problematic. One possibility is that this represents a circular drainage gully surrounding a roundhouse structure, though its width, depth and the sterility of its fills are at odds with such an interpretation. Ring-ditches representing the ploughed-out remains of Bronze Age round barrows with no surviving mound are common in the region, though it is acknowledged that generally they are of significantly larger size than the ring-ditch at Laurel Farm (Lawson et al. 1981; Lawson 1986; Ashwin and Bates 2000). Examples of ring-ditches of similar size include that excavated at Sweet Briar Road, on the north-western outskirts of Norwich, interpreted as a ploughed-out barrow (Bown 1986) and an example at Bowthorpe, to the west of Norwich with a surviving central burial pit (Lawson 1986, 20). Round barrows are prolific in the area; as well as the large barrow cemetery thought to have been located in the fields now covered by the Dussindale Park housing estate, adjacent to the western limit of the Laurel Farm site, and depicted on the 1589 map of Thorpe St Andrew (Fig. 69) as the "Gargytt Hylls", there

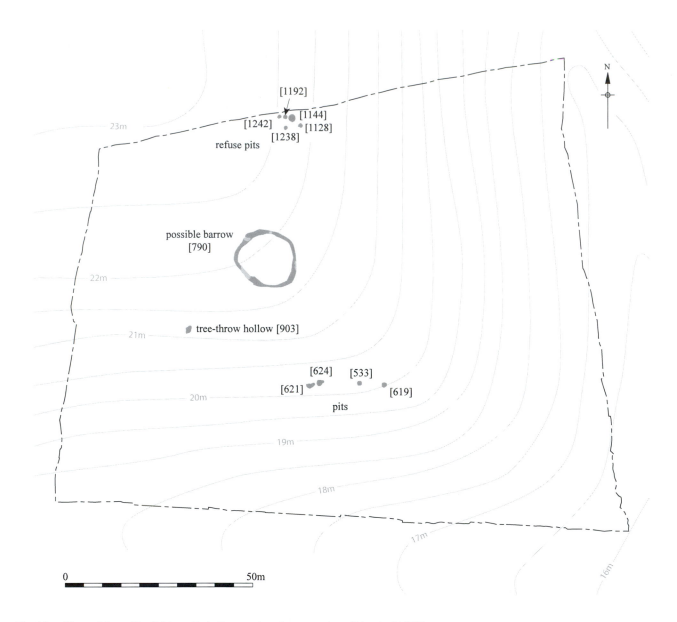

Fig. 32   Phase 4, later Neolithic to Early Bronze Age features, Area B (scale 1:1000)

are numerous suspected ploughed-out barrows identified as crop marks on aerial photographs listed in the HER. The Laurel Farm ring-ditch is therefore considered to be best interpreted as the remnants of a small ploughed-out round barrow. The fact that there was no human bone recovered is not surprising given the extensive truncation combined with the acidic nature of the sandy soils; the investigations as a whole produced only a tiny assemblage of animal bone. The Laurel Farm ring-ditch is positioned on the brow of a hill, overlooking a stream in the now dry valley, which would have been a prime location for a landscape monument of this type, and the lighter sandier soils are preferred for the construction of such monuments in this region (Lawson *et al.* 1981).

The western limit of a Phase 5 Iron Age boundary ditch [784], which extended across the eastern side of the ring-ditch on a west-south-west–east-north-east alignment towards the central portion of the ring-ditch, did not have a true terminal but faded out, with the boundary ditch becoming raised at this point

and shallower until all traces were removed through ploughing (Fig. 9). This suggests that a central mound still existed as an earthwork feature when the ditch was dug and may have acted as a focus for this later boundary. Similar evidence was recorded at the Sweet Briar Road barrow where a ditch bisected the barrow ditches and petered out in the central area suggesting that the mound was extant when the ditch was dug (Bown 1986, 61).

To the north of the Laurel Farm ring-ditch was a Post-Medieval boundary feature comprising two ditches on the same alignment as the Iron Age boundary with an entrance between the two located less than 1m away from the ring-ditch, roughly in line with the centre of the internal area. This suggests that traces of the mound survived until ploughing in the Post-Medieval period eventually obliterated it and therefore supports an interpretation of the ring-ditch as a ploughed-out barrow. A group of tree-throw hollows were situated on the southern side of the ring-ditch and its internal area. It is possible that if the mound in this area was relatively slight by the time that these trees were growing then traces of their root bowls could survive. The barrow mound thus appears to have been occupied by a small clump of trees and it is an often-noted phenomenon that trees were planted on prehistoric tumuli in the historic period, or at least small clumps of trees were allowed to grow on these features. The mound itself probably did not form the focus for an entranceway within the field system, as by this stage it is unlikely to have been a particularly prominent feature within the landscape, however, a clump of trees may have been such a landscape marker.

Pits and tree-throw hollow

An oval pit [1144] measuring 1.90m by 1.60m and 0.40m deep was located adjacent to the northern limit of excavation within Area B. Its fill [1143] contained occasional inclusions of burnt flint along with eight struck flints, including a type of scraper diagnostic of the Beaker period, although much of the remainder may have been residually deposited and could have originated from the Early Neolithic feature [1146] that it truncated (see Chapter 3). Adjacent to this pit was a small circular pit [1192], which produced thirteen struck flints from its single fill [1191]. This material also appears predominantly residual, the only retouched implement being an edge-trimmed blade. A small fragment of Grooved ware pottery of Later Neolithic date was also recovered. A short distance to the west was a small oval pit [1242] that produced two struck flints of Late Neolithic or Early Bronze Age date. Two similar oval features [1238] and [1128] each produced two struck flints of the same broad date.

Some distance to the south-east of the ring-ditch was a sub-circular pit [624], which measured 1.48m by 1.40m and up to 0.45m deep. Two sherds of Beaker pottery dated to the Late Neolithic to Early Bronze Age period were recovered from its fill [625] along with ten struck flints of Neolithic to Bronze Age date. Close by was pit [621] which measured 2.32m by 1.04m and up to 0.48m deep and although it produced no datable artefactual material, it has been placed within this phase of activity due to its proximity and similarity to pit [624] and its unusual content. The pit contained over twenty round, fist-sized flints, though the purpose of these was rather enigmatic; they may represent a store of raw material, flints of this size and shape were used as hammer stones and grinders in this region, or they may represent a structured deposit within the pit. A short distance to the east was a circular pit [533], with vertical edges and a fairly flat base, which measured 1.10m in diameter and 0.40m deep. The upper fill [531] contained lenses of dark brown slightly humic material, along with occasional charcoal and burnt flint. Three Neolithic to Bronze Age flakes were recovered from this, and although these were not refitting, they did appear to have originated from the same nodule. A single sherd of prehistoric pottery, not closely datable, was also recovered. To the east was a pit [619] of similar size that produced two struck flints of the same period.

A sub-oval feature [903] located towards the western side of Area B is interpreted as a tree-throw hollow due to its irregular shape and profile. Six struck flints were recovered from fill [904], including a crudely made piercer, which would not be out of place within Beaker period assemblages, along with two sherds of Beaker pottery.

4.2 Late Neolithic to Early Bronze Age Flintwork

Barry Bishop

Compared to the preceding Early Neolithic period, there are considerably fewer struck flints that can be confidently assigned to the Later Neolithic or Early Bronze Age, from either stratified or unstratified contexts.

The most notable feature of this date is the ring-ditch, which produced nine struck flints in total. These are mostly undiagnostic but their condition suggests a likelihood that they are predominantly residual and their technological traits suggest that they most probably derive from the Early Neolithic activity at the site. Of interest, however, is the axe from fill [872] (Fig. 33.1). The axe had snapped transversely roughly along its mid-point and this surface had then been struck, resulting in a large plunged flake that preserved much of one side and its base. It is made from a mottled translucent black and opaque grey flint not unlike that used for manufacturing axes at Harford Park and Ride during the Early Neolithic (Bishop forthcoming b). It appears finished; its edges have been bevelled through fine trimming although no polishing is evident. As only its base was present, however, it could potentially have had a polished cutting edge. Due to its fragmented state it is not closely datable. Early Neolithic axes tend to have all-over polish whilst Later Neolithic examples are frequently only polished around their cutting edges, suggesting that this may be more typical of Later Neolithic types. However, the cutting edge of this example is missing so it is uncertain whether it was in fact finished; it may even have broken during manufacture and therefore not been polished. As its precise dating cannot be established, the circumstances surrounding its deposition are elusive. It may have been residually introduced or deliberately placed as a significant and perhaps prestigious object. Although the evidence from here is far from convincing, it should be noted that during the Later Neolithic and Early Bronze Age periods, axes were occasionally deliberately flaked-down or burnt prior to burial, perhaps as an attempt to symbolically 'kill' or control their metaphorical potency. A burnt axe of similar form to the example here had been buried in a pit in the entranceway to a Beaker period enclosure at Harford Park and Ride (Percival with Trimble in prep.) whilst at Rothley Lodge Farm in Leicestershire a Later Neolithic pit contained a re-flaked stone axe that may have been 'ritually "undressed" before burial', and another close-by pit produced a burnt axe (Pitts 2005, 9; L. Cooper, pers. comm.).

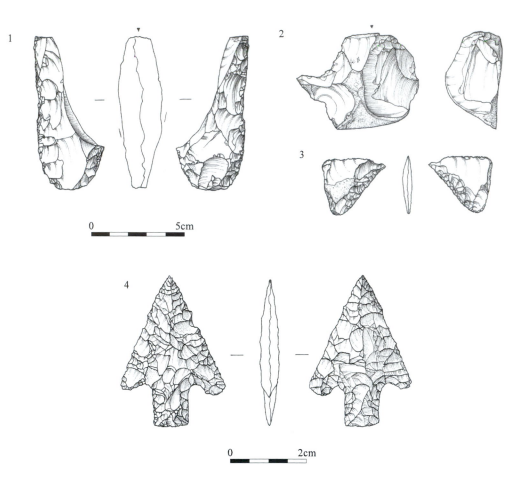

Fig. 33   Late Neolithic to Early Bronze Age flint (scale 1:2/1:1)

Few other features from these periods were identified. Pit [1144], located adjacent to the northern limit of excavation within Area B, produced an assemblage of eight struck flints that included a semi-invasively retouched thumbnail scraper. These are diagnostic implements of the Beaker period although much of the remainder of the assemblage, which included blades, one of which may have been serrated, may well have been residually deposited. The struck flint from nearby pit [1192], comprising thirteen pieces, also appears predominantly residual, its only retouched implement being an edge-trimmed blade. Pit [624] towards the central part of Area B contained an assemblage of ten struck flints including a side scraper whilst pit [903] to the north-west produced six struck flints including a substantial, although somewhat crudely made, piercer (Fig. 33.2). The scraper is not particularly diagnostic but the piercer would certainly not be out of place within Beaker period assemblages.

The unstratified material and that recovered from fieldwalking likewise contained few struck flints that can be confidently placed within the Later Neolithic or Early Bronze Age. Those that can include a Later Neolithic chisel-type transverse arrowhead that was recovered from topsoil deposits located in the north-western part of Area B (Fig. 33.3). It was competently made on a possible 'Levallois' flake and had been bifacially thinned. These are often associated with Woodlands type Grooved ware

and Peterborough ware pottery types, both datable to the Middle to Later Neolithic period. This is confirmed by Green's extensive survey of flint arrowheads, which suggest a date range of *c.* 3500–2250 BC for this type (Green 1984, 19). They are found in settlement contexts, which have perhaps provided the largest numbers, but they are also frequently associated with ritual or ceremonial sites, particularly henges (Green 1980 235–236; Healy 1984, 13). The only other chronologically diagnostic piece from this period is a possible crude or unfinished plano-convex knife, recovered from close to the central southern limit of the main excavation area.

The most notable piece of Early Bronze Age date consists of a finely made Sutton C or Conygar Hill type (Green 1980) barbed and tanged arrowhead with a prominent squared tang (Fig. 33.4; see Fig. 67). This was recovered as a residual find from a colluvial deposit [1177] in Area D (see Chapter 7.1). These are most commonly associated with Beaker or Food Vessel style pottery (*ibid.*), are well-represented in the East Anglian region (Green 1980, table IV.3) and have been dated to *c.* 2300–1500 BC (Green 1984, table 1). Although commonly found as stray finds and occasionally within settlement contexts, the quality of manufacture of this piece is notable and may tentatively suggest that it was used ceremonially rather than just for practical use, and possibly associated with funerary activity (Devaney 2005, 17).

4.3 Late Neolithic to Early Bronze Age Pottery

Sarah Percival

The methodology used to analyse the Later Neolithic to Early Bronze Age pottery was as set out above (Chapter 3.3). Seventeen sherds of pottery from this period weighing 130g were recovered from six contexts. The majority of this very small assemblage is Beaker, with a small quantity of Grooved ware. Phase 4 pit [624] contained two sherds with a total weight of 13g whilst pit [1192] contained a single sherd weighing 5g and tree-throw hollow [903] contained two sherds weighing 81g. The remaining sherds were recovered from the deposits infilling the artefact-rich Phase 3 tree-throw hollows, and are considered to be intrusive in these contexts, or were collected from topsoil.

Fabrics

Three fabrics were identified. Flint-tempered sherds, perhaps from a single vessel, make up 62% of the assemblage by weight (81g). Two grog-tempered fabrics were also identified (Table 16). Grog is commonly found in Later Neolithic to Earlier Bronze Age fabrics and is often, although not exclusively, used for finewares. Flint is more likely to have been chosen for coarse, chunky vessels often with fingertip-impressed rusticated surfaces.

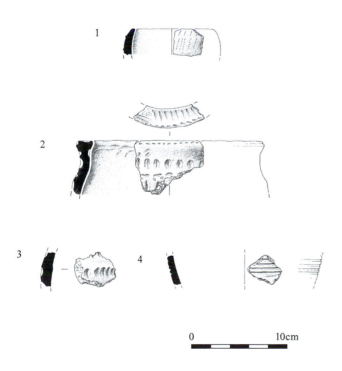

Fig. 34   Late Neolithic to Early Bronze Age pottery (scale 1:4)

Form and decoration

Eleven sherds weighing 23g are formless undecorated body sherds. Beaker sherds include two from the body of a fine vessel with impressed decoration perhaps accomplished using a cockle shell (Fig. 34.1; Simpson 2004, fig. 4) and two sherds with fingertip-impressed decoration, a form common among 'domestic' Beaker assemblages in East Anglia (Fig. 34.2, Fig. 34.3; Bamford 1982; Gibson 1982). One fingertip-impressed rim sherd has cable motifs on the rim top and running down the body of the vessel (Fig. 34.2; cf. Healy 1996, fig. 97, P301).

A single sherd of possible Grooved ware in grog-tempered fabric G101 has incised channels running across the body of the vessel (Fig. 34.4; Healy 1988, fig. 80). The presence of the channelled decoration may suggest that it is of the Durrington Walls substyle (Longworth 1971), though this interpretation must remain tentative due to the small size and poor preservation of the sherds.

Deposition

The single sherd of Grooved ware from pit [1192] may represent a contemporary deposit along with the material from pit [624] and tree-throw hollow [903]. The remainder of the Later Neolithic to Earlier Bronze Age pottery is probably either intrusive or residual within the topsoil (Table 17).

Discussion

Beaker pottery often forms a small component of many excavation assemblages from within and around Norwich. A small beaker assemblage was recovered from excavations along the Norwich Southern Bypass at both Harford Farm and Bixley (Ashwin and Bates 2000) and a larger quantity was found at Harford Park and Ride (Percival with Trimble in prep.). The Beaker assemblages from both Harford Farm and Harford Park and Ride were found in 'domestic' contexts, while food vessels were chosen to accompany burials at Harford Farm (Bamford 2000). This suggests that the Beaker sherds found at Laurel Farm were of domestic origin and represent low-intensity use of the site during this period.

Grooved ware is rarely found in Norfolk, compared to the numerous domestic Beaker assemblages recovered. Only fifteen sites are listed for the county in the Grooved ware gazetteer compiled in 1999 (Longworth and Cleal 1999). Few finds have been made in the Norwich area, although several sherds were found during excavations adjacent to the Norwich Southern Bypass at Markshall, Caistor St Edmund (NHER 9584; Percival 2000), and at Trowse (Percival 2000, fig. 123, P54). Beaker and Grooved ware are believed to overlap chronologically, with Beaker being current from around 2600 until 1800 BC (Kinnes *et al.* 1991). Grooved ware dates broadly from the period 3000–2000 BC (Garwood 1999, 152).

Fabric	Description	Quantity	% quantity	Weight (g)	% weight
F100	Moderate medium angular flint; moderate quartz sand.	2	11.8	81	62.3
G100	Common fine to medium sub-rounded grog; common quartz sand	11	64.7	29	22.3
G101	Common medium to coarse sub-rounded grog; common quartz sand	4	23.5	20	15.4
Total		17	100	130	100

Table 16   Quantity and weight of Late Neolithic to Early Bronze Age pottery by fabric

Phase	Feature type	Feature	Quantity	Weight (g)
Late Neolithic/Early Bronze Age Features				
4	Pit	624	2	13
4	Tree-throw	903	2	81
4	Pit	1192	1	5
Intrusive Material				
3	Tree-throw	744	3	17
3	Tree-throw	787	8	6
Topsoil		1	1	8
Total			17	130

Table 17   Quantity and weight of Late Neolithic to Early Bronze Age pottery by period and feature

4.4 Stone Identification

Kevin Hayward

A Sarsen Nodule (Tertiary – Reading Beds) of a kind well-known from southern and eastern England was recovered from fill [1066] of ring-ditch [790]. This weighed 10kg and was not worked. It may be from the surrounding Tertiary sediments or an alternative possibility is that it was an erratic brought into this region from the local Anglian Tills which would have been the product of glaciation and transportation of stone from western and northern England.

Chapter 5

Phase 5 Middle to Late Bronze Age Activity

5.1 The Middle to Late Bronze Age Archaeological Sequence

As with the Later Neolithic activity, evidence for Middle and Late Bronze Age activity was rather sparse. Features of Middle to Late Bronze Age date were only located in the south-western corner of the development site and were first identified during the evaluation phase in Trenches 35, 36 and 194 and the area around these was subsequently enlarged to form Area A during the excavation (Fig. 35). Activity from this period comprised an enigmatic group of features; a hearth, a number of postholes and a tree-throw hollow which were found lying adjacent to a large circular feature that was over 3m deep. Following the partial infilling of this feature with redeposited natural sediment, quantities of pottery, struck flint, quernstones and burnt material were deposited within the upper part of the feature.

Middle Bronze Age shaft

A circular feature [158] was located within the south-western corner of Area A at a level of 23.55m OD. This was the most elevated of the four areas of higher ground defined by the valleys of former streams running through the development site. The feature was circular in plan and measured 2.40m in diameter and 3.32m deep. It had near

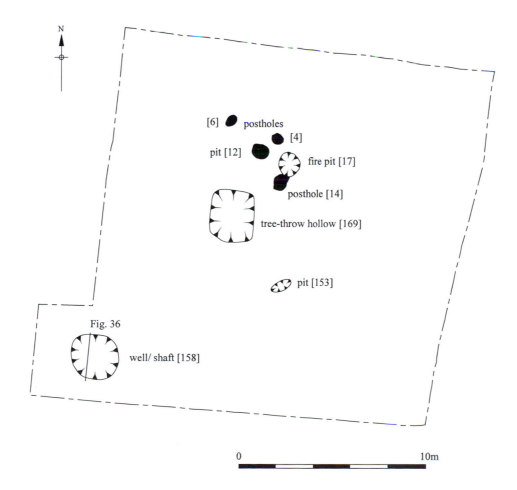

Fig. 35   Phase 5, Middle to Late Bronze Age features, Area A (scale 1:200)

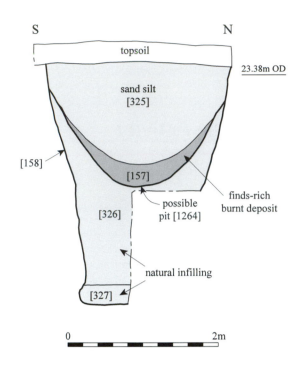

Fig. 36   Section through Phase 5 Middle Bronze Age shaft [158] (scale 1:50)

vertical sides and a flat base and was slightly undercut by c. 0.10m up to a height of c. 0.25m from the base (Fig. 36). Due to its depth, excavation of this feature was stepped down by machine in spits to allow the excavated half to be bottomed. The primary fill [327], which was up to 0.25m thick, comprised mid brown silty sand that was devoid of inclusions, probably representing accumulated material eroded from the sides of the feature, the shallow depth indicating that it was probably not open for long. This was overlain by deposit [326], up to 2.50m thick and comprising greyish brown silty sand with very occasional flint pebbles, presumably representing redeposited natural sediment that had collapsed into the feature. The upper part of this deposit slumped inwards towards the centre of the shaft so that in the middle it was only 1.60m thick, perhaps formed from the deliberate cutting of a pit [1264] into its centre. The overlying fill [157] was up to 0.30m thick and also slumped down towards the centre. This was of notably different composition to the earlier fill and comprised black charcoal-rich silty sand that contained abundant cultural material including quantities of burnt flint and large quantities of burnt daub and clay. Over 2kg of sandstone fragments, mostly burnt, were recovered from this deposit, many of which had flat surfaces and could represent burnt quernstones and grinding stones. An assemblage of 30 unburnt struck flints characteristic of Middle Bronze Age and later industries were also recovered from the pit along with nine fragments of Middle Bronze Age Deverel-Rimbury pottery. One of the sherds came from the same vessel that was represented in posthole [6] (see below). Charcoal fragments recovered from a bulk soil sample taken from

this fill have been identified as oak (*Quercus* sp.), hazel (*Corylus avellana*) and Maloideae and a single fragment of barley/wheat grain was also recovered. Following the dumping of the artefact-rich material, the feature was completely infilled with a deposit of greyish brown silty sand [325], which contained very occasional struck flint and burnt clay flecks.

The size and profile of this feature is consistent with a well. However, this is considered to be an unlikely explanation as the base was higher than the present day water table and a plentiful water supply would have been more easily accessed in the very near vicinity in the base of the Dussindale valley. In addition, as discussed for similar features recorded beneath a round barrow excavated at Eaton Heath, south-west of Norwich, there was no sign of a clay lining and so the feature could not have held water as it was cut through porous natural material (Healy 1986, 57). Another possibility is that this feature may have been a shaft dug deliberately for ritual purposes. It has been suggested in relation to the features at Eaton Heath that the excavation of a vertical-sided shaft through unstable sand and gravel would have posed significant difficulties (Healy 1986, 57). These have been interpreted as natural solution holes, examples of which were also recorded on several of the Norwich Southern Bypass sites (Ashwin and Bates 2000). A large group of similar features was also excavated during a previous investigation at Eaton Heath and at the time these were interpreted as forerunners of Iron Age ritual shafts or as wells or for water storage (Wainwright 1973, 12–25). These features were later interpreted as solution holes and the presence of pottery sherds, struck flint and charcoal fragments at depths of up to 8m is thought to be due to periodic slumping of the solution holes in areas where occupation debris was present on the ground surface (Healy 1986, 58). For the purposes of this report the term 'shaft' has been used to describe the feature; it is acknowledged that this could be naturally formed or deliberately dug.

The fact that the vertical sides of this feature had not suffered erosion or collapse indicates that it was probably not open for any great length of time. The primary fill at the base of the feature indicates natural silting but this was a shallow deposit that could have accumulated rapidly. The homogeneity and substantial thickness of the overlying fill indicate that it had rapidly infilled with the surrounding natural sand and gravel before being infilled with specifically selected cultural material. The significance of this infilling is discussed below (see Chapter 10.4).

Postholes and pits

To the north-east of the shaft was a group of four postholes [4], [6], [12], [14], all similar in shape and form, being between 0.50m and 0.80m in diameter and surviving to a depth of 0.20m. A short distance to the south was another, more oval shaped example [153]. Artefactual evidence was only recovered from posthole

[6], which produced twelve sherds of Middle Bronze Age Deverel-Rimbury pottery, from only two vessels, one of the vessels also providing two of the sherds recovered from the shaft. Three struck flints, all crudely produced and similar to those from the shaft, were also present.

Feature [17] appeared to slightly truncate the edge of posthole [14], although the relationship was not certain and they may have been contemporary. This oval feature had gradually sloping edges and a fairly flat base and measured 1.15m by 0.85m and was 0.20m deep. The primary fill, which comprised a mixture of black and orange silt, charcoal and burnt clay with occasional flint inclusions, was slightly convex on the surface and was likely to represent *in-situ* burning within a small fire pit. The upper fill, sand silty with frequent charcoal flecks, appeared to be a dump of burnt waste material deposited following the burning activity below.

Features [4], [6], [17] and [153] formed an arc, which if projected measured *c.* 11m across, and postholes [12] and [14] could have formed part of an inner concentric arc, as discussed further below. In the area defined by these arcs, towards the centre, was a shallow sub-rectangular feature [169] with an undulating base, interpreted as a tree-throw hollow. The only cultural material recovered from this was a single, undiagnostic, struck flint flake, however, the position of this tree-throw hollow suggests association with the arcs of features, with an arc of posts perhaps surrounding an uprooted tree (see Chapter 10.4).

Other features

Flintwork, predominantly of Middle Bronze Age or later character, was recovered from pit [223] and linear feature [221], both located within evaluation Trench 144 in the eastern portion of the development site. The pit also produced Romano-British pottery. A small collection of flakes from fills [755] and [767] of Phase 6 pit [754], located within the central part of Area B, was also of interest as the assemblage had Middle Bronze Age or later characteristics and was found in association with a large assemblage of Iron Age pottery, thereby presenting good evidence that flintworking continued into this period (see Bishop, Chapter 6.2).

5.2 Middle to Late Bronze Age Flintwork

Barry Bishop

Although struck flint with later prehistoric (later second and first millennium BC) characteristics was present amongst the topsoil deposits, the fieldwalked material and as occasional and probably residually deposited material in later features, only a few cut features contained what may be *in-situ* deposits.

The shaft

The most notable assemblage likely to date to this period was recovered from fill [157] of the shaft or solution hole. This produced 30 struck flints (Table 18) as well as other cultural debris, including over 2kg of mostly burnt sandstone fragments (see Hayward, Chapter 5.4).

Although the assemblage was not large, a wide range of raw materials was employed, including thermally fractured nodular flint cobbles as well as smaller, rounded alluvial flint and chert pebbles of much poorer knapping quality. These all would have been available at or close to the site and it appears few attempts at selecting better quality raw materials had been made. No refits were present and the flakes had been made using many cores. The sieved bulk samples produced only three small flakes, probably incidentally produced during knapping but not in sufficient quantities to indicate knapping occurring *in situ* or close by.

The types of debitage and tools present, along with the techniques used to manufacture them, are typical of industries dating from the Middle Bronze Age to the Iron Age (cf. Brown 1991; Herne 1991; Young and Humphrey 1999; Humphrey 2003).

The flakes are very variable in shape and size but are mostly rather crudely struck, being thick and squat with wide obtuse striking platforms and often retaining significant cortex on their dorsal faces. The only blade present consists of a narrow cortical flake, which was

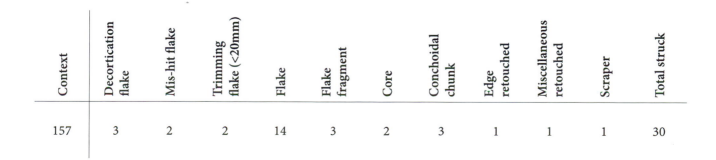

Context	Decortication flake	Mis-hit flake	Trimming flake (<20mm)	Flake	Flake fragment	Core	Conchoidal chunk	Edge retouched	Miscellaneous retouched	Scraper	Total struck
157	3	2	2	14	3	2	3	1	1	1	30

Table 18   Composition of the Bronze Age struck flint from shaft [158]

retouched but may have been fortuitously produced; it had evidently been hard hammer struck using a cortical striking platform. The flakes were also hard hammer produced, many having prominent impact points and pronounced bulbs of percussion.

Two cores were recovered. One weighs 70g and has been extensively reduced, having produced a variety of different shaped flakes, and also exhibits numerous incipient Hertzian cones from failed attempts at flake removal (Fig. 37.1). The other consists of a split alluvial pebble fragment that has a series of small but quite narrow flakes removed from around the scar, which, along with damage visible around the striking platform edge, indicates its use as a scraping type core-tool (Fig. 37.2). Reduction was very opportunistic, there are no indications that the cores were pre-shaped to enable reliable flake production or that striking platforms were modified to enable repeated flake production.

Three flakes had been retouched. One consists of the distal end of a thick cortical flake with moderate shallow convex retouch around its distal end (Fig. 37.3), another, a blade with crude fine retouch or heavy use-wear along one lateral margin and cortical 'backing' along the other (Fig. 37.4), was probably for use as a knife-like implement. The remainder consists of a large flake with a slight notch on one lateral margin and a more pronounced notch on the other (Fig. 37.5). The latter also has many incipient Hertzian cones around the area of the notch, indicating further unsuccessful attempts at extending the notch or otherwise modifying the flake. A short area of damage or use-wear around the flake's distal end may indicate that it had also been used for chopping or scraping.

Discussion

The struck flint assemblage from the shaft or solution hole [158] is typically later prehistoric in date and comparable to other contemporary assemblages from the area, such as that from the Middle Bronze Age settlement at The Oaks which is characterised by crudely produced flakes and simple retouched implements (Bates 2006). Although some advances have been made (e.g. Humphrey 2007), the definition of the specific typological and technological changes in struck flint industries through the late second and the first millennia BC are still poorly documented and understood. Furthermore, the nature and significance

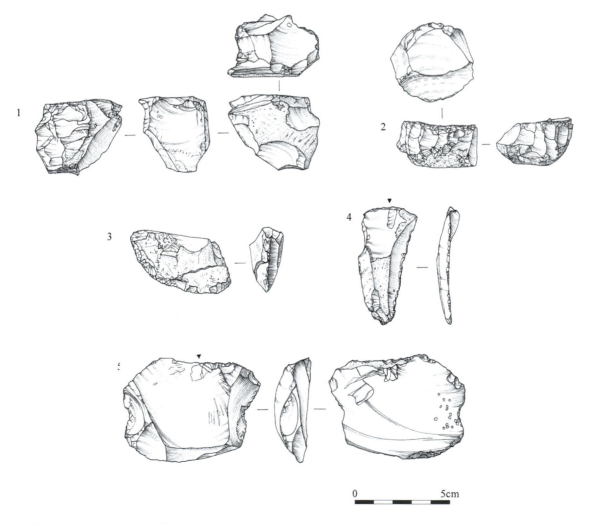

Fig. 37   Middle to Late Bronze Age flint (scale 1:2)

of struck flint production and use have also been little explored and there has been even less emphasis placed on understanding the social significance of flintworking during these periods. The assemblage recovered from the partially infilled shaft is typical of those from the later second millennium BC, being composed of irregular flakes, simply reduced cores and expediently made retouched implements, including core-tools. It was the product of numerous knapping events, elements of which were gathered up and dumped, along with quantities of other artefactual material, into the pit, seemingly as a deliberate act. The size of the struck assemblage and the context of its deposition is more notable, however, as flintworking during this period is usually considered to have been *ad hoc* and largely confined to the domestic sphere (Edmonds 1995; Young and Humphrey 1999). Typical later Bronze Age assemblages are small, have a high use rate and are present in low densities scattered within settlements or across the field systems, representing opportunistic and short-lived knapping episodes. By and large it would seem that, when required, pieces of readily to-hand raw materials were struck with little overall strategy or proficiency until suitable edges were procured, once the task was completed the flint would be discarded with little formality (Young and Humphrey 1999, 232–233). "*By the mid second millennium there is little evidence to suggest that stone tools were customarily selected for inclusion in acts of formal deposition, or that complex conventions surrounded their routine use and disposal*" (Edmonds 1995, 177). However, consideration of the circumstances surrounding the deposition of the struck flint may indicate that on certain occasions such mundane items may have been incorporated into ceremonial activities (see Chapter 10.4).

5.3 Middle to Late Bronze Age Pottery

Sarah Percival

The methodology used to analyse the Middle to Late Bronze Age pottery was as set out above (Chapter 3.3). A small assemblage of 22 sherds weighing 591g was identified as being of this period. The pottery was recovered from three contexts and is mostly in poor condition.

Fabric

Two fabrics were identified. The majority of the assemblage comprises grog-tempered fabric G100. A number of flint-tempered sherds were also found (Table 19). The mix of grog- and flint-tempered fabrics is similar that found within the Deverel-Rimbury assemblage from Grimes Graves (Longworth *et al.* 1988).

Form and decoration

The form and decoration of the vessels suggest bucket- or tub-shaped forms with applied decorated cordons of the Deverel-Rimbury tradition. One flint-tempered vessel has an applied fingertip-impressed band which finds parallel among the assemblage from Grimes Graves (Longworth *et al.* 1988, fig. 25). A second vessel, in heavily grog-tempered fabric, has slashed decoration along the rim top, piercings below the rim and an applied cordon again decorated with slashed lines (Fig. 38). Vessels with similar decoration have also been found at Grimes Graves (Longworth *et al.* 1988, fig. 32, 252, 253), Mildenhall fen (Clark 1936b, fig. 5, 6, 10) and at the Frettenham Lime Company Site, Caistor St Edmund (Percival 2000, fig. 170, P146).

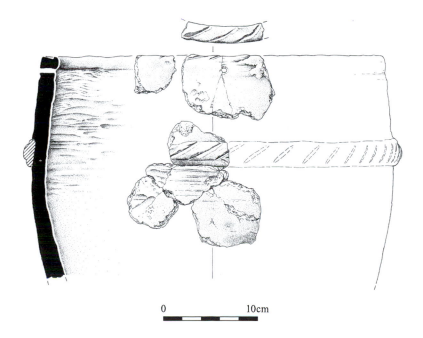

0   10cm

Fig. 38   Middle to Late Bronze Age pottery (scale 1:4)

Fabric	Description	Quantity	% quantity	Weight (g)	% weight
F100	Moderate medium angular flint; moderate quartz sand.	9	40.9%	149	25.2%
G100	Common medium to coarse grog; common quartz sand	13	59.1%	442	74.8%
Total		22	100%	591	100%

Table 19   Quantity and weight of Bronze Age pottery by fabric

Deposition

The majority of the Deverel-Rimbury sherds came from Phase 5 shaft or solution hole [158] and posthole [6] (Table 20). One large flat base sherd in flint-tempered fabric was found in as an intrusive sherd in layer [744] within the Phase 3 Early Neolithic tree-throw hollow.

Discussion

The Deverel-Rimbury pottery from Laurel Farm is extremely similar to the large contemporary assemblage from Grimes Graves (Longworth *et al.* 1988). Thirteen radiocarbon determinations on samples associated with the pottery from Grimes Graves suggest that the Deverel-Rimbury occupation spanned the period from *c.*1375–845 BC (Longworth 1988, 48). Closer to Norwich a broadly contemporary assemblage was recovered from The Oaks, Thorpe St Andrew (Percival 2006) and from the Frettenham Lime Company Site, Caistor St Edmund (Percival 2000, fig. 170, P146).

Phase	Feature	Cut	Quantity	Weight (g)
Late Bronze Age Features				
5	Pit	158	9	406
	Posthole	6	12	88
Intrusive Material				
3	Tree-throw	744	1	97
Total			745	842

Table 20   Quantity and weight of Bronze Age pottery by period and feature

5.4 Stone Identification

Kevin Hayward

Samples of the two types of stone found within fill [157] of shaft or solution hole [158] were submitted for stone identification. The most frequent type was Lower Greensand: flaggy fine micaceous sandstone. Greensand erratics from Thetford were used as whetstones or smoothstones at prehistoric sites in this region. The second type was a banded micaceous metamorphic rock: schist or phyllite source from western Britain.

Both types of stone may be erratics from the local Anglian Tills which would have been the product of glaciation and transportation of stone from western and northern England.

5.5 Analysis of Middle Bronze Age Archaeobotanical Remains

Phil Austin and Louisa Gray

The methodology used to analyse the archaeobotanical remains from Middle Bronze Age features was as set out above (Chapter 3.4). Only one sample taken from a Middle Bronze Age feature produced remains that warranted full analysis.

Sample {4} taken from context [157] the fill of the shaft or solution hole [158] contained only three taxa: oak (*Quercus* sp.), hazel (*Corylus avellana*) and Maloideae (see Appendix 1). Again this indicates the continuing presence of oak and Maloideae in the locality. Hazel is recorded for the first time though it is likely that it was present in earlier periods. Ring growth was again noticeably slow in the few fragments for which these could be studied. Most of the fragments in this sample were small and poorly preserved. Oak woodland with hazel and occasional members of the Maloideae is likely. It is possible that hazel became more readily available than previously, perhaps through the management of this species as coppice. This sample also contained a fragment of grain identified as the distal end of a barley/wheat (*Hordeum/Triticum* sp.) grain.

Chapter 6

Phase 6 Middle to Late Iron Age Activity

A number of features, including roundhouses, associated structures and elements of a co-axial field system, are likely to have formed part of a farmstead which was occupied during the last few centuries BC (Fig. 39).

Dating of this activity was confirmed by the presence of Middle to Late Iron Age pottery, dating from the third–first centuries BC, recovered from across Area B. Notable assemblages were present in three pits, which also returned radiocarbon determinations confirming occupation during this period. However, most of the Iron Age pottery was present as small quantities in scattered features, some of which were likely to be significantly

later than the pottery, which must therefore have been residually introduced. Nevertheless, the pottery assemblage does indicate activity at Laurel Farm during this period. The focus for occupation in this period was on the higher ground to the western side of the Dussindale Valley and the earlier barrow/ring-ditch seems to have played a significant role in the setting out of the Iron Age settlement and field system. At this time the barrow could still have been an upstanding monument and may have been used as a landscape marker. The Middle Iron Age settlement at Harford Farm, Caistor St Edmund, was also laid out amidst a group of upstanding barrows (Ashwin

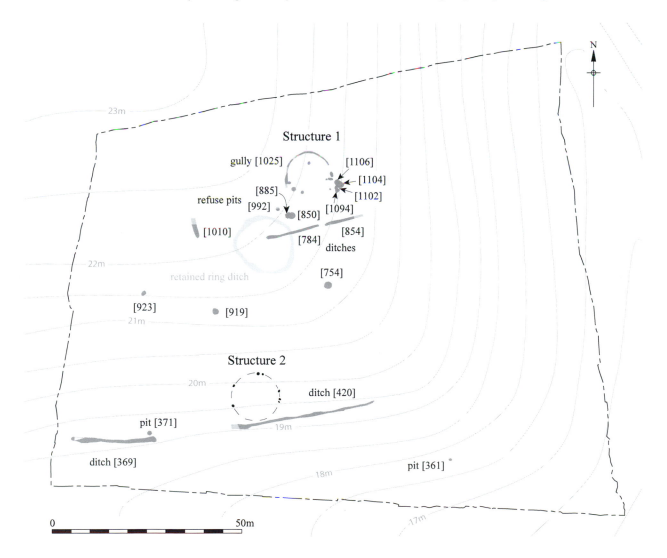

Fig. 39   Phase 6, Iron Age features, Area B (scale 1:1000)

and Bates 2000, 135–137). A radiocarbon date obtained from one of the Laurel Farm circular structures suggests the possibility that occupation of this settlement may have continued into the Roman period.

6.1 The Iron Age Archaeological Sequence

Structure 1

A semi-circular gully [1025], measuring 12m in diameter by *c.* 0.35m wide and 0.15m–0.21m deep, was located in the central northern portion of Area B (Fig. 39). This had steeply sloping sides and a concave base and its single fill comprised silty sand derived from the natural deposits that it was cut into. No cultural material was recovered from the feature but its form and size suggest that it was part of the encircling drainage gully, the 'eaves-drip' gully, surrounding a roundhouse (Structure 1) (Fig. 40). The gully formed the northern half of a presumably penannular feature and, as the ground sloped down from the north to the east and south, would have had the effect of channelling any ground water, which would have naturally flowed south and eastwards, away from the structure.

Five features [957], [982], [1005], [1055] and [1083], ranging in depth from 0.24m to 0.36m, may have been postholes representing the surviving structural elements of a ring of timber posts from the roundhouse wall, which would have been internal to the drainage gully. There were no traces of the drainage gully surrounding the southern part of the projected roundhouse circle, but it is possible that the gully only ever encircled the northern part of the structure as the topography of the land was such that water would have drained naturally from the southern part of the building. Two small circular features [980] and [971] were recorded internally, these were most likely to have been postholes, possibly forming elements

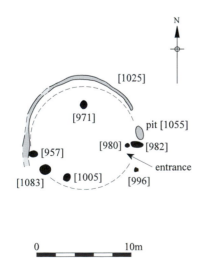

Fig. 40   Phase 6, Iron Age roundhouse Structure 1, Area B (scale 1:400)

of an inner ring of roof supports *c.* 8m in diameter. Iron Age roundhouses most frequently have their entrances facing between east and south, and an entrance on this side seems most likely for Structure 1. Posthole [996], located a short distance to the south-east of the projected line of the roundhouse wall, may have formed part of a porch structure for a south-east facing entrance. This posthole produced a large fragment of pottery that was prehistoric but unfortunately not closely datable.

Features associated with Structure 1 produced very little artefactual material; they were all filled with deposits very similar to the natural silts and sands they were cut into, although most contained small quantities of charcoal and burnt flint, presumably deriving from occupation-type activities. Pit [1005] also contained a small assemblage of abraded Early Neolithic pottery and struck flint fragments, which were likely to be residual. No contemporary pottery was recovered and interpretation of the structure being of Iron Age date is based on its form and dimensions, which are typical of this period, and because other features and finds from the site indicate an Iron Age presence. All of the features were shallow and it was evident that the area had been subject to a high level of horizontal truncation, both from erosion and agricultural activities, leading to a potential loss of shallower features and emphasizing the sturdiness of those that survived.

Structure 2

A group of postholes [413], [415], [438], [440], [535], [581], [676] and [678] located in the southern part of Area B may have formed part of a circular structure (Structure 2) *c.* 12m in diameter, thus comparable in size to the arc made by the semi-circular gully of Structure 1 (Fig. 41). These postholes were relatively small, measuring between 0.35m and 0.70m in diameter, and had very steep sides and dark fills, suggesting that the posts may have rotted *in situ* rather than having been salvaged. Posthole 'pairs' [438]/[440] and [413]/[415] could conceivably have formed an east-facing entrance to the postulated structure. A single sherd of Iron Age pottery was recovered from posthole [422]. Posthole [581] returned a calibrated radiocarbon date of AD 120–330 from a fragment of oak charcoal (Waikato-22913; see Appendix 1), placing this firmly within the Roman period. If the posthole does indeed date to the period indicated by the radiocarbon determination then it could indicate a long-lived tradition of roundhouse construction; such building traditions are known to have continued in some parts of the province throughout the Roman period. Roundhouses are common throughout lowland Britain in the first and second centuries AD and are also found on a number of sites in southern Britain in the third and fourth centuries (Hingley 1989, 31), with an example close by at Scole in Norfolk (Ashwin and Tester in press). Another possibility is that the material used for the radiocarbon determination was intrusive. Supporting this was the fact that only the lowermost 60mm of the posthole had survived ploughing and erosion and it could easily have been contaminated through these processes.

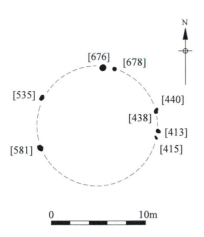

Fig. 41   Phase 6, Iron Age roundhouse Structure 2, Area B (scale 1:400)

Pits

A small group of pits was located within the area between the two postulated structures (Fig. 39). Sub-circular pit [885], which measured 1.80m by 1.60m and 0.45m deep, had near vertical sides and a flat base. No datable material was recovered from its single silty sand fill but it was truncated by a circular pit [850], which measured *c*. 1.80m in diameter and 0.43m deep. Its primary fill consisted of a thin deposit of clean, naturally deposited sand, probably arising from slumped sides or rain-wash. The overlying fill [849] contained large quantities of cultural debris including a mass of charcoal, burnt daub and clay, charred bone, including pig, and a relatively large quantity of pottery. The pottery was dated to the Middle to Late Iron Age, *c*. third–first century BC, and samples of holly (*Ilex aquifolium*) charcoal from the fill returned a 2-sigma calibrated date of 350–290 BC and 220–50 BC (Beta-225548; see Appendix 1). Close to this was another circular pit [992], measuring *c*. 1m in diameter, which was also filled with quantities of charcoal and a small quantity of Iron Age pottery.

Pit [754], which was located *c*. 20m to the south-east of these two pits, measured *c*. 2m in diameter and 0.63m deep and had steep sides and a flat base. Five fills were recorded; the earliest consisted of a mass of charcoal, burnt clay, burnt flint and small burnt bone fragments, and this was covered with further burnt material, including large quantities of ash and occasional burnt bone, but also with unburnt pottery. The following three fills continued this pattern, with dumps of reddened sand mixed with burnt clay and animal bone, being followed by a very humic fill containing burnt flint, clay and bone and, lastly, a sandy fill with just occasional charcoal flecks, burnt clay (including one fragment with slag attached) and pottery. A bulk sample taken from an intermediate fill [766] produced evidence for iron working in the form of flakes and spheres of hammerscale along with a fragment of vitrified hearth lining (see Appendix 3). Micro-slags from the pit could have been produced by smelting or primary smithing and the small quantity of hammerscale provides evidence for secondary smithing (see Keys, Chapter 6.3). A large assemblage of pottery, 52 sherds in total, was retrieved from the pit and dated to the Middle Iron Age. Twelve struck flints were also recovered and this material dated from the Neolithic to the Middle Bronze Age, Maloideae charcoal from the lowest fill returned a calibrated radiocarbon date of 370–160 BC, firmly placing it in the Middle to Late Iron Age (Waikato-22909; see Appendix 1).

Pit [919], located *c*. 30m to the south-west of [754], measured *c*. 1.60m in diameter and 0.23m deep. Its single fill similarly contained abundant charcoal fragments along with fragments of animal bone identified as cattle. The pit also contained a relatively large assemblage of pottery comprising 44 sherds of Middle Iron Age date. A radiocarbon sample obtained from hazel (*Corylus avellana*) charcoal returned a calibrated date of 200–10 BC (Beta-225549; see Appendix 1).

A sub-rectangular pit [923] was located *c*. 18m to the west of [919] and this measured 1.36m by 0.92m and 0.26m deep. Its single sandy fill contained occasional burnt flint and a total of ten sherds of Middle Iron Age pottery were recovered from this pit, along with residual Neolithic to Bronze Age struck flint.

To the east of Structure 1 was a group of four consecutively dug pits [1094], [1102], [1104] and [1106]; only one, [1104], produced a single sherd of Middle Iron Age pottery.

Ditches

Two segments of ditches aligned approximately north-east–south-west were located *c*. 7m to the south of Structure 1. The western segment, recorded as ditch [784], extended for a distance of 14.50m and was up to 0.90m wide but only survived to a maximum of 0.20m deep. Its western end was traced to the central part of the earlier Phase 4 barrow or ring-ditch where it became progressively shallower. This suggests that there was an upstanding mound within the ring-ditch that may have acted as a focus, or an alignment upon which the ditch was laid out. The ditch contained a single fill, a dark-brownish grey silty-sand, which probably represented a waterlain primary fill, and it produced three struck flints and a single fragment of Iron Age pottery. The eastern segment, ditch [854], which was of similar width, survived for a distance of 8m and was 100mm deep; its eastern end petered out, probably due to the combined effects of ploughing and erosion, the latter being particularly marked in this area. A 1.5m wide gap between the ditches may have formed an entrance, perhaps to allow access between a habitation area to the north and fields to the south.

Located 47m to the south-east was a parallel ditch [420], 1.25m wide and 0.44m deep, which survived for a distance of 36m, truncated at both ends by quarry pits of Anglo-Saxon date. Another segment of ditch [369] on the same alignment as [420] was located *c*. 20m to the west.

This measured 22.60m by up to 1.45m wide and 0.65m deep and generally had steeply sloping sides and a concave base. There was little indication that the boundary continued to the east beyond the later truncation, although severe erosion along the eastern side of the excavation area may have, like its northern counterpart, removed any traces. A small pit [371] was located a short distance to the north of the eastern terminal of [369] and this measured 0.95m diameter and 0.18m deep. A sherd of Iron Age pottery was recovered from this pit along with two residual Early Neolithic flints (see Bishop, Chapter 3.2). An isolated pit [361] was situated near the southern boundary of Area B, *c.* 26m south-east of the western boundary of ditch [420]. This measured 0.75m by 0.45m and 0.30m deep and produced a sherd of Iron Age pottery along with two Early Neolithic struck flints.

These ditches are interpreted as field boundaries, most likely parts of a co-axial field system. A very similar series of ditches of Early to Middle Iron Age date forming part of a rectilinear system of land boundaries was recorded at the Norwich Southern Bypass site at Valley Belt, Trowse (Ashwin and Bates 2000, 159). The boundaries in the southern side of Area B were traced for a distance of *c.* 80m whilst those in the northern area were traced for a distance of 27m. No perpendicular 'returns' to this system were identified, however, the only possible contender being a short 4m long stretch of ditch [1010] located *c.* 17m to the west of ditch [784]. It was perpendicular to this ditch, of a similar form and contained a similar fill, but it was truncated to the north by a Post-Medieval ditch and was not traced beyond this point. It was noted, however, that it became shallower to the north and therefore may have been completely removed by ploughing and erosion further north.

6.2 Iron Age Pottery

Sarah Percival

The methodology used to analyse the Iron Age pottery was as set out above (Chapter 3.3). A small assemblage of Iron Age pottery comprising eighteen vessels was recovered from fourteen excavated features. One hundred and ninety-five sherds weighing 1,890g were recovered and the sherds were mostly small and abraded with a mean sherd weight of 9g.

Fabric

The majority of the assemblage is made of sandy fabrics (88% / 729g) with a small number of flint-tempered sherds (Table 21). The sand is almost certainly naturally occurring within the clay matrix. The use of both flint-tempered and sandy fabrics occurs throughout the Iron Age; however, assemblages with a high proportion of flint-tempered sherds tend to be earlier Iron Age, while those which are predominantly sandy are later Iron Age, usually post third century BC.

Form

The assemblage contains the remains of a minimum of eighteen vessels, all of which are jar forms. The majority of the jars are small, with a diameter at the rim of 12cm or less. One vessel has an angular shoulder, but this is the exception with the remainder having slack shoulders and short upright or slightly everted necks (Fig. 42). Rims may be flattened (five examples; e.g. Fig. 42.8, Fig. 42.9), rounded (eleven examples; e.g. Fig. 42.2, Fig. 42.5,

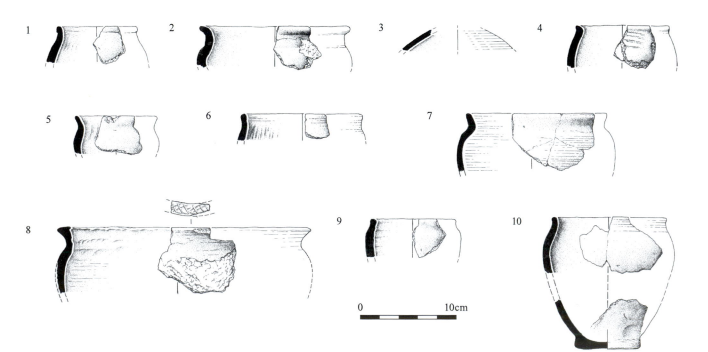

Fig. 42   Iron Age pottery (scale 1:4)

Fabric	Description	Quantity	% quantity	Weight (g)	% weight
F1001	Moderate medium angular flint, moderate rounded quartz sand	8	8.5	99	12.0
Q1000	Sparse rounded clear and coloured small to medium quartz grains	10	10.7	69	8.3
Q1001	Moderate rounded clear and coloured small to medium quartz grains	30	31.9	141	17.0
Q1002	Moderate rounded clear and coloured medium to large quartz grains	1	1.1	4	0.5
Q1004	Common rounded clear and coloured quartz small to medium grains	21	22.3	153	18.5
Q1005	Common rounded clear and coloured small to medium quartz grains	24	25.5	362	43.7
Total		94	100	828	100

Table 21   *Quantity and weight of Iron Age pottery by fabric*

Phase	Feature	Cut	Quantity	Weight (g)	% Weight
Iron Age Feature					
6	Ditch	420	2	9	0.5
		784	1	4	0.2
6	Pit	361	1	2	0.1
6	Pit	371	1	23	1.2
6	Pit	754	52	356	18.8
6	Pit	850	50	631	33.4
6	Pit	919	44	579	30.6
6	Pit	923	10	35	1.9
6	Pit	992	3	12	0.6
6	Pit	1104	1	16	0.8
6	Posthole	422	1	9	0.5
Intrusive Material					
1	Palaeochannel	739	1	1	0.1
3	Tree-throw	735	1	11	0.6
3	Pit	804	2	8	0.4
4	Ring-ditch	790	1	8	0.4
Residual Material					
7	Layer	1218	1	9	0.5
8	Pit	30 (T43)	1	23	1.2
10	Tree-throw	818	1	1	0.1
10	Tree-throw	1068	1	3	0.2
10	Colluvial layer	671	1	7	0.4
Unphased					
	Ditch	68 (T102)	1	10	0.5
	Topsoil	1	18	133	7
Total			195	1890	100

Table 22   *Quantity and weight of Iron Age pottery by feature and phase*

Fig. 42.6, Fig. 42.7, Fig. 42.10) or have an external lip or bead (three examples; e.g. Fig. 42.1). Decoration is rare. One vessel has fingernail-impressed decoration on the rim top (Fig. 42.8) and a second has a combed band below the neck (Fig. 42.3).

Deposition

The Iron Age pottery was spread through a number of Iron Age features (Phase 6) and was also found in unphased features (Table 22). The majority of the sherds came from three pits [754], [850] and [919], which produced 82.8% of the total Iron Age assemblage (1,566g), including the majority of the rims and bases. The remaining features produced very small assemblages.

Discussion

The small Iron Age assemblage is almost certainly later Iron Age, around the third–first centuries BC. The assemblage is comparable to that from Park Farm, Silfield, near Wymondham, which was dated typologically to the third– mid first centuries BC (Percival 1996, 265). The assemblage is likely to post-date those from other sites from the Norwich area, such as Harford Farm (Percival 2000) and Harford Park and Ride (Percival with Trimble in prep.) which are primarily earlier Iron Age.

The pattern of uneven distribution of pottery between Iron Age pits is common to many Iron Age sites with some sites containing significant assemblages whilst others are empty of artefacts (cf. Ashwin and Bates 2000). The explanation for the patterning, however, remains uncertain. It seems reasonable to suggest that the material within the pits represents *in-situ* Iron Age deposits, while that from other features is probably redeposited. The composition of the assemblage, containing multiple incomplete vessels, each represented by low numbers of sherds, is comparable to that of the earlier prehistoric assemblages comprising incomplete vessels represented by small, abraded sherds typical of curated material. The small quantity of Iron Age pottery found perhaps suggests a short-lived, low-intensity occupation.

6.3 Ironworking Slag

Lynne Keys

Activities involving iron are represented by micro-slags alone rather than bulk slags. Sample {62} from pit [754] (fill 766) produced small magnetic ore fines and some micro-slags (see Appendix 3). The latter consisted of spheroids, occasionally irregular and distorted (which could represent either smelting or primary smithing),and a minute amount of flake hammerscale from secondary smithing.

6.4 Analysis of Iron Age Archaeobotanical Remains

Phil Austin and Louisa Gray

The methodology used to analyse the archaeobotanical remains from Iron Age features was as set out above (Chapter 3.4). Charcoal from seven samples ({39}, {45}, {61}, {62}, {70}, {71} and {82}) recovered from Iron Age deposits were studied resulting in the identification of eight taxa, making it the second taxon richest phase (see Appendix 2). Holly (*Ilex aquifolium*), not represented in earlier periods, and willow/poplar (*Salix/Populus* sp.), represented in this period only, were identified along with oak (*Quercus* sp.), oak/chestnut (*Quercus/Castanea*), hazel (*Corylus avellana*), Maloideae, honeysuckle/privet (*Lonicera/Ligustrum*) and *Prunus* sp. Oak is clearly the most common wood represented. The impression gained is that shrub taxa were more widely exploited. The fires in this phase probably include fires used predominantly for domestic purposes, hearths or ovens for example, for which wood choice is not necessarily critical, this may partly explain the greater apparent diversity. Oak woodland with an under-storey composed of hazel, holly and, possibly hawthorn and cherry is likely. It is plausible that hazel coppice or scrub was present and that open areas were not uncommon.

Sample {71} context [918], fill of refuse pit [919] contained an emmer/spelt (*Triticum dicoccum/spelta*) grain. Further identification of this grain was not possible because no chaff was recovered to support any identification to ploidy level.

Chapter 7

Phase 7 Roman Activity

A substantial assemblage of Roman pottery recovered from a colluvial deposit within Area D in the south-eastern quadrant of the development site indicates that a settlement of some form was located in the near vicinity during the Roman period. The assemblage included waste products arising from second- to early third-century pottery production. Roman pottery kilns have been excavated in the near vicinity at Heath Farm, Postwick. A few scattered features of probable Roman origin were recorded across Areas A and D, assigned to Phase 7 activity.

7.1 The Roman Archaeological Sequence

Colluvial deposits, Area D

A layer of colluvial material [1177] (not illustrated), recorded as [48] in evaluation Trench 45, was observed over the whole of Area D, continuing beyond the limits of excavation. This comprised brown silty sand with frequent lime or chalk flecking, occasional flecks of ceramic building material and flint pebbles. A small assemblage of Romano-British pottery was recovered from this layer including large parts of two individual vessels, both of late second-century AD date, along with a single Early Neolithic blade and an Early Bronze Age barbed and tanged arrowhead (see Chapter 4.2).

Colluvial layer [1197], recorded and sampled as [46] during the evaluation, overlay [1177] in the north-western corner of Area D. It was recorded over an area measuring 6.70m by 6.60m, continuing to the north and west beyond the limits of excavation and was up to 0.30m thick (Fig. 43). This comprised greyish brown silty sand with occasional flint pebble inclusions. The layer had been damaged by ploughing at its eastern extent with several plough marks pulling material uphill from the deposit. A very large assemblage of Romano-British pottery, nearly 1,400 sherds, was recovered from this deposit and this dates from the second to early third century AD. Although it is clear that layer [1197] was deposited in this area through a natural colluvial process, the crucial question is the provenance of the substantial pottery assemblage. Some of the material within the assemblage represented waste material or 'seconds' from pottery production, but many of the vessels were sooted which means they had been used and

the assemblage is not simply a pottery production waste dump (see Gerrard, Chapter 7.2). An unusual feature of this assemblage was the very high proportion of jars and it may be that this assemblage represents dumped waste from an unknown but specific activity that required the use of a large number of jars.

The only other evidence for Roman activity north of Area D comprised a single pit [149] excavated in Trench 84, located *c.* 80m to the north-west, which produced a small assemblage of Roman pottery. The upper fill of the pit contained a large quantity of charcoal, some of which was identified as oak (Poole *et al.* 2007) and a few fragments of hammerscale were also recovered (see Keys, Chapter 7.4).

Features within Area D

Several features in Area D contained Romano-British pottery, but this was mostly in very abraded condition and only present in small quantities, and may therefore

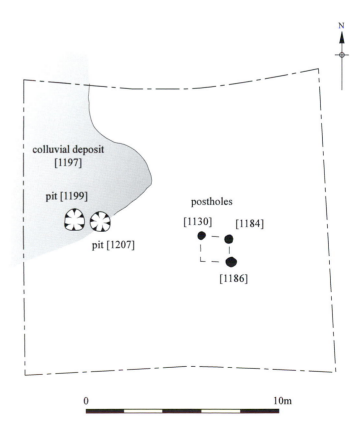

Fig. 43   Phase 7, Roman features, Area D (scale 1:200)

be residual. A few features produced slightly larger quantities or material that was in much better condition and which may be of contemporary date to the pottery. The most convincing of these was perhaps [1199], a small pit located in the western part of Area D, which produced over 50 sherds of pottery (Fig. 43). This assemblage was closely linked to the material from layer [1197], indeed sherd links were noted indicating that the material came from the same source. In close proximity to the east was another small pit [1207], which also produced a small quantity of Romano-British pottery. A series of postholes were also recorded in this area, which given the predominance of Roman activity in this area and paucity of otherwise-dated activity may be contemporary.

Towards the south-eastern corner of Area D was a group of three postholes [1130], [1184] and [1186]; these appeared to form three points of a square. The posts were positioned approximately 1m apart forming parts of a four-post structure, and a fourth posthole may have been removed by the digging of Post-Medieval pit [1205].

Features within Area B

A few scattered features recorded across Area B contained small quantities of often rather abraded Romano-British pottery. A sub-circular pit [359], located approximately 12m from the southern limit of Area B, measured 1.0m by 0.70m and 0.18m deep (Fig. 44). This contained quantities of charcoal fragments. Although quite small and shallow, it appears likely that this feature represents the base of an eroded or plough-damaged refuse pit. To the east was pit [630], this measured 0.64m by 0.50m and 0.10m deep and also contained a small quantity of pottery of similar date. Adjacent to the west was pit [632] of very similar size and profile. To the south and adjacent to the southern limit of excavation was a very substantial tree-throw hollow [320].

A deposit of material [1218], located towards the north-eastern corner of Area B, measured *c.* 0.75m in diameter and 70mm thick. This comprised silty sand with very occasional charcoal flecking. It may represent

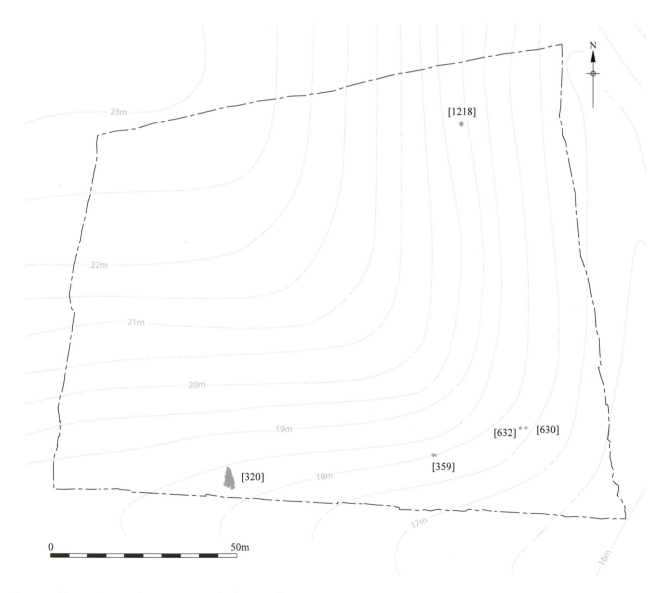

Fig. 44   Phase 7, Roman features, Area B (scale 1:1000)

the very base of a refuse pit or the remains of a midden. A colluvial deposit [488] was also identified within the south-western part of Area B. All of these features and deposits produced pottery dated to after AD 120.

7.2 Romano-British Pottery

James Gerrard

The total Romano-British pottery assemblage amounted to 1,641 sherds weighing 15.327kgs from a mere 31 contexts. However, only four contexts provided assemblages of any significance and the pottery from the remaining contexts is highly abraded and of little use beyond its value as dating evidence. All the pottery from the site was recorded in a database that is available for consultation in the site archive.

Fabrics

The majority of the pottery appears to be typical of the types of fabrics produced and used within Norfolk during the Roman period (A. Lyons, pers. comm.). Much of the pottery is sandy, slightly blue in colour and has occasional flecks of mica or visible clay relicts. This would seem to indicate production in Central Norfolk at Brampton (BSHGW: Bates and Lyons 2003, 44–51; Green 1977), Postwick (Lyons 2003, 47) or Scole (Lyons and Tester forthcoming). The close proximity of the Postwick kilns to the site and the presence of 'seconds' in the assemblage may suggest that these fabrics represent very local production at nearby and as yet undiscovered kilns. Non-local and imported fabrics represent a very minor component of the overall site assemblage (Table 23).

The groups

Group 1

The largest group of pottery from the site came from layer [1197]/[46]. 1,384 sherds, weighing 12.843kg was recovered from this deposit and amounted to 12.63 EVEs based on rims. By sherd count and weight this accounts for 84% of the total Roman period pottery assemblage from the site. The majority of the pottery in this group is in a local grey and slightly micaceous fabric (BSHGW) (Fig. 45). Some vessels have occasional clay relicts (VGW) and were probably produced at the nearby Postwick kilns (Bates and Lyons 2003), while others – lacking these inclusions – may have been made slightly further afield at Brampton (Green 1977). Two jar rims display firing defects and can probably be classed as 'seconds' while another sherd has a firing blister, which reinforces the impression that the users of these pots were receiving vessels directly from the kilns. Other fabrics include Sandy Grey wares, a few fragments from a Dales ware jar, and a number of sherds from a Lower Nene Valley Colour Coated beaker.

The greyware forms suggest a date in the second to early third century for this group (A. Lyons, pers. comm.). However, this dating should be refined by further comparison of the forms with the few traded and imported sherds. They suggest that a tighter dating is possible. Three roughcast sherds from Cologne can be dated AD 130–200/250 and a sherd from a Nene Valley beaker with underslip *en barbotine* scroll decoration is probably datable to the mid second to early third century (Perrin 1999, 93). A single fragment of a rouletted Moselkeramik beaker favours a slightly later date (AD 200–275) as do a small number of beaded and flanged bowl sherds in SGW. On balance a late second to early

Fabric	Name	Sherd Count	Weight (g)	Reference
BSHGW / VGW	Brampton / Postwick Grey ware	1,048	10,070	Lyons 2004, 32; Bates and Lyons 2003
DAL SH	Dales ware	8	102	Tomber and Dore 1998, 157
KOL CC	Cologne fine ware	3	6	Tomber and Dore 1998, 57
LNVCC	Nene Valley Colour Coated ware	21	91	Tomber and Dore 1998, 118
MISC	Unidentifiable sherds	248	1,531	Prob. BSHGW / VGW
MOS BS	Moselkeramik	1	2	Tomber and Dore 1998, 57
SAM	Samian	4	41	Tomber and Dore 1998, 25–41
STW	Non-local tempered wares	7	50	Bates and Lyons 2003, appx 4
SGW	Sandy Grey wares	232	2,160	Bates and Lyons 2003, appx 4
VGW	Visible Clay Relict Grey ware	69	1,274	Bates and Lyons 2003, appx 4
Total		**1,641**	**15,327**	

Table 23   Number of sherds and weights by fabric for the entire site assemblage of Romano-British pottery

Jar	11.57	92%
Bowl	0.91	7%
Dish	0	0%
Beaker	0.15	1%
Total	12.63	100%

Table 24   Quantification of the pottery from [1197]/[46] by vessel form

third-century date for this group seems appropriate.

The most interesting aspect of the pottery recovered from [1197/46] is the high proportion of jars present in the group. Quantification of the material by EVE reveals that jars form 92% of the assemblage, bowls 7% and beakers 1%. Other forms (such as flagons, dishes, large storage vessels) are not present even as body sherds. Comparison with data collected by Evans (2001, fig. 5) demonstrates that this is an unusually high proportion of jars even for a rural site. During analysis of the pottery it was noticeable that despite many of the sherds being abraded, rim sherds could still be refitted to make complete or semi-complete circumferences and this suggests that a relatively small number of vessels are present.

The odd composition of the group and its apparent isolation at the site means that any interpretation of this group must be tentative. The fact that many vessels are sooted indicates that they were used and that the assemblage is not simply a group of dumped pottery production waste (as might be indicated by the 'wasters' or 'seconds'). Possibly the assemblage is the dumped residue from a specific activity that required the use of a large number of jars. The lack of firm evidence for Romano-British settlement makes makes establishing the nature of this activity problematic.

Group 2

The pottery from Group 2 was recovered from the fill [1198] of pit [1199]. It is closely related to the pottery in Group 1 and totalled 51 Romano-British sherds weighing 764g (2.14 EVEs). The key sherd is a fragment of Dales ware jar that is probably derived from the same vessel as the example in Group 1 and indicates that this group of pottery is derived from the same source.

Group 3

The final group is small (53 sherds, 740g, 0.88 EVEs) but includes large parts of two individual vessels from layer [1177]. The first vessel is a necked jar in micaceous VGW suggesting that the vessel may have been produced at Wattisfield (A. Lyons, pers. comm.). The second vessel is a necked jar with cordons in BSHGW/VGW. This vessel has a firing blister, which suggests that it is a waster. Interestingly, no vessels of this type were found at the Postwick kilns (A. Lyons, pers. comm.). Both are likely to be of mid to late second-century date.

Conclusions

The relative dearth of Roman pottery from the site would seem to indicate that activity in the area during the Roman period was of low intensity. This makes the large group of pottery from [1197]/[46] all the more significant, especially given its unusual functional composition. The presence of local fabrics is to be expected and some connections with the nearby kilns seem assured. However, the small proportion of non-local imports would appear to indicate relatively low status.

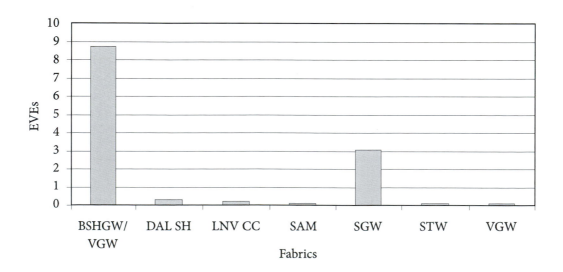

Fig. 45   Quantification of the pottery from [1197]/[46] by fabric and EVE.

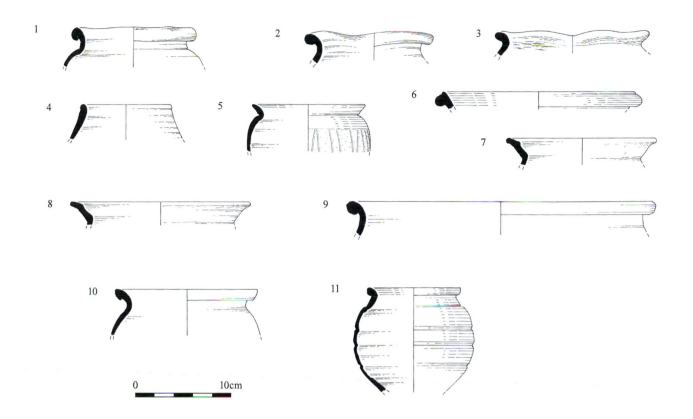

Fig. 46   Romano-British pottery (scale 1:4)

Catalogue of illustrated Romano-British pottery

Group 1

Fig. 46.1. Necked jar in BSHGW, sooted externally (Lyons 2004, appx 1, Type 4.5). Mid second to late third century. [1197]

Fig. 46.2. Warped necked jar in BSHGW (Lyons 2004, appx 1, Type 4.5). Mid second to late third century. [1197]

Fig. 46.3. Warped necked jar in BSHGW (Lyons 2004, appx 1, Type 4.5). Mid second to late third century. [1197]

Fig. 46.4. Plain bag-shaped beaker in BSHGW (Lyons 2004, appx 1, Type 3.6). Later second–third century. [1197]

Fig. 46.5. Jar with vertical burnished lines in BSHGW. Similar to a small vessel described as a beaker from Snettisham (Lyons 2004, fig. 27.43) but seemingly derived from a second-century Black Burnished form (Monaghan 1987, 3J2). [1197]

Fig. 46.6. Beaded and flanged bowl in UBB. The vessel is similar to an example in ?BB2 fabric from Caister (Darling and Gurney 1993, fig. 153, 540). The bead is poorly developed suggesting a third-century date. [1197]

Fig. 46.7. Lid seated jar rim in DAL SH. Similar to an example from Caister (Darling and Gurney 1993, fig. 140.114). This sherd is probably part of the same vessel as P8. [1197]

Group 2

Fig. 46.8. Lid seated jar rim in DAL SH. Similar to an example from Caister (Darling and Gurney 1993, fig. 140.114). This sherd is probably part of the same vessel as P7. [1198]

Fig. 46.9. Necked jar in BSHGW. (Lyons 2004, appx 1, Type 3.6). Later second – third century. [1198]

Group 3

Fig. 46.10. Necked jar in MRW. (Lyons 2004, appx 1, Type 3.6). Later second–third century. [1177]

Fig. 46.11. Necked jar with multiple cordons in BSHGW. [1177]

7.3 Romano-British Small Finds

James Gerrard

Few Romano-British items were recovered from the site and this is surely linked to the low-level nature of any Roman period activity. The most notable item was an intact but undecorated crossbow brooch with onion shaped terminals (<349>, [671]). Various typological classifications of these objects have been attempted (Swift 2000, 13–88) with varying degrees of success (Cool 2010, 278). What seems certain is that this item is of fourth-century date. It also seems clear that crossbow brooches were worn by members of the Late Roman military and elite (Janes 1996; Swift 2000, 3–4; 2003, 21–23; Cool 2010, 278). It is presumably a casual loss and the same can probably be said of the fragments of two other brooches from the site: a piece of an early Roman bow brooch <11> and a terminal from a Fowler Type A penannular brooch <244>.

Fig. 48   Fourth-century crossbow brooch

Eight Roman coins were recovered of which four were first- or second-century types. Only one of these was closely datable, an *as* of Antoninus Pius, struck between AD 138–161. The remaining four coins include two irregular radiates of 'Tetricus I' and 'Victorinus' (*c.* AD 270–290) and two *antoniniani* of Carausius (AD 286–293). Full details of these coins are available in the archive.

7.4 Ironworking Slag

Lynne Keys

There was scant evidence for ironworking during the Roman period. The recovered evidence is from micro-slags, but only two spheroids were present in the tiny amount (1g) of sieved material from pit [149] (see Appendix 3). This hammerscale would have come from secondary smithing activities. Some ore fines, a tiny sliver of iron and small pieces of fired clay (total 8g) were recovered from colluvial layer [488] and a small quantity of burnt coal was recovered from tree-throw hollow [320].

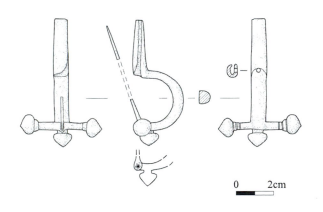

Fig. 47   Fourth-century crossbow brooch with onion shaped terminals <349> [671] (scale 1:2)

Chapter 8

Phase 8 Anglo-Saxon and Early Medieval Activity

During the later Saxon and early Medieval period (Phase 8) there was a marked change at the Laurel Farm site; extensive evidence for industrial activity was recorded across Area B. Dating for this was largely provided by radiocarbon analysis (see Table 25), along with the recovery of a few pieces of Thetford-type ware, of possible tenth-century date (see Sudds, Chapter 8.5). A large number of features from this period have been identified as being associated with the initial stages of iron extraction and production. This is of considerable significance due to the scarcity of similar evidence in the archaeological record. There was an absence of associated settlement-related evidence, however, with no certain domestic structures recognized and very little contemporary pottery or other artefactual materials recovered; it therefore seems that during the Anglo-Saxon period the site was used solely for industrial activity. Laurel Farm was ideally placed for this, with the raw materials needed for the initial stages of iron processing all available at the site, and a market for the products in the nearby developing town of Norwich.

Three principal types of features associated with iron production were identified: a number of substantial quarry pits dug to obtain iron ore from natural deposits; large circular pits used for charcoal burning; and smaller, intensively burnt pits where the ore would have been roasted. As features of this kind have rarely been published in depth before, detailed descriptions and figures are included here. Although no *in-situ* evidence for smelting furnaces was recorded, quantities of industrial residues including tap slag, furnace slag and run slag were recovered. This material would have been produced during iron smelting and its presence indicates that this process was undertaken at Laurel Farm.

The industrial activity extended predominantly across the southern part of Area B, with most features being situated to the south of the Bronze Age round barrow. It is likely that the mound would still have survived as an earthwork at this time, though probably denuded, and as one of the Anglo-Saxon features was recorded cutting the southern side of the ring-ditch, the ditch seems to have been infilled by this time. For the sake of clarity of description the features are discussed as three geographically distinct clusters; one in the east, one in the central part of the excavated area and a third in the west (Fig. 49). In reality the distribution of features

is likely to form more of a continuum than a cluster, and it is important to note that there are no apparent chronological trends in the distribution of features. Very little structural evidence was identified although a small rectangular sunken feature that had a central hearth was dated to this period, but this too is likely to have been related to the iron working process rather than representing habitation.

A substantial V-shaped, palisaded, defensive ditch dating to the eighth or ninth century AD, positioned on the same alignment as the later parish boundary, appears to have been a temporary feature at the site and was both preceded and succeeded by the evidence for iron processing. Although this may simply represent an early boundary ditch, its defensive nature may suggest it was of more importance, and the fact that it was constructed during the same period as the Viking excursions along the River Yare and their settlement at Norwich may be of significance.

8.1 The Anglo-Saxon and Early Medieval Archaeological Sequence

Ditches in the south-eastern corner of Area B

Ditch [615], which was aligned north–south and situated towards the eastern edge of the site, extended for over 35m, continuing beyond the limits of excavation to the south. Its northern extent ended in a slightly squared terminal and there were no indications that it continued further to the north, although this area had been subjected to erosion and was covered with a thick alluvial layer. The ditch varied from between 2.10m to 3.15m in width, its sides were steeply sloping and it had a vertically-sided 0.20m wide slot, reminiscent of an 'ankle breaker', dug into and along its base (Fig. 50). It was filled with silty sand with very occasional charcoal flecks and pieces of residual struck flint and pottery. There were up to four fills recorded [758]–[761], the primary fill may represent some collapsing of the edges of the ditch but there was little to indicate whether it had been backfilled deliberately or had naturally infilled. Its sharp edges, despite it having been cut through loose sandy deposits, suggest that it had not remained open for long before

being infilled, indicating that it may have been backfilled
deliberately not long after it was dug.

The dating of the construction and infilling of this
ditch can be set within reasonably secure parameters.
It truncated pit [579], which has provided a calibrated
radiocarbon date of AD 650–780 (Beta-225543), and had
itself been cut into by pits [617], [597] and [367] which
have provided dates of AD 680–880 (Waikato-22908),
AD 670–880 (Beta-225544), and AD 1020–1200 (Beta-
225541), respectively (see Appendix 1). Taking the
radiocarbon dates at face value, the ditch would appear to
have been excavated after AD 650 at the earliest and been
infilled by AD 880 at the latest.

On the same alignment and located *c*. 2m to the east
of ditch [615] was a much smaller linear feature [692].
This measured 10.40m in length, its northern terminal
being parallel to that of ditch [615], and was up to 0.50m
wide and 0.45m deep. Its edges were near vertical and it
had a flat base, the survival of its edges from weathering
suggests that it was immediately infilled and its size and
shape indicate that this may have been a palisade trench.
It had been truncated by two pits, [546] and [597], the
latter also truncating larger ditch [615] and producing a
radiocarbon date as discussed above.

The profile of the larger ditch, particularly the
'ankle-breaker' type feature in its base, is reminiscent of
defensive ditches and suggests it may have had a military
function. The fact that its profile had survived despite the
loose nature of the sub-strata suggests it was not open
for long. The small ditch most plausibly represents a
palisade and its alignment and position strongly suggests
it was associated with ditch [615], if a defensive function
was accepted for the larger ditch then the palisade could
have operated in conjunction with it. One of the major
drawbacks with suggestions of a military or defensive
function for these ditches would be that they both
terminate to the north, whilst the palisade only extended
for just over 10m. The area to the north and east of these
features, lying on the brow of the adjacent dry valley, was
heavily affected by erosion and it was also covered by
colluvium, potentially masking any features. Suggestions
that this at least partly formed after the Saxon activity
were reinforced by a colluvial layer that contained large
fragments of charcoal and small fragments of iron ore
downhill to the north and east of the ditch. These factors
lead to the possibility that further segments of a north–
south aligned boundary could have existed further north
than those recorded.

Other possible explanations of the function of these
linear features is that as they lie on the same alignment
and very close to the modern Civil Parish boundary
(just within the Thorpe St Andrew side as currently
drawn) they may have been boundary features acting as
a territorial marker delimiting what may have been and
what certainly were later to become, separate parishes.
This possibility would apply regardless of whether or not
the boundary ditch also had any military or defensive
associations. Thorpe St Andrew, or Thorpe Episcopi
as it was called in Medieval times (Nuthall 2002), was

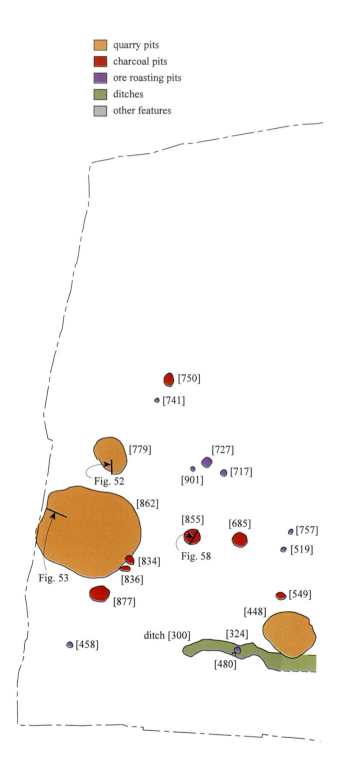

Fig. 49   Phase 8, Anglo-Saxon and early Medieval features,
Area B (scale 1:625)

known to be the location of the Bishop of Norwich's
manor. The boundary could have delimited a manorial
estate directly under the control of the Cathedral and
it is possible that the Bishop in early times would have
had his own manor in which he may have developed a
lucrative ironworking industry.

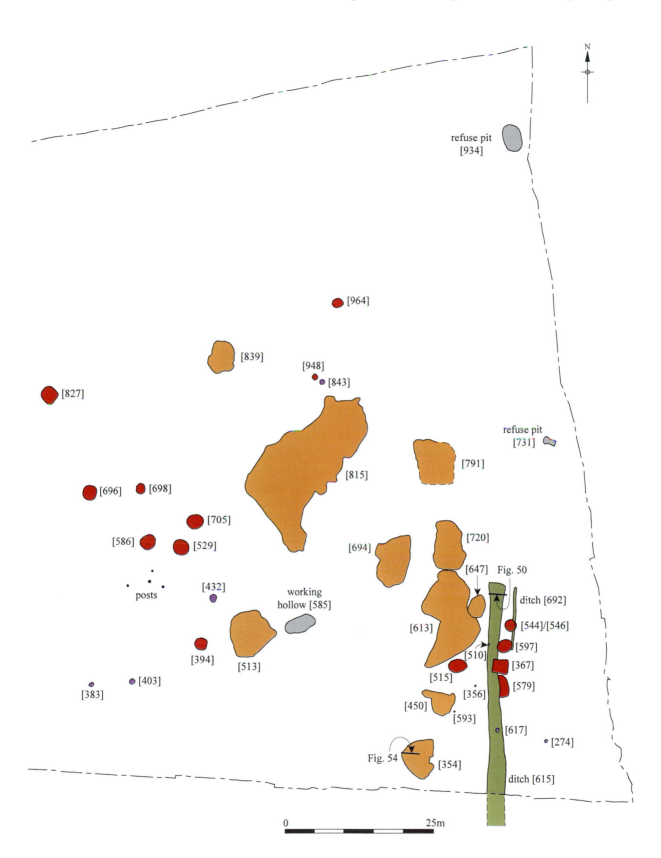

Quarry pits

Thirteen quarry pits were recorded within Area B interpreted as being dug to remove iron ore, which occurs as ironstone nodules, iron panning and carrstone within the natural geological deposits overlying the chalk bedrock in this area (see Hayward, Chapter 8.4). The quarry pits varied considerably in size and shape but were typically irregular in plan, very large in size and often had a complex series of several fills, apparently representing a mix of collapse, natural infilling, deliberate dumping of refuse, deliberate backfilling, and deliberate levelling. It is evident from artefactual material that the final infilling and levelling of the upper

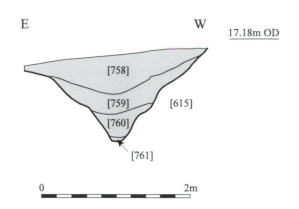

E   W   17.18m OD

[758]

[759]   [615]

[760]

[761]

0   2m

Fig. 50   Section through Anglo-Saxon ditch [615] (scale 1:50)

part of some of the more substantial features took place some considerable time after the features were first dug.

Although thirteen features were identified as quarry pits, it is possible that other features at the site may have been smaller quarries or prospection pits, but as these displayed less conclusive evidence, they have been omitted from this discussion. Due to health and safety considerations and time constraints it was only possible to partially excavate the pits and often not to their full depth. The body of datable material retrieved from the quarries was therefore not extensive, nor was it present in all of the features. The datable material that was recovered derived from numerous periods. A few pits produced small quantities of Post-Medieval pottery, ceramic building material or clay tobacco pipe fragments. Two of the pits that produced this material, [862] and [613], were machine excavated with only one fill being recorded but in the others this Post-Medieval artefactual material was only present in the latest uppermost fills of the features, usually noted as being different to the other fills in the features, and described as slumped or levelled in. It is likely, therefore, that the quarries remained as prominent earthworks for some time and hollows that were either deliberately infilled or ploughed flat much later on when the site was brought into agricultural productivity after enclosure in 1800. That they formed hollows was demonstrated by quarry pit [448] which had much thicker soil horizons present above it and required deeper machining to define its edges. The later Post-Medieval material recovered from the quarries would appear most likely to be associated with the levelling of the uppermost portion, rather than their original excavation or initial infilling.

A single radiocarbon determination was obtained on material from the quarries; a hazel twig from the lower fill of quarry [448] returned a 2-sigma calibrated date of AD 80–250, firmly placing that material within the Roman period. There was little reason to doubt this date, it was obtained on relatively short-lived wood and was recovered from the base of the feature. Nevertheless, the presence of Middle Iron Age pottery alongside Post-Medieval pottery from the upper fills of the feature and the presence of struck flint and other materials datable from the Early Neolithic through to more recent periods

from the other quarries illustrates the very real problem of residual material present within the features.

The quarries shared a number of stratigraphic relationships with other features. Quarry [815] was cut by Post-Medieval ditch [583], the same ditch that also cut three of the ore/charcoal roasting pits. Three of the quarries in the eastern cluster were cut by features that, although they did not contain artefactual material, were thought to be associated with Post-Medieval tree and scrub clearance. Quarry [862] was cut on its very eastern edge by two ore/charcoal roasting pits dated by association with other features to the Saxon period. Two quarries, [448] and [513], cut Middle Iron Age ditch [420], but no other quarries were recorded as truncating features. The stratigraphic evidence would therefore indicate that the quarries, taken as a whole, predate the Post-Medieval period but post-date the Middle Iron Age. The locations of the three clusters of quarries coincide with that of three clusters of pits which show evidence for intense burning and have been identified as charcoal firing and ore-roasting pits. These are securely dated to the Saxon period, and they all concentrate along the southern side of the excavated area. It is also notable that although located close to the ore/charcoal roasting pits, the quarries actually avoid the specific areas chosen for this pitting, in the case of quarry [815] this had one straight edge, on its south-western side, which respected the pits, suggesting that a boundary may have been drawn between the area used for quarrying and that for the ore/charcoal roasting.

The quarries cut through the loose glacial sands of the Corton Formation. These consist predominantly of sands but include a great variety of materials, including pebbles, gravels, silts and clays. No systematic analysis of the underlying sediments was undertaken during the excavations, but all of the samples taken were examined for their lithological content and from these it was estimated that approximately a quarter of the natural sediments at the site were composed of gravel-sized or larger clasts. Of these around 5% consisted of ironstone (within many of the Saxon ore/charcoal roasting pits there were much higher proportions, often attaining 100%, indicating this material had been accumulated). In addition to the ironstone, frequent large lumps of iron-rich conglomerate, iron-pan, were also found in many of the samples. The ground engineering report for the development site records ironstone nodules in some of the boreholes investigated, suggesting that the material must have been relatively common within the strata (Whitbybird Limited 2005a; 2005b). Such ironstone nodules and deposits of iron panning are common within the glacial sands and gravels of north-east Norfolk (Tylecote 1967, 187). The loose compaction of the often sandy natural deposits would have meant that significant quantities of ironstone nodules could have been acquired with reasonable ease. Given that the nearest *in-situ* sources of iron ore, iron rich oxides within the red sandstones known as carrstone, are some distance away, the nearest being the Lower Cretaceous sandstones of Hunstanton/Sandringham, *c.* 60km to the west, this may have been the most convenient area to acquire the ore (see Hayward, Chapter 8.4). Vast numbers of pits for the extraction of these iron nodules have been recorded on the north Norfolk coast, including many at Weybourne thought to date from the late Saxon to Medieval period (Norfolk HER 6280).

After extraction the quarries generally appeared to have infilled quite quickly. Initially, a number of them showed evidence of collapsing sides contributing to their infilling, which may have happened quite quickly as they often had vertical or very steep sides and were cut through relatively loose sands. The majority of the material infilling the pits appeared to have been washed in; these deposits were generally very clean with only very occasional fragments of charcoal or artefactual material present, and it may be supposed that these deposits originated from adjacent up-cast or spoil heaps. Some of the fills appeared to have been deliberately dumped but, again, with a few exceptions this material was relatively clean and may have originated from similar sources, the deliberate disposal of up-cast from the quarrying. As many of the quarries were close to each other it is possible that open quarries were used to dispose of the waste from digging new ones. Some of the infill of the pits contained waste from ironworking processes, including charcoal, burnt clay and pebbles, but also occasional pieces of slag and burnt ironstone. In addition, a number of layers and lenses of brown and red sand may have represented the residues from washing the ironstone.

There was evidence that a few of the quarry pits may have been used for a further stage in the iron production process once the ironstone had been quarried. Pits [862] and [779] apparently had a clay lining applied and this may have been to waterproof the pits so that ore could be washed to remove sand and clay accretions. It is also possible that pit [448] may have been used for washing ore; an irregular linear feature [300]/[322]/[411]/[437] extended roughly west–east towards the south side of the quarry pit. This was up to 2.0m wide and 0.70m deep and was recorded for a distance of *c.* 16m. This feature may represent a channel designed to hold a reservoir of water to be used in the pit for the ore washing process (see Riddler, Chapter 8.2).

Ore roasting pits

Eighteen distinctive small, shallow, circular or oval pits, with traces of intense burning and filled with burnt ironstone and charcoal, were recorded within Area B, interspersed with the quarry pits. These have been identified as ore roasting pits, this process being undertaken to improve the iron content prior to smelting (see Riddler, Chapter 8.2).

Ore roasting was undertaken to remove impurities such as sulphur prior to smelting and also to remove water from the ore. The technology involved in the process is relatively straightforward; a fire was lit in

a small shallow pit and the ore was placed on top and left to burn for several hours before being removed. The ephemeral nature of the pits, along with the fact that they were in effect largely dismantled so that the ore could be recovered, means that such features tend to leave little trace in the archaeological record. The charcoal assemblage recovered from bulk soil samples taken from these pits was almost exclusively from oak (*Quercus* sp.), unsurprisingly the fuel of choice for this process, with the only other species being elm (*Ulmus* sp.), spindle tree (*Euonymus europaeus*), blackthorn (*Prunus* sp.) and Maloideae, being present in very small quantities.

Charcoal burning pits

Interspersed with the three clusters of quarry pits and ore roasting pits were a series of pits, 21 in total, measuring *c.* 1.70–3.60m in diameter with evidence for *in-situ* burning and containing large quantities of charcoal. These features have been identified as charcoal burning pits or 'kilns', to make charcoal to be used in the processes of iron production, such as ore roasting and smelting. These pits were characterized by the presence of substantial quantities of charcoal forming their primary fills and burnt edges. The primary fills often survived only as remnants, and irregularities in some of their edges and bases suggest that they had been 'dug over', or, more plausibly, that their original burnt fills had been largely removed after firing and that they had been subsequently backfilled with a mix of 'clean' unburnt sands alongside burnt material deriving from the original fills. The evidence therefore demonstrates that the pits had been filled with fuel in the form of wood, the contents were then ignited and, once consumed, removed and the charcoal recovered. Any debris remaining was then swept back into the pit.

Pit [705] was of particular interest in that a number of stakeholes were recorded in its base. Others were recorded as having 'mottled' bases and this mottling may also represent traces of stakes although they were

Fig. 51   Charcoal burning pit [705] after excavation showing stakeholes which formed the timber superstructure of the charcoal kiln

not recorded as such. Over 80 stakes or stakeholes were recorded in the base of pit [705], mainly arranged in rings around the circumference of its base (Fig. 51, see Fig. 62). These were all around 50mm in diameter and pushed in 100mm deeper than the base. They were set vertically and had pointed ends; in some cases the carbonised structure of the wood was preserved whilst others contained only charcoal fragments similar to those within the primary fill of the pit. There were also two batons of carbonised wood approximately 0.80m long and 50mm wide, which lay beyond the boundary of the feature to the east. These appear to be collapsed burnt stakes, although it was not possible to determine from which stakehole they originated. The stakes and stakeholes suggest that once the pit had been dug a wickerwork frame was set into the pit, possibly standing proud of it. This was filled with the fuel and the structure then ignited. The lower fill [601] of [586] also showed evidence of structuring. It was described as having charcoal circles in section, linear in plan, which looked like the bottom layer of a carefully laid fire of parallel narrow logs.

Bulk soil samples taken from these pits unsurprisingly produced large quantities of charcoal and the assemblages were dominated by oak (*Quercus* sp., see Austin and Gray, Chapter 8.6). Other good types of firewood were represented by beech (*Fagus Sylvatica*) and hornbeam (*Carpinus betulus*) and species of small trees/shrub such as blackthorn (*Prunus* sp.), but these were present in much smaller quantities and it seems that oak was the preferred wood for making charcoal at the site. Twig wood was also recovered from many of the samples, including Traveller's Joy (*Clematis Vitalba*), hazel (*Corylus Avellana*) and field maple (*Acer Campestre*), probably representing material gathered for kindling. Twig wood from honeysuckle (*Lonicera* sp.) and ivy (*Hedera helix*) may have been brought in on larger wood fragments and charred incidentally as these are climbing plants that attach to other species. The charcoal would have been used for fuel in the many ore roasting pits recorded within Area B. Although there was no surviving structural evidence for smelting furnaces within the excavated area, slag recovered from bulk samples indicated that it was carried out in the near vicinity and it is likely that some of the charcoal produced in this area would have been destined for use in smelting furnaces, this being the preferred fuel type for the smelting process. Charcoal burning pits [529], [597], [827], [834] and [877] all produced evidence of waste from iron smelting in the form of tap slag, furnace slag or microslags (see Chapter 8.3).

Catalogue of Anglo-Saxon and Early Medieval Industrial Pits

Quarry pits

Western group

Quarry pit [448] was sub-circular in plan with steep, stepped sides, measuring 9.0m by 7.70m and excavated to a depth of 1.50m. It was predominantly filled with naturally accumulated sand with charcoal fragments and burnt flint present throughout. Red burnt sand, possibly consisting of burnt ironstone residues, was present in the lowest fill recorded. Pottery dated to AD 1500–1800 and fragments of clay tobacco pipe was recovered from its upper fill, likely to have been dumped in the upper part of the pit in to level the feature. A calibrated radiocarbon date taken on hazel wood from its lowest recorded fill produced a radiocarbon date of AD 80–250 (Waikato-22907; see Appendix 1), presumably originating from an earlier period of activity at the site.

Quarry [779] was oval in shape with steeply sloping sides and measuring *c.* 7.0m by 4.50m. This pit was at least 1.70m deep, but it was not possible to excavate to its base (Fig. 52). Five fills were recorded, the earliest [795] comprised a. 0.20m thick layer of sandy-clay, possibly representing a deliberate clay lining to waterproof the pit. After the iron ore had been quarried, the pit may have been made waterproof for use in the subsequent stage of iron production, washing the ore, as discussed further below. The clay lining was overlain by a dump of material [796], at least 0.20m thick but not fully excavated, containing frequent charcoal fragments and burnt daub, representing dumped burnt waste. The overlying

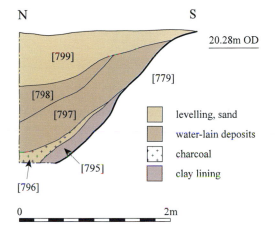

Fig. 52 Section through partially excavated quarry pit [779] (scale 1:50)

fills [797] and [798] consisted of sandy silt-clays over 0.80m in thickness, apparently waterlain, suggesting that the feature had contained water like a pond, presumably due to the presence of the clay-lining, and had naturally silted up.

Adjacent to the western limit of excavation was a substantial quarry pit [862], sub-circular in plan with steeply sloping sides, measuring *c.* 17m in diameter and at least 1.20m deep, although the base was not reached (Fig. 53). A deposit of orange grey silt-clay [861] and greyish brown silt-clay [860] adhering to the steep sides of the pit with a combined maximum thickness of 0.50m may represent a waterproof clay lining. Filling the bulk of the feature were two fills of relatively clean sands [859] and [858] containing patches of red sandy-clay that may represent burnt ironstone

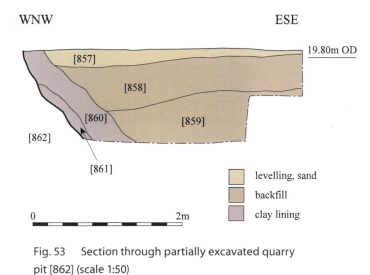

Fig. 53 Section through partially excavated quarry pit [862] (scale 1:50)

residues, possibly arising from the washing of iron ore. The pit was finally sealed with sands containing humic material [857], possibly representing soils formed on the top of the feature, or possibly dumped into it to level it. No artefacts or other datable material were recovered.

Central group

Quarry [513], which measured 7.60m by 7.40m, had variably sloping sides, again its base was not reached and excavation ceased at a depth of 1.20m. A sequence of five fills was recorded; the lowest appeared to represent collapsed sides of the feature whilst the next three were naturally accumulated, consisting of laminated silts and sands, although some deliberate dumping of material may have occurred interspersed with the natural infilling. The final fill, which also consisted of silts and sands but included burnt daub, pottery fragments dated to the Saxon and the Medieval periods, Medieval ceramic building material and five Early Neolithic struck flints, was thought to represent deposits that had either slumped or been deliberately dumped into the feature, perhaps to level it.

The largest quarry pit encountered at the site was pit [815], located just east of the centre of Area B, which was amorphous in plan, extending over 25m by 20m, and may actually represent more than one feature. The excavated portion had steeply sloping sides, but it was not possible to expose the base, with excavation ceasing at a depth of 1.20m. Within the excavated portion, five fills were recorded, all consisting of loose silts and sands. Charcoal fragments were present in the lowest excavated fill, but the only artefactual evidence, which consisted of a few fragments of pottery, ceramic building material and clay tobacco pipe dating to the nineteenth century, came from the top 0.20m of the feature. Again, this material was presumably deposited to infill or level a hollow left in the upper part of the pit.

Quarry pit [839] had irregular sides, measured 5.40m by 4.25m and was excavated to a depth of 0.45m, but was not bottomed. No datable material was recovered from its single silt and sand fill although this was recorded as being red-brown in colour and may have included comminuted burnt iron ore, possibly derived from washing this material.

Eastern group

Quarry pit [354], lying adjacent to the southern limit of excavation, was irregular in shape and measured 6.50m by 5.0m and was 0.90m deep with a gently sloping western side, a steep, slightly undercut eastern side, and an uneven and undulating base (Fig. 54). It contained a series of up to six fills. The earliest [353] comprised clean sands and appeared to represent naturally accumulated material formed by partial collapse of the edges of the pit. This was followed by a series of mostly clean sandy deposits that contained frequent charcoal and more humic material, perhaps representing dumped deposits or material formed from the erosion of the adjacent

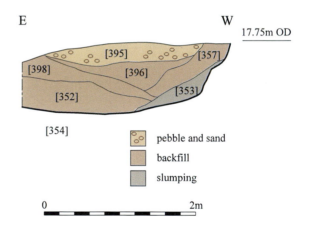

Fig. 54　Section through partially excavated quarry pit [354] (scale 1:50)

land surfaces. The feature was finally levelled with a deposit of pebbly sand [395], seemingly of a different origin from the others and perhaps representing deliberate infilling of the feature.

Quarry pit [450], which was irregular in shape with very steeply sloping sides, measured 5.0m by 2.75m and was excavated to a depth of 0.42m, although its base was not reached. Its fill was similar to the natural deposits but was laminated, indicating infilling from rainwash, and contained an abraded sherd of Saxon or Middle Iron Age pottery.

Quarry pit [613] is thought to consist of at least three intercutting or conjoined sections, all containing similar fills. It was irregular in plan and measured 16.25m by up to 5.60m wide and was at least 1.70m deep with steeply sloping edges, although it was only partially excavated and the base not reached. Its fills consisted of laminated sands and silts of variable colours indicating that the feature had silted up largely from rain-wash. There were also quantities of charcoal present as well as Post-Medieval pottery, glass and clay tobacco pipe fragments although it is not clear from exactly where in the sequence of infilling this material was found but, if following a similar pattern to many of the other quarries, this material may only have been present in the uppermost fills. The fills also produced quantities of charcoal and burnt flint but no further dating evidence was recovered, although it was truncated by a number of features thought to represent Post-Medieval tree and shrub clearance.

Quarry pit [647] was oval in plan and measured 3.65m by 2.80m and was at least 0.85m deep (Fig. 55). It had stepped, near vertical sides and a slightly concave base with a deeper area in the centre. It was filled with laminated silts and sands [646], indicating rain-washed deposits. This feature, although somewhat smaller than the other quarries in this cluster, has been interpreted as another quarry due to its depth and steep sides.

Quarry pit [694] measured 8.75m by 5.80m and was excavated to a depth of 0.60m, although its base was not reached. A single fill was recorded, consisting of mottled sand with no datable inclusions and interpreted as material eroded in from a spoil heap that was probably located immediately to the west of the quarry.

Quarry pit [720] measured over 8.0m by 5.0m, was excavated to a depth of 1.20m, and had very steeply sloping sides. The lowest fill recorded was in excess of 0.28m thick and consisted of silts and sands similar to the underlying natural deposits, whilst the upper fill was similar but also contained lenses of red clay, possibly originating from the washing of iron ore. No finds or other datable evidence were recovered.

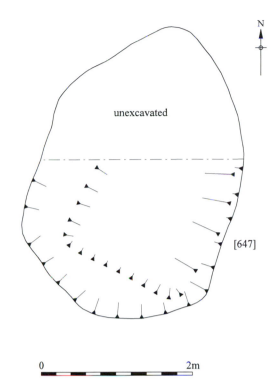

Fig. 55   Detail of partially excavated quarry pit [647] (scale 1:50)

The visible extent of quarry pit [791] was 5.0m by 4.0m, although it was not possible to establish its full extent due to overlying colluvium. It was excavated to a depth of 0.50m, and where excavated had almost vertical sides. The single fill [823] recorded consisted of silty sand similar to natural deposits.

Ore roasting pits

Western group

Pit [324], which measured 1.10m by 0.95m and 0.22m deep, was oval in shape and had gently sloping sides and a flat base. Its single fill [323] consisted of a firmly compacted dark greyish black charcoal-rich sandy silt containing occasional flint pebbles and burnt ironstone fragments.

Pit [458] measured 1.0m in diameter and survived to a depth of 0.30m. It was circular in plan and had steeply sloping sides and a slightly concave base. Its single fill [457] consisted of a fairly compact mid brown silt with some sand, containing frequent charcoal including many large fragments.

Pit [480], also circular in plan, measured 0.60m in diameter and survived to a depth of 100mm. It had gently sloping edges and a flat base. Its single fill [479] comprised dark greyish black, well compacted and heavily burnt silty sand and flint pebbles containing very frequent charcoal fragments, including some large fragments, and occasional ironstone and magnetized particles.

Pit [519], which was sub-circular in plan, measured between 0.90m–1.0m in diameter and survived to a depth of 0.19m with gently sloping edges and a flat base. Scorching around and beneath the cut indicated intense *in-situ* burning. Its single fill [518] comprised dark brown heavily burnt silty sand of friable consistency with very frequent charcoal, distributed in occasional large patches, very occasional flint pebbles and struck flint.

Pit [717], sub-circular with steeply sloping sides and a slightly concave base, measured 1.14m by 0.92m and survived to a depth of 0.15m. Its single fill [716] consisted of a loose dark black brown to black sand and silt containing frequent charcoal, include some very large fragments, burnt flint and occasional undiagnostic struck flints.

Pit [727] circular in plan, its upper edges were disturbed and enlarged whilst the lower sides were gently sloping and the base concave and uneven, indicating that it may have been 'emptied' at some point (Fig. 56). It measured 1.05m in diameter and survived to a depth of 0.23m. Lining the pit was a deposit of burnt 'fired' orange pink clay [726] that was up to 30mm thick. Filling the cut and lining was [725] a deposit up to 0.20m thick of dark greyish brown silt sand with occasional ash and charcoal flecking which was concentrated towards the base of the fill, along with small flint pebbles, burnt flint and struck flint inclusions. The bulk sample taken from this feature produced a quantity of charcoal, all of which was identified as being oak. A radiocarbon date of AD 660–780 (Waikato-22902; see Appendix 1) was obtained from a fragment of charcoal. The presence of the remnants of a clay lining led to this feature initially being interpreted as a possible furnace, however further analysis demonstrates that this is not the case and the feature seems to be an ore roasting pit (see Riddler, Chapter 8.2).

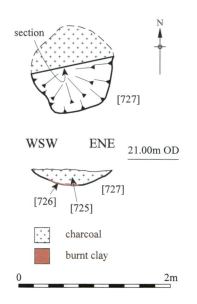

Fig. 56   Detail and section through partially excavated ore roasting pit [727] (scale 1:50)

Pit [741] measured 0.80m in diameter and had moderately sloping sides and an uneven base, surviving to a depth of 0.12m. Its single fill [740] comprised a mottled dark brown and black burnt silt and sand with frequent charcoal fragments, some of which were large, measuring over 20mm in diameter, and burnt flint gravels and pebbles. There was clear evidence for *in-situ* burning in this pit.

Pit [757] measured 0.86m by 0.68m and survived to a depth of 0.11m. It was sub-rectangular in plan with rounded corners, vertical edges and a flat base. It single fill [756] comprised dark black brown heavily burnt silt and sand with frequent charcoal, small angular flints and a single burnt flint.

Pit [901], sub-circular in plan with gently sloping edges and a concave base, measured 0.70m by 0.85m and was 0.15m deep. Its single fill [902] comprised a mid to dark brownish black burnt silt and sand containing occasional small flint pebbles and frequent charcoal flecking.

Central group

Pit [383], which measured 0.88m by 0.62m and 0.27m deep, was irregular in plan and its sides and base were also irregular and heavily pitted by rootholes. Its fill [384] comprised a mix of charcoal fragments and dark orange burnt sand and the natural deposits around its edges were heavily scorched.

Pit [403] measured 0.95m in diameter and was up to 0.39m deep with steeply sloping sides merging to form a tapered base. Its fill [402] comprised burnt mid to dark greyish yellow brown silt sand containing *c.* 20% charcoal, including many large fragments over 15mm diameter, variably burnt flint pebbles and comminuted burnt ironstone fragments. The contents had clearly been burnt *in situ* and the natural deposits around its edges were heavily scorched.

Pit [432], which was sub-circular in plan, measured 1.30m by 1.10m and 0.11m deep and had steeply sloping edges and the base had originally been flat but was subsequently disturbed by root damage. Its fill [431] comprised mottled grey and light yellowish brown silt and sand containing lenses of charcoal and ash, occasional flint pebbles and struck flint inclusions. The natural sub-stratum around the edges of the pit was discoloured and heavily scorched, clear evidence for *in-situ* burning.

Pit [843], circular in plan with steeply sloping edges and a generally flat but pitted base, measured 0.72m in diameter and survived to a depth of 90mm. It contained a single fill [837] comprising charcoal flecks and fragments in a greyish black burnt sand matrix with frequent burnt pebbles. The pit and its contents had evidently been burnt *in situ*.

Eastern group

Pit [274] measured 0.56m by 0.50m and was 0.12m deep. It was sub-circular in plan with steep edges and a flat base and scorched bands of reddened sand extended beyond the edges of the feature (Fig. 57). Its fill [273] comprised mottled grey/brown silty sand with frequent ironstone fragments, representing around 15% of the fill, charcoal fragments and burnt flint.

Pit [356], which measured 0.28m in diameter and 60mm deep, had gently sloping sides and an uneven base. Scorching extended beyond the feature's edges turning the natural sand reddish yellow. Its fill [355] comprised coarse sand that been burnt black in colour.

Pit [510], sub-circular in plan and measuring 0.30m by 0.23m and 0.18m deep, had vertical edges and a flat base. Its fill [509] comprised orange brown sandy silt with very frequent charcoal, some pieces measuring over 150mm in size, and a large ironstone fragment.

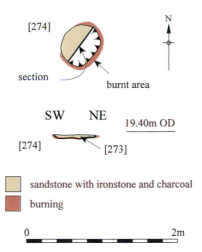

Fig. 57   Detail and section through partially excavated ore roasting pit [274] (scale 1:50)

Pit [593] measured *c.* 0.25m in diameter and was 90mm deep with gently sloping sides merging into a concave base. Scorching extended beyond the edges of the feature and its fill [592] comprised fine to medium grained sand burnt red to black in colour with charcoal.

Pit [617], which measured 0.60–0.68m in diameter and was 90mm deep, was sub-circular in plan with gently sloping sides merging into a concave base. Scorched bands of reddened sand extended beyond the edges of the feature and its fill [616] comprised fine to medium grained sand burnt mid brown to black in colour, containing frequent ironstone fragments and four fragments of pottery of Thetford-type tradition. This is broadly dated from the mid-ninth to mid-twelfth century; different production centres had variable dates (see Sudds, Chapter 8.5). A radiocarbon determination taken on Maloideae (apple family) charcoal returned a date of AD 680–880 (Waikato-22908; see Appendix 1).

Charcoal burning pits

Western group

Pit [549] was oval in plan with gently sloping sides and a concave base and measured 1.70m by 1.24m and 0.25m deep. Its single fill [548] consisted of heavily burnt friable dark brown silty sand with abundant charcoal evenly distributed throughout, and very occasional flint pebbles.

Pit [685] was circular in plan, measuring between 2.40–2.50m in diameter and 0.30m deep, and had stepped vertical sides and a flat base. Its single fill [684], also recorded as [20] during the evaluation phase, comprised burnt dark brownish black sandy silt with frequent charcoal flecks and fragments and occasional burnt and unburnt flint pebbles. Early Neolithic flintwork was recovered from this pit, presumably deriving from the tree-throw hollow that it truncated. A fragment of carbonised bark from the pit produced a radiocarbon date of AD 660–810 (Beta-225545; see Appendix 1), overlapping at the younger end of the range with the date provided for pit [877].

Pit [750] was oval in plan with steeply sloping sides and an uneven base and measured 2.30m by 1.36m and 0.48m deep. Its single fill [749] comprised mottled brown, grey and black burnt silt and sand with abundant ash and charcoal, forming 20% of the fill.

Pit [834], 1.75m by 1.40m and 0.22m deep, was oval in plan with steeply sloping and slightly irregular sides, and a concave, pitted base. Its single fill [833] comprised light brown silty sand with frequent charcoal flecks and large fragments, very occasional flecks of fired clay, flint pebbles and fragments, 'globular' slag, and residual struck flint dated to the Neolithic or Bronze Age.

Pit [836], oval in plan with steeply sloping edges and a flat base, measured 1.87m by 1.0m and 0.25m deep. Its single fill [835] comprised light yellow sand with frequent charcoal flecks and fragments, occasional flint pebbles and residual Early Neolithic struck flints.

Pit [855], sub-circular in plan with steeply sloping edges and a flat base, measured 2.82m by 2.62m and 0.48m deep (Fig. 58). There were patches of scorching to its edges and primary fill [856], which was up to 50mm thick, consisted of loosely compacted charcoal with burnt clay. This was overlain by [886] a 0.16m thick deposit of mid brown sand with occasional pockets of clay and burnt flint which produced six Early Neolithic struck flints. It was banked up against the side of the pit and probably represents collapse of part of its western side where it cut through the artefact-rich Early Neolithic tree-throw

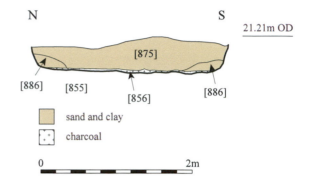

Fig. 58   Section through partially excavated charcoal burning pit [855] (scale 1:50)

hollow. The remaining fill [875] was up to 0.45m thick and comprised a dumped deposit of loose orange sand with frequent pockets of burnt red clay, occasional flint and quartzite pebbles, and further Early Neolithic struck flints, presumably also derived from the tree-throw hollow.

Pit [877], which measured 3.10m by 3.50m and 0.96m deep, was sub-circular in plan with steeply sloping edges and a slightly concave base with a deeper step in the centre (Fig. 59). The primary fill [881], which was up to 0.20m thick, consisted of compacted charcoal, including some pieces over 20mm in diameter, and also occasional slag fragments and burnt flint pebbles. A piece of oak charcoal from this fill produced a radiocarbon date of AD 780–980 (Waikato-22904; see Appendix 1). This was overlain by fill [880] comprising a dumped deposit up to 0.13m thick of dark brown sandy silt with occasional charcoal flecks and fragments, soft yellow ironstone and large quantities of 'runny' slag and burnt flint. The third fill [879] was up to 0.42m thick and consisted of a dumped deposit of yellow sand with frequent patches of burnt purple-brown sand, frequent slag fragments and occasional charcoal flecks and fragments and burnt flint. It was in turn overlain by [878] a further dumped deposit up to 0.29m thick comprising burnt mid reddish brown sand and silt with occasional burnt flint pebbles and very occasional charcoal flecking with 'runny' slag and pieces of ironstone and burnt clay.

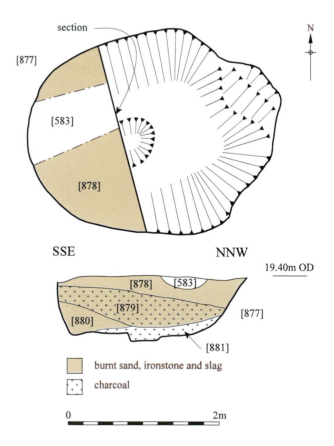

Fig. 59   Detail and section through partially excavated charcoal burning pit [877] (scale 1:50)

Central group

Pit [394], which measured 2.0m in diameter and 0.18m deep, had steeply sloping sides and a flat base (Fig. 60). The primary fill [393] was up to 60mm thick and consisted of charcoal with occasional burnt flint incorporating frequent lenses of grey ash. Its upper fill [392] was up to 100mm thick and comprised light greyish brown silty sand with frequent lenses of grey ash, charcoal fragments, occasional flint pebbles, burnt flint, a pottery sherd dated either to the Middle Iron Age or Anglo-Saxon period, along with two residual Early Neolithic struck flints.

Pit [529], which measured 2.60m in diameter and 0.25m deep, had moderately sloping edges and a slightly concave base (Fig. 61). The primary fill [536] comprised a 60mm thick deposit of loose black charcoal and occasional burnt flint, surviving as patches on the base of the pit. The upper fill [530] consisted of a 0.25m thick dumped deposit of mid to dark brown silty sand with frequent charcoal fragments, flint pebbles and occasional struck flints.

Pit [586] was sub-circular in plan with gently sloping sides that merged into a concave base. It measured 2.48m by 2.70m and was 0.25m deep. The primary fill [601] comprised a 0.12m thick deposit of orange brown sand with very frequent charcoal inclusions and occasional burnt flint, burnt clay and burnt sand. The pit showed evidence of having been 'cleaned out' but still retained remnants of charcoal and evidence of scorching to its base and sides. Its middle fill [600] was 0.21m thick and comprised orange brown sand with frequent charcoal, occasional burnt flint, struck flint and burnt sand. This appeared to be material dumped into the pit and may have been mixed with remnants of the primary fill. Its upper fill [587] was 0.18m thick and comprised light orange brown sand, with occasional charcoal fragments, flint pebbles, some of which were burnt, and struck flint inclusions.

Pit [696], which was sub-circular in plan with steeply sloping edges and a flat base, measured 2.50m by 2.30m and 0.35m deep. Scorching was evident around the edges of the feature. Its single fill [695] comprised dark greyish brown sandy silt containing abundant charcoal fragments, which increased in size and frequency towards the base, frequent flint and quartzite pebbles, occasional burnt flint, struck flints, over a third of which had been burnt, and an abraded sherd of Roman pottery.

Pit [698] was sub-circular in plan, though rather irregular, with variable steeply sloping edges and an uneven base, representing the remnants of a more regular pit that had been 'dug over' and much of its contents removed. It measured over 1.72m in diameter and was up to 0.16m deep. Its single fill [699] comprised dark orange brown coarse sand with frequent charcoal flecks and fragments, occasional burnt flint, very occasional struck flint and an abraded Roman pottery sherd.

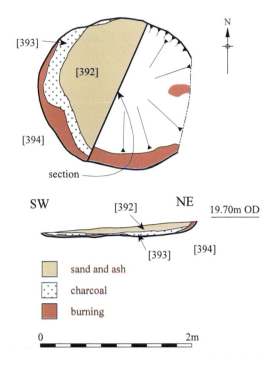

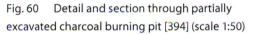

Fig. 60   Detail and section through partially excavated charcoal burning pit [394] (scale 1:50)

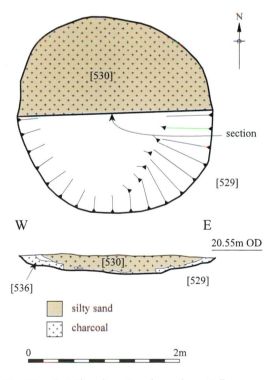

Fig. 61   Detail and section through partially excavated charcoal burning pit [529] (scale 1:50)

Pit [705], sub-circular in plan with sloping edges and a flat base, measured 2.70m by 2.40m and was 0.19m deep with a number of stakeholes cut into its base (Fig. 62, see Fig. 51). The primary fill [706] was up to 0.15m thick and consisted of compacted charcoal, including many large pieces, and a few burnt flint pebbles. Overlying this was [707], a 0.19m thick deposit of dark greyish brown sand with frequent charcoal flecking, occasional flint and burnt flint.

Pit [827] was sub-square in plan with rounded corners and had very steeply sloping edges and a slightly concave base. It measured 2.90m by 2.80m and 0.65m deep. Five fills were recorded within this pit. Its primary fill [1019], which was up to 0.13m thick, comprised light yellow to brown sand with occasional flint pebbles. This represented sand that had collapsed from the edges of the pit, presumably during its construction. Its second fill [1018] was up to 70mm thick and comprised mid greyish to mid brownish red burnt silt, sand and very small ironstone fragments, resembling brick dust, with very frequent charcoal fragments, and this material had clearly been burnt *in situ*. Overlying this was [1017] a

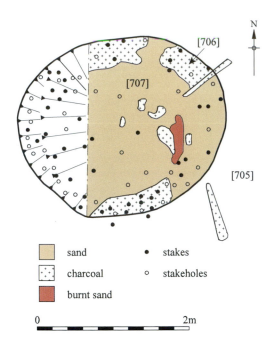

Fig. 62   Detail of partially excavated charcoal burning pit [705] (scale 1:50)

0.25m thick deposit of mid greyish brown silty sand with moderate charcoal fragments and occasional flint pebbles. This also consisted of burnt waste but appeared to have been dumped rather than burnt *in situ*. This was overlain by [832], which was up to 0.20m thick and comprised a dumped deposit of dark brownish red burnt sand, burnt flint pebbles and burnt ironstone fragments and slag with frequent fragments of charcoal, occasional burnt flint, limestone and unburnt ironstone. A fragment of charcoal recovered from this fill produced a radiocarbon date of AD 900–920 or AD 950–1040 (Beta-225547; see Appendix 1). This was overlain by the latest fill [826] which was up to 80mm thick and comprised a dumped deposit of mid to dark brownish red burnt silt and sand (resembling brickdust and very magnetic) containing abundant charcoal fragments, frequent fragments of iron-rich stone, occasional burnt and unburnt flint pebbles, fragments of 'runny' slag, burnt clay or daub and a single Early Neolithic flint. The edges of this pit were burnt and it was noted that the heat-affected flint recovered from upper fill [826] was heavily burnt, implying a particularly high temperature activity.

Pit [948], which measured 1.05m by 0.91m and 90mm deep, was sub-circular in plan and had gently sloping edges and a slightly concave base. Its single fill [947] consisted of black burnt sand with frequent charcoal fragments and burnt clay flecking.

Pit [964] was oval in plan with near vertical sides and a flat base and measured 1.96m by 1.50m and 0.33m deep. Its primary fill [966], up to 0.12m thick, consisted predominantly of charcoal fragments with dark grey burnt silty sand and very occasional burnt flint pebbles. Oak charcoal from this fill produced a radiocarbon date of AD 970–1160 (Waikato-22903; see Appendix 1). This was overlain by a 0.21m thick deposit [965] of yellowish brown silty sand with occasional flint pebbles.

Eastern group

Pit [579], the western side of which was truncated by the north–south aligned ditch [615], was oval in plan and measured 3.60m by at least 1.80m and 0.40m deep. It had near vertical edges and a flat base with a deeper step cut in the middle of its base. A series of four fills were recorded. The primary fill comprised a remnant of what appeared to be its original fill [578] mostly comprising pieces of charcoal, including many large fragments over 10mm in dimension, in a burnt sandy gravel matrix. A carbonised hazel twig from this deposit produced a radiocarbon date of AD 650–780 (Beta-225543; see Appendix 1). The overlying fill [577] comprised a dumped deposit of mid orange brown silty sand with a moderate quantity of charcoal. The two upper fills [576] and [575] comprised silty sands and gravel that had probably accumulated naturally.

Pit [367] was sub-square in plan with vertical sides and had a pock-marked, but otherwise flat, base with a deeper step cut into its centre (Fig. 63). It measured 2.75m by 2.46m and was 0.64 deep. A complex series of seven fills were recorded within this pit. The earliest [366] consisted predominantly of charcoal within a sandy matrix. The edges of the pit were also scorched and it was clear that the pit had contained an *in-situ* fire. Charcoal recovered from this fill produced a radiocarbon date of AD 1020–1200 (Beta-225541; see Appendix 1). Overlying this were three fills [469], [468] and [364] that comprised a mix of charcoal and burnt sand and stones, including some pieces of burnt ironstone, which had been tipped in from the eastern side. The remaining three fills [365], [467] and [363] comprised naturally accumulated sands interspersed with a further dump of burnt material.

Approximately 5m west of this was a similarly shaped and sized pit [515], which measured 3.10m by 2.31m and was 0.51m deep. It had vertical, sometimes undercut, sides and a flat base and a complex series of seven fills was also recorded. The first two [570] and [569] comprised sands and gravels and were relatively clean, probably representing erosion and collapse to its edges, it being cut into loose natural sands. The third [568], however, comprised *c.* 20% large charcoal fragments in a sandy gravel matrix, and four further fills [567]–[564] of predominantly clean gravelly sand were recorded in the upper part of the pit.

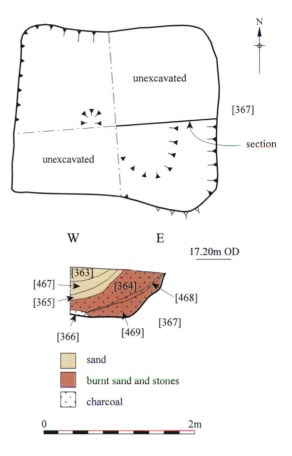

Fig. 63   Detail and section through partially excavated charcoal burning pit [367] (scale 1:50)

Only a small fragment of pit [546] survived truncation by pit [544]. It measured 1.40m in diameter and survived to a maximum depth of 0.19m. Two fills were recorded; the first [545] consisted almost entirely of charcoal fragments, including many large pieces, spread around the base and sides of the pit. There was evidence of *in-situ* burning within the pit, including sporadic burning to its edges, reddened sand and fire cracked gravel and pebbles, although its edges were not heavily scorched. Overlying the charcoal layer was a deposit of gravelly sand [559] showing few traces of burning and containing only occasional charcoal flecks, representing the deliberate backfilling of the pit.

Pit [546] had been largely truncated to the west by pit [544], which also truncated the north–south linear feature [692]. This was sub-circular in plan, measuring 1.74m by 2.00m and 1.26m deep and had near vertical sides and a flat base. The primary fill [560] comprised gravelly sand probably representing material collapsed from its edges. The second [543], which was up to 0.55m thick, comprised yellow white sand with very frequent flint pebbles and quantities of charcoal. The third fill [542], up to 1.14m thick, comprised dark brown sand silt with frequent flint pebbles, represented the deliberate infilling of the upper part of the pit. The latest fill [541] appeared to represent naturally accumulated wind-blown sand.

Pit [597], which truncated ditch [615], was circular in plan and had very steeply sloping edges and a flat base. It measured between 2.34m and 2.52m in diameter and was 0.39m deep. The earliest fill [596] was present in patches along the base of the pit and predominantly consisted of compacted charcoal, including many large fragments, and burnt sand and pebbles, clearly represented the remains of an *in-situ* fire. A fragment of hazel charcoal produced a radiocarbon date of AD 670–880 (Beta-225544; see Appendix 1). The overlying fill [595] comprised pebbly sand containing frequent charcoal that appeared to have been deliberately tipped into the pit and this in turn was sealed by naturally accumulated sands and gravels [594], interpreted as its natural silting and levelling.

Context	Feature	Sample	Feature type	Calibrated 2 sigma range
578	579	44	Charcoal burning pit	AD 650–780
536	529	42, 85	Charcoal burning pit	AD 660–780
725	727	57	Ore roasting pit	AD 660–810
684	685	51	Charcoal burning pit	AD 660–810
596	597	47	Charcoal burning pit	AD 670–880
616	617	50	Ore roasting pit	AD 680–880
881	877	80	Charcoal burning pit	AD 780–980
706	705	0	Charcoal burning pit	AD 890–1030
832	827	66	Charcoal burning pit	AD 900–920 and AD 950–1040
966	964	81	Charcoal burning pit	AD 970–1160
601	586	48	Charcoal burning pit	AD 980–1160
584	585	46	Working hollow hearth	AD 1010–1160
366	367	35	Charcoal burning pit	AD 1020–1200
393	394	31	Charcoal burning pit	AD 1020–1210

Table 25   Radiocarbon dates obtained from iron processing features

Dating of the iron processing activity

The radiocarbon dates obtained from the iron processing features could be interpreted as indicating two separate phases of industrial activity relating to iron processing – one dating to *c.* 700 cal AD and the other to *c.* 1020 cal AD. Alternatively there could be a continuum of this iron processing activity, the evidence is not conclusive.

Working hollow [585]

Located between the eastern and central clusters of industrial features was a small sub-rectangular feature [585] (see Fig. 49). This comprised an oval pit aligned roughly north-east–south-west, which measured 5.60m in length by 2.40m wide and survived to a depth of 0.45m. The edges of the feature were moderately sloping and broke imperceptibly with a slightly concave base. The earliest fill recorded [584] comprised an approximately square patch of burning measuring 0.60m by at least 0.40m, located centrally within the base of the feature. This deposit consisted of intensively burnt gravels, pebbles and sands, mixed with patches of large charcoal fragments, along with magnetized burnt ironstone and ore fines. It was sealed by a dump of silty sand [598] that lay along the southern edge of the cut and which was thought to represent the collapse of the sides of the feature. Overlying this and filling the remainder of the feature was a similar deposit [599] comprising silty sand with patches of charcoal. This most likely represents the gradual infilling of the feature from surrounding deposits, with the patches of charcoal suggesting that activities involving fire were also conducted in the immediate vicinity.

Although in shape and dimensions this structure resembles the sunken-featured buildings more commonly associated with the Early Anglo-Saxon period, it is most likely to represent some form of working hollow, as demonstrated by the presence of the hearth within the feature. Prunus charcoal recovered from the hearth deposit produced a radiocarbon date of AD 1010–1160 (Waikato-22906; see Appendix 1), placing it within the range of the later Saxon to early Medieval ironworking activity recorded across the site. The proximity of this feature to the ironworking features suggests that whatever activity was undertaken within the shelter of the hollow it was associated with the iron processing activity represented in this part of the site. This is further supported by the presence of ore fines in the hearth deposit, and this may even represent an ore roasting pit within the hollow. This feature may have functioned as a windbreak, and may have been surrounded by a bank, a low wall, or may have had a light wooden superstructure.

Four postholes [516], [527], [539] and [561] were situated *c.* 20m to the north-west of the working hollow. They measured between 0.30m and 0.37m in diameter and were up to 0.40m deep. Pottery retrieved from [527] was dated to AD 1100–1500. The former three postholes may have formed an L-shaped structure, perhaps some form of windbreak to provide shelter for some activity related to the industrial processes undertaken in this area.

Refuse pits

Pit [731], which was situated close to the centre of the eastern edge of Area B, was sub-rectangular in plan with a rounded bulbous end at the north-west and measured 2.14m by 1.42m. Its fill comprised dark to mid brown sandy silt with abundant (20%) charcoal and occasional small flint pebbles. There was no evidence of *in-situ* burning and the feature, despite its unusual shape, seems likely to represent a pit excavated for the disposal of burnt waste material and has therefore been placed with this phase of activity.

A substantial pit [934] was situated away from the main area of industrial activity, in the north-eastern corner of Area B and at the bottom of the dry valley. This was oval in plan with gently sloping, slightly stepped sides and a concave base and measured 4.45m north–south by 3.50m east–west and was 0.65m deep. Its primary fill [933], which was up to 0.25m thick, comprised yellowish brown silty clay with very occasional fragments of slag. This was overlain by a 0.40m thick deposit [932], comprising greyish brown burnt silty clay containing very frequent fragments of slag, fragments of ironstone, occasional burnt and unburnt flint pebbles and an incomplete iron horseshoe. Over 35kg of slag was recovered from the excavated portion of the pit, which comprised just over 20% of the feature. Although the pit contained large quantities of burnt material, the pit had not been burnt *in situ* but had clearly been used for the disposal of industrial waste solely from iron smelting and this included tap slag, run slag and dense slag (see Keys, Chapter 8.3). No debris from ore roasting or charcoal production was disposed of in this pit and no slags diagnostic of smithing were recovered; there was no hammerscale present. Small quantities of vitrified hearth lining were also disposed of in this pit and this material may have originated from a smelting furnace in the near locality. The only potentially datable material retrieved from the pit was a horseshoe from the upper fill, this was examined by Ian Riddler and found to be of thirteenth–fourteenth-century date (see note below).

The horseshoe

Ian Riddler

A little under half of an iron horseshoe came from pit [934]. It includes three nail holes, which are rectangular in shape and set close to the rounded outer edge. The horseshoe has smooth edges and belongs to Clark's type 3, which dates to the thirteenth to fourteenth century and is centred about the period *c.* AD 1270–1330 (Clark 1995, 96). Similar dating for the type has been established for both Winchester and York (Goodall 1990, 1056; Ottaway and Rogers 2002, 2,965 and fig. 1530.13283).

8.2 Anglo-Saxon and Medieval Ironworking

Ian Riddler

Laurel Farm is of considerable significance for the evidence that it provides of the early stages in iron production. In the past these stages have sometimes been overlooked in discussions of ironworking. More recently, however, the preparatory stages in iron production, prior to smelting, have been identified and discussed in the light of an increased quantity of archaeological evidence (Hinton 2011, 186–190). Comparable sites of broadly contemporary dates have been found both in Ireland and France, as well as Middle and Late Saxon England, and they enable the nature of the site to be clarified and understood. This particular site is of significance in part because of its sheer size, which has enabled a

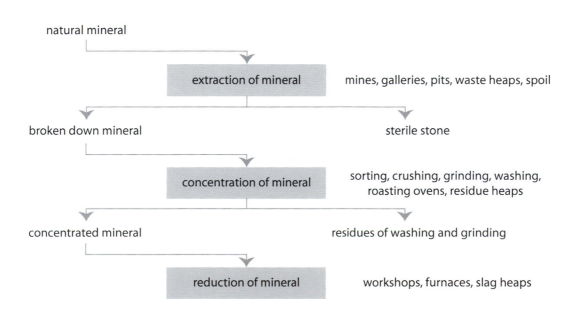

Fig. 64   The early stages in iron production

broad landscape of ironworking features to be examined. Tylecote's description of the Stamford High Street site, where '*the scarcity of metal objects underlines the highly specialised nature of the activity in the excavated area, concerned only with mass-producing iron and divorced from all forging and ancillary operations*' (Tylecote *et al.* 1982, 142) could equally be applied to this site, although the circumstances of production are a little different. The Medieval pit, with its horseshoe and metallurgical residues, adds a further dimension to the story.

The features

The principal features of Anglo-Saxon date across the site occur in three clusters, at the west, the centre and the east of the site as described above (Chapter 8.1). Each cluster includes a number of quarry pits. Close to these quarry pits are groups of charcoal burning pits and the third component within each cluster of features consists of smaller ore roasting pits. It is clear from the summary above that the relative quantity of features of each type varies across the three areas. In order to understand these features, it is useful to summarise the early stages in iron production.

Preparatory stages in iron working

The initial stages in iron production have been described by Mangin (2004, 25–48) and are summarised in Fig. 64. In the first instance, it was necessary to gather together the raw materials for smelting. This included both the iron ore and a copious supply of wood; a water supply would also have been required, as was access to a clay source to provide the superstructure of the furnace. The conjunction of all of these raw materials in this area of Norfolk, alongside its proximity to a market for smelted iron nearby at Norwich, provided an excellent site for iron smelting. The steep sided, large quarry pits were dug to collect iron ore. The ore would have been readily visible at or near the ground surface and the irregular shape of the pits reflects the quarrying of the raw material within the natural site geology. Ore would also have been visible in the nearby streambeds and in the sections leading up to the sloping landscape of the site itself. On some sites the excavated spoil remains close to the edge of the pits, providing an undulating landscape.

Thirteen large quarry pits were scattered across the southern part of the site in three clusters, with a particular concentration in the south-eastern area, where five quarry pits were located. The largest quarry lay some 12m to the north-west of this group, with further quarry pits in a group to the west. The three clusters of quarry pits coincide with the grouping of other Anglo-Saxon features and they appear to be of a broadly similar date, concentrated across the Middle Saxon period.

Crushing and washing ore

Once gathered, the ore would have been prepared and enriched before it was smelted. Several distinct processes were undertaken during this stage, including the separation of the ore from the remainder of its matrix and the concentration of the ore by roasting it. The separation itself involved two processes, namely the crushing of the stone or clay and the washing of the ore. The crushing of the parent material would enable the ore to be separated from its matrix. This was particularly important with ores consisting of hydrated iron oxides formed around a clay or stone core, as was the case at West Runton in Norfolk (Tylecote 1967, 187). Elsewhere, at Stamford, it has been argued that crushing was not necessary and that roasting alone would reduce the size of the ore (Tylecote *et al.* 1982, 141). Archaeological evidence for this initial process consists merely of small debris, which would not necessarily occur in any great concentrations across the site and is not always easy to discern. At Stamford a quantity of iron ore nodules discovered in a layer was interpreted as a remnant of a heap set in one part of the site, left there to weather and break down in size (Burchard 1982, 114 and 141). At Laurel Farm the ore occurred either as carrstone, as an iron pan or as nodules attached to a sand matrix. As a result, initial processing would have been centred on breaking down the material into smaller pieces and there may not have been a great requirement to wash the ore, although there is some evidence to suggest that this took place. Once crushed, the ore could be separated from the remainder of the sand and stone and moved to the next stage, its washing.

Washing the ore removed accreted sand and clay and an abundant water supply was an essential prerequisite for this treatment. One method of separation involved the use of gravity, with the ore and its accretions set on an inclined wooden surface and running water used to push the material down a slope, with lighter fragments travelling further than heavier, ore-laden pieces (Mangin 2004, 43). The water itself would then run into a ditch and be dispersed. The Post-Medieval site at La Montbleuse (Haute-Saône) shows how a washing installation of this type worked, with reservoirs of water retained in ditches and feeding into washing tanks with accompanying sediment baths and ditches to move water away, down the slope (Mangin 2004, fig. 14). Earlier sites, however, may simply contain ditches and sediment pits, as well as areas stained by the ore to a red or orange colour, as at Boecourt, for example (Eschenlohr and Serneels 1991). The west–east aligned ditch [437]/[322]/[300] runs towards a large pit [448] and this may have been a reservoir for the washing process. Further to the west, the quarry pit [862] was lined with clay, suggesting that it was used to hold water, after the ore had been removed. An analogy can be drawn with the late Saxon smelting site at Mersham in Kent, where three ditches ran towards a large pit, 8m in diameter, also thought to have been used in the washing process (Andrews 2004).

Ore roasting

The washed ore was then ready for its next treatment, the roasting process, designed to improve the iron content. The ore was heated to a temperature of several hundred degrees, thereby removing water, as well as sulphur and carbon dioxide as gases, and transforming the ore into fractured pieces of iron oxide. The removal of the gases enriched the iron and allowed it to be smelted more efficiently at lower temperatures. It also provided a better quality of iron. To achieve this state, the ore was heated in a fire for several hours. It is a difficult process to detect because, when successful, the ore is removed from the pit to be smelted and the fire is dismantled. All that usually remains is evidence of the fire and small remnants of the ore. The size and shape of pits is important in distinguishing their function, as well as a close examination of their contents. In particular, some pits retain iron 'fines', effectively a fine powder of ore particles produced during the roasting process (Scott 1990, 152).

A series of small pits, 1.70–3.60m in diameter, and square, rectangular or oval in shape are described above as 'ore-roasting pits' (see Chapter 8.1). Each of these showed signs of *in-situ* burning and retained copious quantities of charcoal, some retained fragments of ironstone. In terms of both their size and shape these pits recall the bowl furnaces from Ramsbury in England and Johnstown 1 in Ireland and it is possible that they are the vestiges of smelting furnaces (Haslam 1980, 19–24; Carlin 2008, 91–3 and fig. 5.3). However, they lack any clay lining or residues from iron working, either in the form of slag or furnace bottoms, which would certainly be expected from smelting furnaces. Their fills largely consist of burnt sand and iron fines, with some charcoal and ironstone, contents that are much more redolent of ore roasting.

At both West Runton and Stamford, larger pits of 1.5–2m in diameter, thought to be used in ore roasting, were also found in close proximity to smelting furnaces (Tylecote 1967, 193 and fig. 3; Burchard 1982, 109 and fig. 58). At these sites excavations were by necessity centred on the furnaces and not on the peripheral areas of iron production (Tylecote 1967, fig. 3; Burchard 1982, fig. 58). At Ramsbury, in contrast, it was suggested that an ore roasting hearth was represented by a poorly defined burnt area covered by a layer of reddened iron ore (Haslam 1980, 12). This also lay close to two furnaces. No ore roasting areas were identified at Mersham although there were pits of various sizes within the excavated area. No smelting furnaces were discovered either, although over 500kg of smelting and smithing slag were recovered (Andrews 2004). Closer parallels are provided by numerous small pits, 0.3–0.8m in diameter, which were found at Boecourt, again close to the smelting furnaces, filled with burnt ore and carbonised wood (Eschenlohr and Serneels 1991; Mangin 2004, 32). A pit at Wittering near Peterborough, Cambridgeshire, identified as a possible smithing hearth or furnace, is of similar dimensions to the Laurel Farm examples and, given that it has been discoloured from intense burning, it is more

likely to be an ore roasting pit (Wall forthcoming). It lay just over 5m from two smelting furnaces. Some 5m to the other side of the furnaces lay an oblong pit whose upper fill contained 2kg of burnt ironstone.

It is clear from all of these examples that ore roasting pits were often situated close to smelting furnaces. The implication is that smelting would follow on directly from roasting, possibly after the roasted nodules had been sieved or sorted to an appropriate size. At first sight, Laurel Farm appears to show a variation on this practice, if its pits have been correctly interpreted, because of the absence of smelting furnaces across the excavated area. However, residues from smelting have been identified by Lynne Keys (Section 8.3 below), and there is no doubt that smelting also took place in this landscape, even though the furnaces themselves were not excavated. Slight evidence of smithing was also recovered but it is likely, as noted by Lynne Keys, that the iron was removed from the site in the form of ingots, to be passed on to blacksmiths. It is worth stressing that iron making was carried out here across an extensive landscape, with each cluster of features extending to around 50m² in area.

Charcoal burning

Twenty-one pits, in three clusters across the site contained quantities of charcoal and can be identified as burning pits or charcoal 'kilns' (see Chapter 8.1). They are generally rectangular or oval in shape and around 1.70–3.60m in diameter. One of the pits ([367]) also contained ironstone in a fill above the primary charcoal deposit, but the fills were generally limited to charcoal alone. An additional pit ([877]), of requisite dimensions, also included ironstone and a quantity of smelting slag in its fills. It is one of only two pits on the site to include any iron slag at all. The primary fill included abundant charcoal and a small amount of slag, whilst the three later fills included greater quantities of metallurgical residues. There is a possibility that this is a remnant of a bowl furnace, by comparison with Milbrook in Sussex, where a pit 1.0–0.95m in diameter was packed with charcoal and a small amount of slag, with clay superstructure in the upper fill (Tebbutt 1982, 21). However, there was no sign of any clay superstructure in any of the fills of the pit and it is more likely that the slag had been placed in the pit, having been gathered from a smelting furnace nearby. It does at least indicate that smelting took place in the landscape.

A pit ([727]) in the western area, close to two ore roasting pits ([717] and [901]), retained a clay lining, up to 30mm in thickness. The pit had probably been emptied at some point, removing most of the evidence of its use. The presence of the lining suggested the possibility that this was a remnant of a low-shaft furnace, although no slag was found in its fill, which would certainly be expected. Charcoal from its fill provided a calibrated 2-sigma radiocarbon determination of AD 660–780 (Appendix 1). That period witnessed the introduction of a different type of furnace into England, which included a slag tapping hollow. Furnaces of this type have been found at Milbrook and West Wittering in Sussex and Ramsbury in Wiltshire (Haslam 1980; Tebbutt 1982). With this in mind, a furnace with a tapping hollow would be expected here, with plentiful evidence of its last firing. Neither is present, however, and accordingly it is more likely to have served as an ore roasting pit, the presence of dark grey brown silt sand in its fill probably reflecting the presence of iron fines.

The charcoal was produced by carbonising smouldering wood in an environment with a limited supply of oxygen, and roasting it at temperatures of around 600° C. Charcoal was invariably the preferred fuel for smelting. Recent excavations on a number of Irish sites have revealed charcoal burning pits, largely filled with carbonised oak and alder (Carlin 2008, 89–91, 101 and fig. 5.8). They are rectangular in shape and 2–3m in length. Oak was the preferred wood for smelting in Ireland and in most of France and is easily the most abundant wood in the samples taken from this site as well (Carlin 2008, 101; Mangin 2004, 53). It has also been noted that elm, beech and possibly also hornbeam (cf. *Carpinus betulus*) occur in the Anglo-Saxon and early Medieval wood samples at Laurel Farm and these are all good hardwoods, suitable for fires and as the raw material for charcoal (see Austin and Gray, Chapter 8.6). It is very difficult to distinguish between residues of charcoal burning and fires using dry wood. In the context of this particular site, however, most of the deposits are likely to represent charcoal production and charcoal use. Even the process of ore roasting could utilize charcoal rather than dry wood and it was certainly the preferred fuel for smelting.

On some sites the various stages in iron production are spatially distinct and can be set some distance from each other (Mangin 2004, 45). The burning of charcoal need not necessarily take place in the iron working area, for example, although that clearly appears to be the case here. Indeed, at Laurel Farm all of the pre-treatments of the iron ore, as well as the preparation of the wood fuel, are visible in the same compact landscape. The missing ingredient is the presence of smelting furnaces, but residues from that process were also recovered (see Section 8.3 below).

The post-Roman features at Laurel Farm can be interpreted as an extensive landscape of initial ironworking preparation, leading up to and including the smelting process. The radiocarbon dates suggest that the area was revisited on a number of occasions across the Middle and Late Saxon period, its use thereby coinciding with the emergence of Norwich as an Anglo-Saxon settlement (Ayres 1993, 117 and fig. 7.2; Atkin 1993, 129–131). The clearance of woodland in the area has been stressed for earlier periods, but it should also be noted that woodland was an essential component of the ironworking process. Rackham has noted that the transformation of Thorpe Wood, as it was known in the twelfth century, into Mousehold Heath in the fifteenth century, was caused (in part at least) by grazing animals

eating young trees (Rackham 1994, 9). Fuel collecting, for both domestic and industrial purposes, is also likely to have played a significant part in the reduction of Thorpe Wood. The important point here, of course, is that in the twelfth century there was still a Thorpe Wood.

8.3 Ironworking Slag and Industrial Residues

Lynne Keys

Over 53.3kg of material, iron slag, ore, ore fines, and related debris was recovered by hand on site and from soil samples processed after excavation. 9.5kg of the assemblage were unstratified, having come from topsoil and test trenches in different areas across site. This report deals only with the iron slag, not with ore, ore fines and charcoal production (for which see Riddler, Chapter 8.2).

The assemblage was examined by eye and categorised on the basis of morphology alone. Each slag type in each context was weighed; the smithing hearth bottom was separately weighed and measured for statistical purposes. A magnet was run through the soils adhering to slag to detect small pieces of hammerscale flake and tiny spheres. Quantification data are given in the table in Appendix 3 in which weight (wt.) is shown in grams.

Explanation of terminology and processes

Activities involving iron can take two forms from the early Iron Age until the late Medieval period.

1. *Smelting* is the manufacture of iron from ore and fuel in a furnace. The resulting products are a spongy mass called an unconsolidated bloom (iron with a considerable amount of slag still trapped inside), and slag (waste). Smelting slag took various forms depending on the technology used: furnace slags, run slag, tap slag and dense slag.

Tap slag is a dense, low porosity, fayalitic (iron silicate) slag with a ropy flowed structure. It is formed as the liquid slag is allowed to flow out continuously or intermittently through a hole in the furnace side into a specially made channel leading to a hollow in the ground. Removal of slag during or towards the end of smelting facilitated retrieval of the bloom after the operation. This tapping innovation is believed to have made its appearance at the beginning of the Roman period in England but disappeared again during the Early to Middle Saxon period and re-appeared in the early Medieval period as iron smelters adopted more efficient technological methods.

Dense slag is of low porosity like tap slag, but without the flowed surface; it too represents smelting activity and is often encountered in assemblages with tap slag.

Run slag is what its name suggests, and was produced by smelting. If tap slag is very fragmentary it can be hard to

Activity	Slag type	Weight (g): strat.	Weight (g): unstrat.	Total weight (g)	Comment
smelting	tap slag	16757	191	16948	
unknown	undiagnostic	6633	5063	11696	
smelting	furnace slag	5940	1800	7740	
smelting	run slag	2554	284	2838	
smithing	smithing hearth bottom	0	1230	1230	one example
smelting	dense slag	934	0	934	
	Total weight	32818	8568	41386	

Table 26   Bulk slag types by weight (g)

identify as such and the term 'run slag' is then used.

The term *furnace slag* is used for slags produced during the Iron Age and Early Anglo-Saxon periods in particular when slag tapping was not carried out; it may also refer to slag which has the appearance of having once formed part of slags produced by smelting. Furnace slag may be furnace slag bottoms (plano-convex lumps resembling smithing hearth bottoms but generally very much larger) and *slag blocks* which can be massive in size. This slag type is more common in Iron Age Continental Europe and, in the past, the German name *Schlackenklotz* was often used for it. It was produced in a furnace built over a pit to allow slag to collect below, rather than it being tapped or run out of the furnace at some stage. It is a very distinctive slag when found intact or in large pieces but broken up it can be difficult to differentiate from miscellaneous smelting slags produced in any furnace. For example, runs from the surface of slag blocks often break off and, in isolation, resemble tap slag. Other smelting slags encountered are *prills*, *slag runs* and occasional non-magnetic *slag spheres*. The latter can easily by confused with smithing spheres so their context and the rest of the slag assemblage must be taken into account when identifying the process that produced them. Furnace slags often contain quite large voids (as compared to smithing slag) left by burnt-out charcoal.

2a. *Primary smithing* took place in periods before the Post-Medieval development of casting iron. It involved the hot working (by a smith using a hammer) of the unrefined iron bloom on a stringhearth (usually near the smelting area) to remove excess slag. Slags from this process include the *smithing hearth bottom* and micro-slags, in particular tiny *spheres*.

2b. *Secondary smithing* involved the hot working (using a hammer) of one or more pieces of iron to create, or to repair, an object. As well as bulk slags, including the *smithing hearth bottom* (a plano-convex slag cake which builds up in the hearth base), smithing generates micro-slags. These can be *hammerscale flakes* from ordinary hot working of a piece of iron (making or repairing an object)

and/or tiny *spheres* from high temperature welding used to join or fuse two pieces of iron.

Much slag cannot be assigned to either smelting or smithing on grounds of its morphology or because broken up during deposition, re-deposition or excavation; these are described as undiagnostic slags. If, however, there are particular diagnostic slags present in the assemblage, it is sometimes possible to suggest that larger broken undiagnostic fragments with some distinctive features could also represent the process. Other types of assemblage debris may derive from a variety of high temperature activities - including domestic fires - and cannot be taken on their own to indicate iron working was taking place. These include fuel ash slag, fired clay, vitrified hearth lining and cinder.

Discussion of the assemblage

The diagnostic slags, virtually without exception, indicate iron smelting. The presence of ores and the evidence for ore roasting and production of charcoal on the site (see Riddler, Chapter 8.2) attest to preparations for one or more smelting operations which almost certainly took place somewhere nearby.

There is very little definite evidence for smithing: the one smithing hearth bottom was found in site topsoil in the south-western corner of the development site (Trench 15) and only the tiniest quantities of hammerscale flakes and spheres were recovered from a few soil samples across the whole site. Hammerscale flakes were recovered from only two features: Phase 6 Iron Age pit [754] and an unphased tree-throw hollow [10]. It is, of course, possible that iron blooms produced by the smelt were removed from site to be worked up by smiths elsewhere which could indicate some authority controlling operations from start to finish. The distribution of activities such as charcoal production and ore roasting may support this thesis.

No *in-situ* evidence for furnaces was recovered. Very little in the way of furnace or hearth lining was found elsewhere on the site. The furnace superstructure may have been a portable type removed, re-sited, repaired and re-used each time a smelt took place and this would leave very little evidence. Having said this, it appears, on the basis of some slag and the few pieces of vitrified material, that the wall/lining of the furnace(s) or hearths may have been tempered with silica, which would have facilitated smelting by acting as a flux at high temperature.

The spatial distribution of material from different stages (charcoal preparation, ore roasting, iron smelting) of the smelting process strongly suggest a streamlined and highly organised operation involving a number of people.

Anglo-Saxon to early Medieval slag

Industrial residues and slag were recovered from a few of the features that could be definitely assigned to the Phase 8 Anglo-Saxon and early Medieval phase of activity. Iron slag came from charcoal burning pit [597] and consisted of a tiny quantity of smelting micro-slags. A minute quantity of micro-slag came from charcoal burning pit [529]. More evidence for smelting in the form of tap slag came from charcoal burning pit [877]. The upper fill [878] contained a small quantity of tap slag and undiagnostic slag which, because of its high vesicularity, is probably furnace slag; mid fill [880] also contained some tap slag. Charcoal burning pit [834] also contained a tiny quantity of tap slag. Fill [826] of charcoal burning pit [827] contained a few tiny slag fragments, fired clay and possible ore fines, not enough or significant enough to indicate any smelting or smithing activity, whilst fill [832] produced a tiny amount of tap slag.

Of significance for the site as a whole is fill [932] of pit [934], which contained just over 35.1kg of iron slag, the diagnostic types representing smelting, much of it indicative of slag tapping during the process. The slag appears not to be mixed with debris from ore roasting or charcoal production and so was derived purely from an area in which only smelting was taking place. Also in [934] were small quantities of vitrified hearth lining, one of the few occasions it was recovered on the site. The date of the deposition of the slag in pit [934] has been placed somewhere in the thirteenth or fourteenth century, based on a fragment of iron horseshoe. It is possible the slag lay elsewhere above ground and is earlier than its deposition date, but one cannot say more than that. A similar site is Mersham, Kent, where an even larger quantity of smelting slag was deposited in several large pits some time in the early Medieval period (Willson 2001). There, too, no furnaces were found.

8.4 Ironstone

Kevin Hayward

Samples of ironstone taken from various features and natural deposits at the site were assessed in order to identify (under binocular microscope) whether the proportion of iron in the stone is of sufficient quantity to classify it as an iron ore. This analysis also aimed to identify the type of iron ore and to suggest a geological source.

Context (grid square)	Phase	Ore Description	Number	Weight (g)
1 (225/450)		Dark brown limonite massive	2	39
1 (125/275)		Massive earthy brown limonite	1	49
1 (375/175)		Massive ore rind of harder dark grey/brown limonite	1	25
1 (400/175)		Limonite nodule slightly botryoidal form	1	27
231	1	Massive dark brown limonite	3	10
349	11	Massive limonite concentrating in glassy quartz rich sandstone - Tertiary/Quaternary	5	52
636	3.1	Dark brown massive earthy limonite	2	14
826	8	Blood red Carrstone micaceous	1	30
832	8	Red/brown Carrstone shiny quartz	1	198
879	8	Botryoidal dark brown limonite	1	45
932	8	Massive ochrous light brown earthy mineral	1	46
932	8	Flint belemnite from the chalk infilled with brown limonite iron - post cretaceous Tertiary/Quaternary	1	23

Table 27   Selected samples of ironstone

Eleven examples of ironstone (see Table 27) were selected for detailed examination. The application of a 1kg mason's hammer and sharp chisel to each example ensured that a small fresh fabric surface was exposed. The fabric was examined at x20 magnification using a long arm stereomicroscope or hand lens (Gowland x10).

Ore or ironstone?

Heavy concentrated chunks of botroydal and massive light brown to dark brown ironstone are present as individual nodules (e.g. from contexts [375]/[175], [932], and [879]) that are clearly suitable for ore production.

Type of ironstone

These earthy ironstone nodules are limonite. Limonite, a hydrous ferric oxide occurs in concretions and the earthy light brown colour is a result of hydration or alteration of the iron in a sandstone. Limonite is made up of 60% iron and its characteristic light-brown streak (Read 1947) distinguishes it from the blood-red streak of haematite and black of magnetite. These unburnt examples of limonite are not magnetic, a feature of this earthy iron mineral. However, like haematite, burnt examples become magnetic.

Parent material

It is not easy to determine the parent material from which the ironstone itself was won. The ore concentrates within a brown/blood red friable quartz sandstone, containing numerous grains of glossy quartz which is usually indicative of a Tertiary rock type. Some local ironstones occur within the very young Red Crag coastal deposits of the (Pliocene) of Ipswich. Another local alternative is a bog iron ore, given the site's proximity to areas of fenland. Finally, the nearest and most likely candidate is the ironstone contained within the pebble beds of the glacial Corton Formation exposed by the dry valley at Thorpe St Andrew. These have been identified as forming 5% of all clasts and would have provided an on-site supply of iron. The quarry pits identified at the site presumably exploited this source of ironstone.

Finally, mention must be made of Carrstone, an older iron rich lower greensand of North Norfolk (e.g. Hunstanton) which is also comparable to the parent material and at 40km from source would seem a very long way with which to transport chunks of relatively low grade ore. It is, however, possible that this is the original geological source of the ironstone pebble clasts identified in the Anglian Glacial outwash deposits of the Corton Formation that outcrop close to the site.

8.5 Saxon Pottery

Berni Sudds

Four small non-diagnostic body sherds of probable Thetford-type ware were recovered from the ore roasting pit [617]. The Thetford-type tradition is broadly dated from the mid ninth to mid twelfth century, although the date range of different production centres varied. If the sherds were produced at Norwich, which is possible given the proximity, a date from the late tenth century might be more likely (Jennings 1983, 91). However, charcoal from the pit returned a 2-sigma calibrated date of AD 680–880 (Waikato-22908; see Appendix 1).

8.6 Analysis of the Anglo-Saxon and Early Medieval Archaeobotanical Remains

Phil Austin and Louisa Gray

Charcoal analysis

The methodology used to analyse the archaeobotanical remains from Phase 8 features was as set out above (Chapter 3.4). The Anglo-Saxon and early Medieval period activity was by far the richest phase of those investigated. All but two, ash (*Fraxinus excelsior*) and willow/poplar (*Salix/Populus* sp.), of all the taxa identified were represented in the 31 samples analysed. Of the 20 taxa identified for the assemblage as a whole, eleven were present only in this phase. Again, oak (*Quercus* sp.) was the most common taxon, being present in every sample. The evidence suggests that oak woodland, with an under-storey that probably included hazel (*Corylus avellana*), holly (*Ilex aquifolium*) and possibly hawthorn (Maloideae) and cherry (*Prunus* sp.), was present locally and was seemingly sustained over centuries. Whatever woodland was present in the area is thought to have been more open, and physically less dense, than had existed in earlier phases. Ring growth patterns indicate that much of the wood was not produced under stress. Many fragments of different taxa exhibited 'normal' or, occasionally, wide rings – indicative of rapid growth. Wood indicative of slow growth was present but not common. It is thought, therefore, that woodland and other sources of potential fuel wood may have been under careful management. Wood may also have been gathered from solitary trees growing in the open. The scale of woodland and the ratio of woodland to non-woodland is not known. Certainly open areas existed in Saxon to early Medieval times as clearly indicated by the presence of light demanding taxa, such as field maple (*Acer campestre*), spindle tree (*Euonymus europaeus*), Traveller's Joy (*Clematis vitalba*) and (possibly) blackthorn (*Prunus* sp.). For nut production hazel requires more light than that available within closed woodland. Hawthorn and blackthorn are also hedgerow plants and may have been present as such. The presence of hazel nutshell (Sample {28}, context [273]) is further evidence of areas of open countryside. Whether or not any of the charcoal examined derived from wood removed during clearance episodes is unknown.

Non-native taxa

The identification of two charred fragments of the non-native horse chestnut (*Aesculus* sp.) in a deposit from the Saxon to early Medieval period of site activity (fill [536] of charcoal burning pit [529], Sample {42}; Cal AD 660–780, Beta-225542; see Appendix 1) is surprising. A native of the Balkan Peninsula, this tree is known to have been introduced to England in AD 1612 or 1615, as a cultivar, and is not recorded from the wild until as recently as AD 1870 (Preston *et al.* 2002). Unless the identification made is incorrect, it is presumed that the wood of this taxon was introduced in some form. What that form was is unknown. However, with apparently no other evidence to support its presence at this time in England; it seems more likely that it was introduced incidentally, perhaps as an artefact (or as driftwood, even).

Wood form, relative maturity and growth patterns

Wood form was evaluated principally by fragment size, growth ring count and ring curvature. The vast majority of fragments examined derived from stem/branch wood. In the case of oak a great many of these fragments were remnants of heartwood. The tree taxa beech (*Fagus sylvatica*) and ash (*Fraxinus excelsior*) were only represented by mature wood. Sapwood, in oak denoted by the lack of tyloses in vessels, was also present though not as frequently. The greater incidence of heartwood or innermost wood is not necessarily significant in itself. The outermost wood of a branch, for example, is more likely to be destroyed during exposure to an open fire because the chance of combustion occurring increases with the greater availability of oxygen. Rather than being preserved as charcoal, for which little or no oxygen is a prerequisite, the wood is reduced to mineral ash leaving no record of its presence. The presence of bark in several samples suggests that in many instances, stem/branch wood was almost certainly burnt in the form of round-wood rather than as converted or otherwise modified timber. Sample {43}, fill [545] of charcoal burning pit [546], in particular contained a high quantity of bark fragments. Why it was so abundant in this context is unclear.

Twig-wood was also present, particularly in the Phase 8 Anglo-Saxon samples, mostly derived from small twigs of approximately <3mm diameter. The few fragments of oak twig-wood that were identified tended to be larger in size than that of twig-wood of other taxa. This is no doubt due to the relatively large diameter of oak twigs compared with many other taxa. Honeysuckle (*Lonicera*)

and Traveller's Joy, for example, are climbers/scramblers that typically produce wood of small diameter, including that of their stem wood, and so it is not surprising that these taxa were represented exclusively by twig-wood. Ivy (*Hedera helix*), hazel and holly were also represented as twig-wood.

A significant proportion of the oak fragments exhibited a regular and/or narrow ring growth pattern. Occurrences of widely spaced rings were few in oak and all the other taxa identified. Even within twig-wood fragments, narrow rings were typical rather than an exception. Inter-annual ring growth patterns provide information as to the conditions under which wood forms. Closely spaced rings, with much reduced late wood, are produced under conditions where growth is compromised whereas widely spaced rings, with much increased late wood, are produced where growth occurs in optimum conditions. These are reliable indicators of periods of rapid growth, producing low density wood, and slow growth, producing high density wood, respectively. Variation in inter-annual rings has many causes ranging from local environmental conditions to world wide climatic change (Schweingruber *et al.* 2006). One of the most significant factors is the suppression of growth through lack of light and competition for water and nutrients. Whilst it seems clear that much of the wood represented in this assemblage especially that of oak, grew under constraint, it is thought that this is possibly because it was growing in (closed) woodland conditions, where shading and relentless competition from other trees and shrubs can be a significant handicap to growth. Interestingly, a few larger than average fragments showed periods of fast growth following on from that of prolonged slow growth. It is thought that this may represent the response to an improvement in local environmental conditions through an event such as an opening up of the canopy. The climbers identified here, honeysuckle and ivy, also exhibited slow growth indicating that they shared similar environmental conditions to that evident in the tree taxa. It is thought, therefore, that these too would have been present in woodland, most likely in direct association with the oak.

Preservation: thermal and biological degradation

The general condition of fragments was often poor due mainly to the consequences of thermal degradation in combination with mineral deposits embedded throughout fragments, which tended to obscure anatomical features. Extensive radial and, occasionally, tangential splitting typically in association with high levels of thermal degradation, were clearly evident in a significant quantity of fragments. Radial/tangential splitting and high levels of thermal degradation were consistently a feature of twig-wood fragments. The severity of thermal degradation included many fragments that were partly 'vitrified' or close to 'vitrification'. None were actually wholly 'vitrified'. This material was recovered from features associated with charcoal production for iron processing. The temperatures reached and, perhaps more significantly, that could be maintained in a pit, oven or furnace almost certainly would have exceeded the average temperatures possible to achieve in open fires used for domestic purposes.

Fungal mycelium was frequently observed in the vessels of charred wood, and was not restricted to any particular taxon. The presence of fungal degradation indicates that some of the wood, at least, was probably in some state of decay when burnt. Fragments containing evidence of possible decay are thought to represent wood gathered as deadwood. Recording of the presence of mycelium was somewhat inconsistent (especially in oak fragments which could be identified confidently without fracturing to view all three planes –TS, TLS and RLS) and it is thought that more fragments contained mycelium than were actually recorded. Insect bore-holes were observed in few fragments and were by no means common. Insect attack tends to follow fungal attack. That bore-holes were also present in some fragments supports the suggestion that the wood was dead or decaying when charred. However, it cannot be discounted that the onset of fungal attack occurred at a later stage, for example when wood was stored. It is unclear if any of the wood was 'green', that is unseasoned, when burnt. Of the taxa identified only ash is noted for its ability to burn efficiently when 'green'.

Fire events and wood use

The charcoal from most contexts almost certainly represents the remains of wood gathered for fuel. *In-situ* burning was evident in at least five of the Phase 8 pits associated with industrial activities. It is likely that the charcoals from these deposits are the relatively undisturbed remains of fires. The relatively large dimensions of the fragments support the view that the charcoal was relatively undisturbed until excavation. Though these pits reflect industrial use, there is little in the condition of the charcoal to differentiate between charcoal that was used in a domestic context and that from an industrial activity. Thermal degradation was consistently high.

Taxon representation: wood acquisition – preference and avoidance

In accordance with the 'principle of least effort' the woods identified most probably would have been collected locally and therefore provide evidence of the local vegetation. However, factors such as physical inaccessibility, political restrictions and cultural beliefs may each influence the woods considered available, and thus the woods gathered for fuel (Asouti and Austin 2005). Unfortunately, it cannot be determined with any great certainty, if at all, which of these factors may have affected collecting behaviour on this site at different times or how they may have influenced wood acquisition.

What is clear is that oak is the most sought-after fuel wood. It is consistently the most abundant wood, by weight, fragment count and in terms of its 'ubiquity', that is the number of samples in which it is present. The taxa identified alongside oak are best considered minor components. It is thought that most of the non-oak fragments, mostly shrub/small tree taxa, were probably gathered more opportunistically, principally perhaps for use as kindling. The twig-wood that survived in a number of contexts almost certainly represents wood used for kindling. However, it is possible that fragments of honeysuckle and ivy could have been charred incidentally. These climbers typically attach themselves to other plants as a support and therefore may have remained attached to the oak wood when that was burnt. A single fragment of rose (*Rosa* sp.) twig-wood with thorns still attached, recovered from Anglo-Saxon to early Medieval charcoal burning pit [597] (Sample {47} [fill 596]) is probably an incidental inclusion. However, it is possible that rose was deliberately used for some reason. The fragment is a remnant of a thin stem; one that once may have supported a flower in bloom, for example.

Whilst it is tempting to conclude that oak may have been the only good firewood available, the presence of elm, beech and possibly hornbeam (cf. *Carpinus betulus*) in the Saxon to early Medieval samples suggests otherwise. The wood from these large timber trees are particularly good firewoods, with burning properties different from, but on par with, oak. Elm, for example, is valued for its slow burning properties. Among the small trees/shrub taxa, the Maloideae and Prunus spp. include taxa that produce good fuel wood. It is perhaps significant that the wood of these alternative good fuel woods were not better represented. This might indicate that they were not available in any great quantity, that they were reserved for other uses or that they were not considered appropriate for use as fuel. The poor representation of hazel is also notable. This taxon is often amongst the most ubiquitous taxon represented, typically alongside oak, on dry sites of most periods throughout the UK. That it is not well represented here suggests that it was not readily available or reserved for other purposes.

Habitat types

The assemblage as a whole indicates the ongoing presence of deciduous woodland and scrub. Though water runs close to the site, there is little evidence of exploitation of riverine or wetland taxa. Alder (*Alnus glutinosa*) and willow/poplar, for example, are not represented in the Phase 8 Anglo-Saxon samples. Taxa preferring or tolerant of damp woodland conditions, alder buckthorn (*Frangula alnus*) and elm, for example, suggest the presence of such conditions. There is no compelling evidence indicating the presence of heathland (or any other distinct habitat type other than deciduous woodland and scrub) at any time in the site's history. Though alder buckthorn can be found in heathland environments, no taxa more clearly indicative of heathland, heather (*Calluna* sp.) and gorse (*Ulex* spp.) in particular, were identified. The wood of these taxa can make good kindling and if present in the past it is believed they would have been used as such.

Woodland management

No direct evidence of silviculture or of woodland management practices was recovered during the analysis of the wood charcoal. However, the oak woodland represented in this assemblage was almost certainly managed in Medieval times, wood management is relatively well documented for this period (Rackham 2006). Alder Buckthorn, like alder, was traditionally grown for charcoal production (Preston *et al.* 2002), and it is possible that its presence was associated with the industrial activity at the site. Hazel is a well-known traditional coppice wood and it is possible that it was more valuable as coppice product than as charcoal or fuel wood, hence its poor showing in this assemblage. Of the taxa represented: oak, field maple, beech, willow/poplar and (possibly) hornbeam are among those with a long established history of management.

Plant macrofossils

Sample {47} context [596], the lower fill of charcoal burning pit [597] contained an uncharred seed resembling sheep's sorrel (*Rumex* cf. *acetosa* type). Sample {50} context [616] from the fill of ore roasting pit [617] contained two types of charred plant macrofossil consisting of one vetch (*Lathyrus* sp.) seed and three, more poorly preserved, fragments of vetch/tare/vetchling/pea (*Vicia/Lathyrus/Pisum* sp.). The sample also contained five uncharred taxa including seeds of knotgrass (*Polygonum aviculare* L), fat hen, water-pepper (*Polygonum hydropiper* (L.) Spach) and fragments of wild cabbage/mustard seed (*Brassica/Sinapis* sp.) testa.

Sample {30} context [392], the upper fill of charcoal burning pit [394] contained one charred bud resembling an oak (cf. *Quercus robur/petraea*) bud. The pit also contained fragments of wild cabbage/mustard testa and seeds of fat hen and water-pepper. Sample {31} context [393] from charcoal burning pit [394] contained a fragment of uncharred seed resembling water pepper. Sample {49} context [600] a fill of charcoal burning pit [586] contained a charred ?hawthorn (cf. *Crataegus monogyna* Jacq.) seed and an uncharred knotgrass seed. Sample {80} from the lower fill [881] of charcoal burning pit [877] contained one charred ?hawthorn seed. Sample {64} context [837] the fill of pit [843] contained a poorly preserved fragment resembling part of a charred ?hawthorn seed.

The uncharred seeds are from plants that would have frequented areas of disturbed or cultivated ground. The water-pepper seeds, if contemporaries of the dated material, could be from plants growing near the river and stream (Poole *et al.* 2007). Fragments of ?hawthorn and oak charcoal were observed in the charcoal assessment (*ibid.*) so the possible oak bud and charred ?hawthorn could have entered the deposit with the wood used in the fire pits. The emmer/spelt grain is not unusual for the date although bioturbation needs to be considered as an Iron Age farmstead has been recorded in the area of the site (*ibid.*) and this type of grain would be typical of deposits of this period.

Chapter 9

Phase 9 Later Medieval and Post-Medieval Activity

Evidence for later Medieval activity (Phase 9) was limited to the recovery of a few sherds of pottery that suggest the presence of settlement in the vicinity, but no actual settlement evidence was recorded at the site. As described in Chapter 1.2, by the later Medieval period the site was situated on the margins of an extensive area of heathland, Mousehold Heath. The heath supported small-holdings and sheep farmers and was exploited throughout the Post-Medieval period for a wide range of resources. Agricultural features of later Post-Medieval date were recorded across the development site within the evaluation trenches. A few features from this period were recorded within Area B (Phase 10), also associated with the agricultural use of the land. The upper parts of the substantial quarry pits associated with the iron processing activity that were scattered across the site had been backfilled and levelled by c. AD 1800, presumably to reinstate the land prior to ploughing, when a series of field-ditches were constructed across the site reflecting the layout of the present field system and established as a consequence of the enclosure of Mousehold Heath.

A large quantity of metal artefacts was recovered from across the development site during the fieldwalking and metal detecting surveys. The majority of this material was of eighteenth- and nineteenth-century date and in the absence of any associated settlement evidence is presumed to have arrived at the site via manuring or through casual loss. However, amongst the assemblage was a collection of late Medieval to early Tudor finds and as material of this date is generally under-represented in the archaeological record, these are described in this chapter and some items have been illustrated.

9.1 The Later Medieval and Post-Medieval Sequence

Ditch [583], aligned east-north-east–west-south-west, was recorded for a distance of 115m, continuing beyond the limit of excavation to the west (Fig. 65). Residual Medieval pottery and struck flint was recovered from the ditch, the latter presumably being incorporated into the backfill as the ditch cut through two Neolithic tree-throws towards the central part of Area B. The pottery assemblage recovered from this ditch was also extremely mixed, comprising Early Neolithic, Roman and Medieval material. Pottery dating from AD 1600–1800 and AD 1740–1780 was also recovered along with glass of seventeenth- to nineteenth-century date and clay tobacco pipe.

To the north of ditch [583] were two segments of ditch [931] and [949] aligned approximately parallel with [583]; adjacent to the western limit of excavation the distance between them was c. 40m and in the east this narrowed to c. 30m. Ditch [949], the westerly of the two, continued beyond the limit of excavation, while ditch [931] ended as it went down the slope to the east. The two features were separated by a 4m gap and in total extended for a distance of c. 85m. Pottery dated to AD 1745–1910 was recovered from ditch [931] along with seventeenth- to nineteenth-century glass, pottery and clay tobacco pipe.

A group of six postholes located in the south-eastern corner of the site formed a row aligned east-north-east–west-south-west (Fig. 65). The posts were positioned at regular intervals of approximately 4m and extended for a distance of c. 25m. This fenceline was on the same alignment as plough scars and the current fence of the field to the north.

These ditches and fenceline are interpreted as field boundaries of Post-Medieval origin; nineteenth-century mapping shows that the redevelopment area, which currently comprises a single large open field, was originally divided into smaller parcels of land and these boundaries are on the same alignment as these sub-divisions.

A narrow curvilinear feature [912] was situated a short distance to the north of the eastern end of field boundary [583]. This was roughly U-shaped in plan, measuring c. 5m north–south and up to 3m east–west, and c. 0.35m wide and 0.45m deep. Pottery dated to AD 1600–1800 was recovered from this feature along with clay tobacco pipe and fragments of ceramic building material. To the west was a short linear feature [936] and a group of six small stakeholes were also recorded in the vicinity. The only dating evidence was a piece of Post-Medieval ceramic building material recovered from [936]. This group of features may represent the remains of ephemeral structural features, perhaps a small lean-to or other wooden structure, presumably associated with the Post-Medieval agricultural use of the site. A few isolated features located some distance to the west of this group produced Post-Medieval material; clay tobacco pipe was recovered from pit [963], pottery dated to AD 1700–1900 from pit [1100], and Post-Medieval ceramic building material from pit [1138].

Other features thought to date from the Post-Medieval period comprise a group of tree-throw hollows located within the southern part of the Bronze Age barrow (Fig. 9). As discussed in Chapter 4.1, prehistoric barrows were often planted with trees and became a landscape features in later periods, though this evidence for tree roots must indicate that by this date the mound was much denuded. The trees growing on the Laurel Farm barrow are likely to have been felled during the Post-Medieval period when the land became enclosed, although datable material was only recovered from [1072], which produced a fragment of clay tobacco pipe and ceramic building material. Tree-throw hollow [818] located between the barrow and the putative structure produced Post-Medieval ceramic building material. In the south-eastern corner of Area B, tree-throw hollows [387] and [424] produced eighteenth-century pottery whilst tree-throw hollow [478] produced pottery dated to AD 1850–1950. Tree-throw hollow [523] produced ceramic building material that could be broadly dated to the Medieval/Post-Medieval period and

[486] produced Post-Medieval bottle glass. A substantial tree-throw hollow [653] produced pottery dated to AD 1800–1880. Tree clearance would have been undertaken in order to prepare the land for agricultural use. It is also likely that at this time the upper parts of the partially infilled Anglo-Saxon quarries were backfilled and levelled, as discussed in Chapter 8.1. This would also have been undertaken as preparation of the land for ploughing.

A group of small pits truncated an infilled Phase 8 quarry pit in the south-eastern corner of the site and are presumably of Post-Medieval date. A small pit [655], which truncated the edge of another Phase 8 feature, contained a small quantity of residual struck flint dated to the Late Neolithic to Bronze Age period. Also in the south-eastern corner of Area B was an irregular north–south aligned linear feature [464], which produced a small assemblage of ceramic building material and pottery dated to AD 1740–1780. Another linear feature in the vicinity [466] produced Post-Medieval clay tobacco pipe.

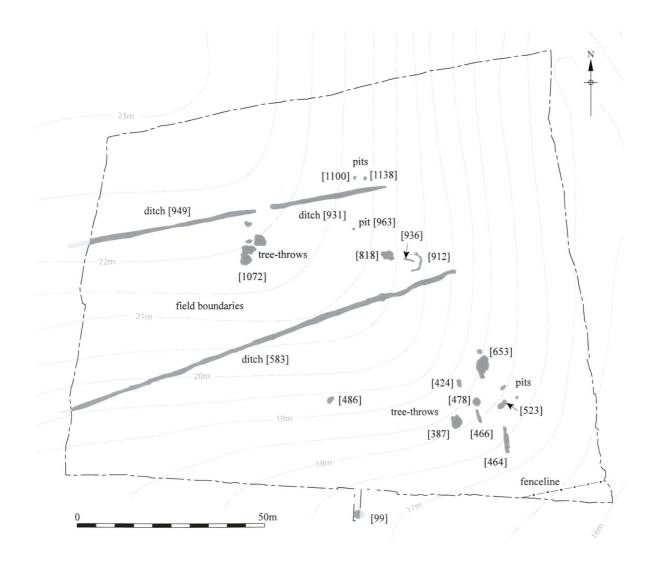

Fig. 65   Phase 9, Post-Medieval agricultural features, Area B (scale 1:1000)

9.2 Medieval and Post-Medieval Pottery

Berni Sudds

A small assemblage of Medieval and Post-Medieval pottery was collected through fieldwalking and excavation at Laurel Farm. The Medieval material comprised thirteen fragments from the same number of vessels and the Post-Medieval assemblage comprised 98 sherds from 88 vessels. The Norfolk Archaeological Unit pottery type codes were used to classify the ceramics. The material was quantified for each context by fabric, vessel form and decoration using sherd count (with fresh breaks discounted) and estimated vessel numbers. A ceramic database cataloguing these attributes has been generated using Microsoft Access and this forms part of the project archive.

The small Medieval assemblage is characterised by fabrics common to the region, namely Local Medieval unglazed wares (LMU; LMU-V; LMU LATE). The glazed vessels are represented by Grimston-type ware and a single import, Mottled green Saintonge ware. The latter, deriving from the south-west of France, is a relatively rare find across Britain but has a predominantly coastal distribution extending down the eastern seaboard and along the south coast.

With just under 100 sherds the Post-Medieval and modern assemblage is also small. The stratified material is frequently abraded and feature groups are usually comprised of no more than one or two sherds. Local glazed and unglazed red earthenwares, creamwares and refined white earthenwares account for nearly half of the group although German and English stonewares and Chinese porcelain were also recovered. Material dating to the seventeenth century, although residual, includes Frechen stoneware and Iron-glazed blackwares. Most of the material, however, dates to the eighteenth, nineteenth or early twentieth century. Staffordshire-type products occur with most frequency, including eighteenth-century salt-glazed stonewares, red stonewares, Staffordshire-type slipwares and nineteenth-century Sunderland-type ware and Yellow ware.

9.3 Medieval and Post-Medieval Ceramic Building Material

Berni Sudds

The Medieval and Post-Medieval ceramic building material assemblage is comprised of abraded roof tile, brick and floor tile. The majority of the roof tile is of the peg type and Post-Medieval in date although a few with coarse moulding sand are probably Medieval. A small number of pantiles were also recovered, first introduced to Britain during the early seventeenth century from Holland and Belgium. They remained popular, particularly in East Anglia and London, until the late eighteenth century.

Three fragments of uncertain form and date in a white-firing fabric were excavated from Post-Medieval and modern deposits (topsoil [1]; [174], an alluvial deposit in Trench 196 located in the south-eastern corner of the development site; and [1072] a tree-throw hollow located within the prehistoric barrow). Few surfaces remain and only one example demonstrated a measurable dimension, a thickness of 22mm. It is possible that the fragments derive from Medieval or early Post-Medieval floor tiles, perhaps of non-local or continental origin although the white-firing fabric is not typical to any of the major tile industries supplying the south and east of England, namely Westminster and Penn or those coming in from Flanders. The brick recovered from site is fragmentary but is comprised entirely of localised Post-Medieval oxidised orange sandy examples. The absence of diagnostic features, and in most cases surfaces, precludes close dating. Outside of the major urban conurbations oxidised, unfrogged bricks continued to be made and used into the nineteenth century.

Although probably derived from field marling and in-wash, the later building material also attests indirectly to the presence of Medieval and Post-Medieval settlement activity in the general vicinity.

9.4 Post-Medieval Metal Small Finds

Märit Gaimster

Altogether some 350 metal objects were retrieved from the site, mostly through metal detecting. With the exception of a small group of Roman coins and brooches (Gerrard, Chapter 7.3), those objects that could be identified were all Post-Medieval; they included categories such as buttons, shoe buckles, lead cloth or bag seals and a large group of around 40 finds of household fittings and utensils (Gaimster and Gerrard 2007). As no Post-Medieval buildings or other settlement features were recorded on site, these finds are likely to represent casual losses, rubbish dumping or manuring. The vast majority date from the eighteenth and nineteenth centuries; with the exception of a possible clog fastener of similar date, however, this report will focus on a small group of finds straddling the transition from the late Middle Ages into the early modern Tudor period. This is a period that is seldom well represented in excavation assemblages (Egan 2005, 3; Egan and Forsyth 1997). Significantly, no military weapons or armaments were recovered that could be associated with the Battle of Dussindale.

The group includes a crudely cast and possibly unfinished double-oval lead shoe buckle (<228>: Fig. 66.1); this type of buckle is likely to date from the fifteenth or early sixteenth centuries (Grew and de Nergaard 1988,

75 and fig. 110 g–h; cf. Egan 2005, fig. 17 no. 93). The copper-alloy plate from a folding clasp (<31>: Fig. 66.2) represents a characteristic late Medieval form, with clasps appearing from the late thirteenth and probably into the early sixteenth centuries (Egan 2007, 108). The Norwich plate is decorated with a simple pattern of punched 'X' shapes, separated with incised double lines. A small, solid-cast copper-alloy button with domed head and integral loop is likely to date from the late fifteenth or early sixteenth centuries (<102>: Fig. 66.3; cf. Egan 2005, fig. 33 no. 183; Bailey 2004, 23, fig. 7.6).

Two small mounts with double prongs for fixing are thought to date from the sixteenth or seventeenth centuries (<234> and <281>: Fig. 66.4, Fig. 66.5; cf. Williams 1996, fig. 13 nos 93–100). At this time the fashion for decorated belts, flourishing in the fifteenth century, appears to have subsided, and the mounts are perhaps more likely to have been attached to horse-harness straps (Egan 2005, 39).

Finally, a small copper-alloy clog or shoe fastener, in the form of a rose on a sunburst, deserves mentioning (<558>: Fig. 66.6); although relatively small, it has the characteristic folded-back T-shaped device for fixing into the leather. Very common as metal-detected finds, these clasps date from the eighteenth and nineteenth centuries (Bailey 1992, 13–17).

Post-Medieval small finds catalogue

Fig. 66.1 Lead double-oval shoe buckle; incomplete and roughly cast/unfinished; 12 x 22mm; fifteenth or early sixteenth century. Unstratified, sf <228>

Fig. 66.2 Complete copper-alloy double-sheet plate from a folding clasp; one side decorated with two blocks of dotted x-shapes separated by double vertical lines; W 32mm L 37mm; late thirteenth to early sixteenth century. Context [79], sf <31>

Fig. 66.3 Complete solid-cast copper-alloy button with domed head and integral loop; diam. 12mm; late fifteenth or early sixteenth century. Context [1], sf <102>

Fig. 66.4 ?Gunmetal (leaded bronze or copper) mount; splayed with trilobate end; two integrated rivets for fixing; L 18mm; sixteenth or seventeenth century. Unstratified, sf <234>

Fig. 66.5 Complete copper-alloy mount; circular with trilobate finish/finial at each end; two integral rivets for fixing; sixteenth or seventeenth century. Unstratified, sf <281>

Fig. 66.6 Complete copper-alloy clog or shoe fastener; rose on sunburst; t-shaped bar for fixing and rectangular eye for corresponding hook; diam. c.18mm; eighteenth or nineteenth century. Unstratified, sf <558>

Not illustrated. Near-complete copper-alloy 'rose/orb' jeton of Hans Krauwinckel II (d. 1635). Context [1], sf <157>

obv: *hanns.kravwinckel.in.nv

rev: *gotes.segen.macht.reich.

cf. Mitchener 1988, 443 no. 1553

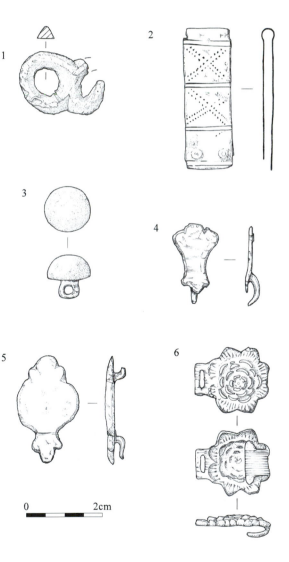

Fig. 66   Post-Medieval small finds (scale 1:1)

9.5 Clay Tobacco Pipe and Glass

Chris Jarrett

A total of 31 fragments of clay tobacco pipes were recovered from the investigations, of which three fragments were unstratified. All the fragments, with the exception of one bowl, are stems and can only be reliably dated to between *c.* 1570–1910, however less affluent communities did not smoke tobacco until the mid seventeenth century when the habit became more affordable. The single bowl with a heart-shaped heel is of Atkinson and Oswald's (1969) type AO20 or fits the shape of Atkin's (1987) No.58 bowl, both dated 1680–1710.

The investigations also produced a total of fourteen fragments of glass. The material is extremely fragmentary and it is very difficult to be precise about the shape of the vessels and their date, but all the fragments are seventeenth century or later in date. The forms mostly identifiable are bottles, and probably cylindrical wine bottles dated from *c.* 1750, but an octagonal bottle is additionally noted that could have been a container for a different type of liquid.

Chapter 10

Discussion

10.1 Phase 2 Palaeolithic Flintworking

A single handaxe deposited within an Early Neolithic pit is the only evidence of a Lower Palaeolithic presence at Laurel Farm, whilst a substantial tree-throw hollow produced an important assemblage of worked flint of Upper Palaeolithic date (see Chapter 2). Elsewhere in the region, evidence for Palaeolithic activity comes from casual finds and scatters of worked flint recorded on the Norfolk Historic Environment Record (NHER). Although Norfolk has produced some of the earliest and most important finds of both Lower and Middle Palaeolithic date in north-western Europe, for example at Happisburgh (Parfitt *et al.* 2010a; 2010b) there have been very few artefacts of this date found within the county. This is partly due to the nature and date of the geological deposits in the vicinity; most of the Palaeolithic remains in Norfolk and elsewhere in Britain derive from riverine terrace deposits of Anglian or later date, but the Laurel Farm site lies on glacial and fluvial deposited sands of Quaternary age that are locally very complex and poorly understood. A few handaxes have been found in the area, along with two 'working sites', containing potentially *in-situ* knapping debris, identified within the River Terrace deposits along the southern margins of the River Yare (NHER 9662 and 9663). Archaeological evidence from the Upper Palaeolithic period is nationally rare but sites are known from the Norwich stretch of the Yare Valley (Robins and Wymer 2006).

The overwhelming majority of Late Glacial/early Post-glacial sites consist of open air flintwork scatters, sometimes preserved in river silts, so the recovery of the material at Laurel Farm within a tree-throw hollow is highly unusual, with only a long blade site at Sproughton in Suffolk also being associated with sub-soil features; in this case from one of two shallow pits that were considered to be remnants of the campsite (Wymer 1976, 3). It is possible that the Laurel Farm material was residually introduced although its position in the tree-throw, within the lowest fills but absent elsewhere, negates this somewhat. Additionally, the apparent absence of similar artefactual material within the overlying topsoil, combined with the relatively unabraded condition of the material (which contrasts with the extensively abraded nature of flintwork recovered from surface deposits), point to a scenario whereby the material was knapped and then deposited into the feature shortly after use. It is possible that the tree-throw afforded shelter to the flintworkers and was subsequently used to dump some of the flintworking waste or that it eroded in not long after manufacture. It has been suggested that the '*visual impact of upturned tree-bowls within woods should not be underestimated. They may have served as landscape markers or as foci for settlement 'camps''* (Evans *et al.* 1999, 249). Whether or not they were imbued with any additional significance, the massed roots of the upturned trees would have afforded protection for activities undertaken within the hollow.

In the absence of firm dating, comparison with other potentially contemporary assemblages would be rather speculative but, based on draft publication texts and an examination of the material by the author (B. Bishop), the strong similarities between this assemblage and that excavated at Carrow Road near the centre of Norwich, some 4km to the south-west, is worth mentioning. This consists of an *in-situ* scatter containing refittable elements that was deposited on the original floodplain of the River Wensum (Adams in prep.). It is manufactured from almost identical raw material to that used at Laurel Farm and presumably has a similar origin. It includes large and very long blades that had often been snapped, along with rejuvenated opposed-platformed blade cores, all with very similar technological attributes to the material here. It also contains microliths, backed blades and 'bruised blades' indicating that it belongs to the final Upper Palaeolithic 'Long Blade' industry, confirmed by an OSL date that provided a *terminus post quem* date of 10,300 BP +/- 300 BP.

As at Carrow Road, Late Glacial and early Post-glacial sites and find-spots do appear to largely focus along the major river valleys, including the Yare (e.g. Robins and Wymer 2006), suggesting that as well as providing suitable settlement locations these may also have been instrumental in enabling population movement from the now-submerged North Sea plains inland into present day Britain. Activity beyond the valleys and onto the interfluves appears more rare but is also attested (e.g. Cooper 2006) and the possibility that streams or springs were present at Laurel Farm may be significant factors in the siting of this activity (cf. Conneller 2009, 167).

Dating by the assemblage alone is difficult as it is small and much of it consists of waste pieces from initial attempts to decorticate and shape the cores; pieces which are the least technologically diagnostic from the various stages of reduction. However, several technological features of this material suggest that it belongs within the Late Glacial or early Post-glacial period, dating to *c.* 12,600–7,700 BC. The calibrated radiocarbon date of 19,550–18,750 BC obtained from the charcoal is thus problematic; during this period Britain was still within the last glacial maximum and would have been too cold for human habitation or for oak to grow. Climatic fluctuations did occur during this last glacial period and sporadic incursions into northern Europe do appear to have taken place between 23,000 and 14,000 years ago (Terberger and Street 2002) and so the possibility that the Upper Palaeolithic material encountered at Laurel Farm may represent such an episode with the wood being brought to the site should at least be considered. Recent work on the timing of the reoccupation of northern Europe after the last glacial maximum indicates this was a complex process (Gamble *et al.* 2004; 2005). Conneller (2007) suggests the mode of reoccupation was also complex, with a variety of mobility and technical strategies used at different times and by different groups, permitting movement into new areas. However, at the time of writing the earliest undisputed evidence for post-Late Glacial maximum activity in Britain dates from 12,940 ± 140BP at Gough's Cave, Somerset with the evidence recovered there indicating that the site was initially used as a hunting camp (Jacobi 2004). On balance, the evidence from Laurel Farm cannot be considered sufficient to support the theory that activity was occurring at the site during a warmer period in the last glacial maximum and the radiocarbon date therefore remains, at present, inexplicable.

10.2 Phase 3 Early Neolithic Habitation

Overall, the evidence for the Early Neolithic period from Laurel Farm indicates that sporadic but fairly persistent occupation occurred at the site during this period (see Chapter 3). Although features of this date were only positively identified within the north-western quadrant of the site in Area B, quantities of Early Neolithic flintwork recovered across the site during the fieldwalking exercise and from colluvial deposits suggest that activity from this period was widespread, and that above-ground middening was occurring. Principal features of this date comprise tree-throw hollows, a conjoined pair of which produced a significant quantity of struck flint and pottery. The remainder of the Early Neolithic features comprised low-density scattered ephemeral features, principally pits, mostly concentrating around the fallen trees. A group of features in the northern part of Area B could represent posts from a semi-circular structure or posts or pits surrounding a central focal feature for which no evidence survives. The Early Neolithic pottery and struck flint assemblage are indicative of material originating from curated sources such as middens. Remnants of a few

hearths or campfires were also recorded and taken as a whole the evidence indicates that the Laurel Farm site is likely to have been the location for domestic habitation during the Early Neolithic period.

Early Neolithic habitation at Laurel Farm in a regional context

The Yare Valley to the south and south-east of present day Norwich is noted for its rich Neolithic ceremonial landscapes, settlements and evidence for axe manufacturing. Great numbers of Neolithic polished flint and stone axes are known from the area and settlement sites are suggested by concentrations of struck flint. In the near vicinity of Laurel Farm, some larger collections of struck flints, which may also indicate the locations of more permanent or larger settlement sites, have been recorded at Postwick, *c.* 1.5km south-east of Laurel Farm, and on the south bank at Trowse Newton (see Chapter 1.2).

The finds-rich tree-throw hollows, combined with the relatively large quantities of flintwork recovered during fieldwalking, may suggest that occupation during this period was relatively intense or of long duration. On the other hand only a few other features could be assigned to this period with complete confidence and many of the features assigned to the Early Neolithic period contained such small quantities of material culture that residuality cannot be completely ruled out. Features of definite or probable Early Neolithic date were not particularly numerous, particularly if compared to some other Early Neolithic occupation sites in the region, such as Hurst Fen (Clark *et al.* 1960), Broome Heath (Wainwright 1972) or Kilverstone (Garrow 2006). These three exceptional East Anglian sites are characterised by significant numbers of pits containing cultural debris, indicating an intensively occupied landscape. At Kilverstone for example, 226 pits were recorded and at Hurst Fen there were 200. Garrow (2006, 59) concluded that the evidence from these pit sites points to a wide variation in the character, permanency and scale of occupation across different places with some re-occupied many times over and with the scale and duration of re-occupation varying greatly. The evidence for cultivation of cereals at Kilverstone demonstrates relatively long-term, though not necessarily permanent occupation (Garrow 2006, 57). The scale of activity at Laurel Farm perhaps has more affinities with the site at Eaton Heath, located on the northern side of the Yare Valley south-west of Norwich; here twelve pits were identified which appeared to be arranged in clusters (Wainwright 1973; Garrow 2006, 27). Similar activity has also been recorded at Bowthorpe, also on the northern side of the Yare Valley, to the west of Norwich. At this site, several features containing Early Neolithic struck flint and pottery have been interpreted as being of periglacial origin or perhaps could represent tree-throw hollows (Percival 2002, 65). The Early Neolithic activity encountered at Laurel Farm perhaps has some affinity with that at Kilverstone Area C, which was characterised by widely dispersed pits. This suggests that dense pit clusters may not always be the norm for Early Neolithic sites or that such clusters are only part of a larger area of inhabitation and that an area of more dense clusters may be present in the vicinity of Area B at Laurel Farm.

The size of the tree-throw hollows at Laurel Farm suggests that they were created by large mature trees; it has been estimated that similar sized examples at sites in Cambridgeshire would have had trunks up to 1m in diameter and root balls up to 5.0m across (Evans *et al.* 1999, 242). The fallen trees would have been a significant feature within the landscape, they would have taken a considerably long time to rot and their roots would have provided a sheltered area. The fills of the two artefact-rich tree-throw hollows suggest that these trees toppled to the south-west, presumably as a result of strong north-easterly winds rather than the prevailing winds from the south to north-west. It may be that a storm or storms from this direction caused several trees to topple as their root systems would have developed to counter the prevailing winds. The upturned roots of these two trees would have lain adjacent to each other, creating a very substantial sheltered area. One of the tree-throw hollows recorded within evaluation Trench 114, a little to the south of Area B, contained a flint assemblage that was indicative of *in-situ* knapping, suggesting that this may have been used as a sheltered area for such activity.

The Early Neolithic struck flint assemblage from the two artefact-rich tree-throw hollows contains material from all stages in the reduction sequence and includes a wide range of implement forms. The quantity of material present is notable and is indicative of a relatively intensive or prolonged episode of occupation involving a broad-based range of activities. The basic technological strategies employed and the typological range of this assemblage are broadly comparable to other Early Neolithic 'settlement' assemblages in the region, such as at Broome Heath (Wainwright 1972), Hurst Fen (Clark *et al.* 1960), Spong Hill (Healy 1988) or Kilverstone (Garrow 2006). The typological composition does, however, contrast with the assemblages from the two most closely dated sites in the area. At Harford Park and Ride, *c.* 8km upstream of the River Yare, a substantial lithic assemblage associated with comparable radiocarbon dates differs from that from the hollows at Laurel Farm in that it is dominated by axe-manufacturing waste. A smaller component of that assemblage is regarded as reflecting the 'domestic' activities of the inhabitants, and this was more comparable in terms of technology and typology to the Laurel Farm assemblage (Bishop forthcoming b). At Colney, also in the Yare Valley but to the west of Norwich, a natural hollow preserved a comparably large lithic assemblage along with Carinated Bowl pottery (Whitmore 2004). The lithic assemblage, although technologically comparable to that at Laurel Farm contained few retouched pieces and was regarded as predominantly the waste from primary flintworking, where tools were made but removed for use elsewhere (Robins 2004).

Most of the Early Neolithic pottery recovered from the investigations came from the two artefact-rich tree-throw hollows; the majority is flint tempered and is comparable to other Early Neolithic assemblages in the Norwich area such as Harford Park and Ride (Percival with Trimble in prep., see Chapter 3.3). It is clear that the Laurel Farm material is likely to have originated from domestic habitation and the composition and condition of the assemblage within the tree-throw hollows suggests that the pottery came from a curated source such as a midden. The assemblages from both Harford Park and Ride and Colney are also indicative of middened material, although as the average sherd size of the Laurel Farm assemblage was larger, it suggests that this material had been subject to less attrition. and may have been deposited after spending a relatively short time within a midden.

Further evidence for middening was provided by burnt flint, charcoal, burnt clay and burnt daub inclusions within the fills of the tree-throw hollows. Dark-coloured humic compounds within the fills also suggest that high quantities of organic material were present, again indicative of midden deposits. Small quantities of burnt and calcined animal bone were also recovered from the tree-throw hollows, although the condition of this material meant that it was not possible to identify the species present.

The struck flint, pottery and other artefactual material such as animal bone had clearly been deliberately deposited into the hollows. The relative paucity of artefactual material from the surrounding topsoil deposits demonstrates that it had been obtained from a source away from the immediate vicinity. The hollows had partially silted up prior to the deposition of artefactual material, indicating that deposition had occurred some time after the trees fell. However, it cannot be demonstrated whether the occupation represented by the recovered finds occurred before or after the trees toppled. It may even have been the presence of the fallen trees or the clearance caused by them that initially attracted occupation to this location (cf. Evans *et al.* 1999).

In contrast to the pottery evidence, a number of factors, including the paucity of obvious and extensive refitting sequences, the varied condition of the assemblage, the high degree of fragmentation and the juxtaposition of burnt and unburnt pieces, all suggest that the lithic assemblage may have been deposited into the hollow after having been exposed for some time to the elements and other agencies, such as trampling and fire. However, the lithic material did not appear to be completely randomly distributed within the hollow, some short refitting sequences were identified and the presence of numerous small flakes and fragments suggest the material had been moved *en masse* within the soil matrix. Within relatively restricted areas of the hollow there was some coherence within the material, such as distinctive pieces of raw materials, the quantities and proportions of struck flint and burnt flint and the distribution of certain flake and tool types. This may indicate that either the hollows were filled through a series of discrete depositional episodes, with the material perhaps originating from varying activities, or that the primary sources from which it was gathered similarly varied in composition.

The majority of Early Neolithic artefact assemblages in the region derive either from plough-disturbed surface scatters or from pits. Tree-throw hollows are frequently encountered during excavation although the vast majority contain little or no artefactual material. Only recently have they received serious archaeological attention and now numerous examples containing artefact assemblages have been published, although few have produced such large assemblages as the examples from Laurel Farm.

Possible examples were excavated at Bowthorpe, close to the River Yare and to the west of Norwich, where a number of often elongated or amorphous features produced Plain Bowl pottery and struck flint assemblages (Percival 2002). Two conjoined amorphous hollows contained a relatively substantial lithic assemblage of 612 pieces, another contained 78 struck flints alongside 20 sherds of Plain Bowl Pottery. Interestingly, the latter was surrounded by a small ring-ditch that may have had a ritual use and which appears to demarcate or draw attention to the hollow (Percival 2002, 83). More definite examples of tree-throw hollows have been recorded at Barleycroft Farm and at Hinxton, both in Cambridgeshire (Evans *et al.* 1999; Evans and Knight 2000, 94–95). At both of these sites, substantial deposits of struck flint and Plain Bowl and Carinated Bowl pottery, which were considered to have been redeposited from surface middens, were recovered from the hollows. A similar scenario was recorded at Eton Rowing Lake in Buckinghamshire, where a number of artefact-rich tree-throw hollows with comparable radiocarbon dates to the Laurel Farm hollows were associated with actual middens that had been preserved beneath alluvium (Lamdin-Whymark 2008). The most prolific tree-throw hollow contained over 1,600 struck flints and pottery from at least 70 vessels, with many of the others also containing significant artefactual assemblages. The assemblages include many different materials and artefact types, suggestive of settlement-type activities. Variability in the condition of the material and a high degree of fragmentation and mixing indicate that it '*was not directly deposited into the feature, but was probably middened or left exposed on the land surface for a period prior to deposition*' (*ibid.*, 86). The material was similar to that in the near-by middens and it seems likely that the deposits in the tree-throw hollows derived from these.

A recent summary of artefact filled tree-throw hollows (*ibid.*, 93–100) indicates that they occur in all prehistoric periods but the practice of deliberate deposition within them reaches its peak in the Early Neolithic and this starts to decline at an early stage, perhaps by around 3,700 BC. This represents a continuation of Mesolithic practices but in the Neolithic the scale of this increases markedly and develops a distinct character, which includes the deposition of a broad range of materials within a charcoal-rich matrix. The position of the artefactual material within the tree-throw hollows suggest that some were filled shortly after the tree had fallen whilst others had evidently been open for some time prior to deposition. The assemblages are usually fragmented with few refitting flints, conjoining pottery sherds or articulated animal bones. There is usually a broad range of flint tool types present '*particularly scrapers and simple edge-retouched flakes*' (Lamdin-Whymark 2008, 95). The deposits are constructed with little formality and there is an absence of carefully selected items. Of particular interest is that the deposits contained in many artefact-rich tree-throw hollows had '*clearly been exposed at another location prior to (final) deposition*' (Lamdin-Whymark 2008, 56).

The Early Neolithic deposits at Laurel Farm share many of these characteristics and are likely to have also been exposed elsewhere prior to final deposition in the hollows. Although not formed *in situ*, they do share some characteristics of middened material, as defined in Needham and Spence's (1996; 1997) analysis of the deposits from Runnymede Bridge, Surrey: '*an occupation deposit relatively rich in refuse, including archaeologically less tangible elements – notably decayed organics and comminuted structural clay – and with evidence for the deliberate and sequential accumulation of refuse at one location*' (Needham and Spence 1997, 80).

Surface deposited middens are rarely encountered in Neolithic contexts. They only survive if protected from weathering and erosion and are easily and rapidly transformed into formless scatters of predominantly lithic material through prolonged ploughing, and thus only rarely survive into the archaeological record. A few, usually protected by alluviation or by being sealed under later earthworks, have been recorded and, interestingly, these are often associated with Carinated Bowl pottery with radiocarbon determinations placing them within the earliest Neolithic, during the first few centuries of the fourth millennia BC (Lamdin-Whymark 2008, 55).

A recurring pattern in the earliest Neolithic, a period associated with Plain Bowl and Carinated Bowl pottery, is therefore becoming apparent. Alongside surface scatters, the earliest Neolithic depositional practices are in many cases associated with tree-throw hollows and surface deposited middens. A similar relationship continues as the Early Neolithic develops but, as Mildenhall ware pottery types become prevalent, purposefully dug pits take over the role of tree-throw hollows as the focus for deposition, although the material often continues to derive from primary sources such as surface accumulations or middens (Pollard 1999; Thomas 1999; Garrow 2006; Lamdin-Whymark 2008). Frances Healy suggests that at Spong Hill the deposits in the Mildenhall ware pits represent '*accumulated midden material*' (1988, 108), although no middens were actually found. A similar situation is recorded at Kilverstone where numerous clusters of Mildenhall ware pits were each filled sequentially from what was described as a single pre-pit context. Variations in the composition of the lithic deposits within these pits were noted and it was suggested that they reflected variation in the nature of the activities conducted throughout the occupation(s) (Garrow *et al.* 2006). In addition to the tree-throw hollows, Early Neolithic pit clusters were also found at Barleycroft Farm although these were associated with Mildenhall ware pottery rather than Carinated Bowls, but nevertheless also appeared to have contained previously exposed material such as from a midden (Evans and Knight 2000, 94–95).

It has become increasingly accepted that the deposition of artefactual material, whether in tree-throw hollows, pits or other contexts, is more than a convenient way to remove unwanted waste material in the manner that we today may dispose of rubbish (Richards and Thomas 1984; Thomas 1999). As in most places, occupation of the landscape around Laurel Farm does not appear particularly dense and it would be hard to envisage what incentive there may have been in actually burying rubbish, unless there were some pervasive cultural reasons for doing so (Hill 1995; Thomas 1999). The deposition of the Laurel Farm material in a tree-throw hollow can therefore be seen as an intentional and meaningful act, and this becomes apparent from its complex structuring. Unlike many of the deposits placed in pits however, its structure does not derive from deliberately arranged fills, nor from the value of items that were included. Rather it derives from the processes that led to it being deposited, the acts of deposition themselves, as well as from the significance of the biographies of the individual materials included (re Gosden 1994; Gosden and Lock 1998). The significance of all of the materials is rooted in their histories; where they came from, who made and used them, how they were used and on what materials, and the circumstances that led to them being discarded in the manner that they were. One obvious point of departure to this, however, is the polished axe. This would almost certainly have been regarded as a prestigious and symbolically charged item, and its placing at the summit of the deposit with its cutting edge pointing upwards is likely to have been highly meaningful. Although the placing of this item can easily be regarded as ritually inspired or as an element of ceremonial practices, it would also be erroneous to separate it from other materials of a more utilitarian nature. Recent work has demonstrated that in pre-enlightenment societies little distinction is afforded between what we may consider as sacred or profane, or the supernatural and the everyday world. More frequently, everyday concerns are incorporated into spiritual or mythological understandings and seemingly utilitarian materials and practices are used as a means of communication or negotiation with these less tangible aspects of life (e.g. Hill 1993; Brück 1999; Bradley 2003). Rather than equating with esoteric practices that have little consequence over the everyday processes of living, for many societies ritual is an eminently practical way of dealing with and relating to things that may otherwise seem beyond immediate control. This can easily extend to a 'ritualisation of the domestic sphere' (Bradley 2003) where the manipulation of what we see as rubbish

and everyday items may have complex metaphorical implications (e.g. Hill 1995).

In this sense, the accumulation of occupation residues and the deposition of portions of this into tree-throw hollows is a purposeful act and one that must carry important meanings to others, be they neighbours, ancestors, descendants or mythological beings. The deposition of this assemblage in the tree-throw hollow may therefore be regarded as an act of communication, even if we do not know precisely what the message says or to whom it is directed.

It has been noted that the receptacles used for deposition appear to change over time. Although the chronology is hazy and the archaeological record not always clear-cut, the deposition of large quantities of material culture into tree-throw hollows is most widely attested during the first few centuries after the inception of the Neolithic. After this, similar patterns of deposition continue but become focused on pits or monumental contexts. Tree-throw hollows therefore appear to have been of particular interest to the earliest Neolithic communities and their practical importance cannot be over emphasised. Although much variation is likely, the landscape at the start of the Neolithic is thought to have been predominantly heavily wooded. Tree-throw hollows are distinctive features of woodland environments and provide invaluable gateways into areas that may have been largely intractable. Clearings are essential for both grazing and cultivation but the felling of large wildwood trees is very difficult, even with the advent of the polished axe (Brown 1997). Probably the most convenient route into the forest would have been through naturally created clearings, such as could be formed from the toppling of mature wildwood trees from wind or lightening, opening up gaps in the canopy which could then be more easily maintained through chopping down of smaller trees and shrubs and through grazing (Brown 1997). The tree-throw hollows that formed the object for deposition at Laurel Farm were very large and deep and must have been caused by the toppling of equally substantial trees which must have made an impact on the forest canopy. There is further evidence, from Laurel Farm and elsewhere, which suggests that once clearances have been created by fallen trees, they are easier to maintain as open spaces and frequently remained a focus for repeated occupation over an extended period (Brown 2000; Lamdin-Whymark 2008, 93). This illuminates an important aspect of human/woodland relationships and the deposition within tree-throw hollows of 'domestic' cultural material may not be a coincidence. Through toppled trees, occupation is enabled, and the residues from occupation are subsequently returned to the entities that allowed it to occur.

Although clearances may allow occupation, it is through occupation and the undertaking of everyday tasks that the clearances are maintained and cultural landscapes created (Ingold 1993). Through the relationships that develop from the movement and use of raw materials, plants and animals, reference is made to many other people, places and times (e.g. Ingold 1986; 2000; Edmonds 1997; Edmonds *et al.* 1999; Chapman 2000; Conneller 2000; 2008). These elements are brought together through the activities conducted in places such as woodland clearances. The deposits placed in tree-throw hollows and other features may have significance that transcends the immediate and local; they can form anchor points that link wider landscapes of occupation and activities for what are otherwise highly transient and dispersed communities. In this way, the placement of the debris from particular episodes of occupation, along with their attached memories and associations, may also facilitate the creation of a sense of place and history. They mark another point in the landscape that had been wrested from intractable and perhaps dangerous forces, and brought into the human domain.

Place and history are also two vital ingredients in establishing identity, arguably this is of particular concern at the very beginnings of the Neolithic. Many prehistorians consider the Neolithic to be above all about transformation (Edmonds 1999; Whittle 1996; 1999). Again, tree-throw hollows figure strongly in this; they transform what could be seen as dark impenetrable woodlands into open, light social arenas and allow grazing and cultivation, still defining elements of what constitutes the Neolithic. Although tree-throw hollows had been utilized long before the Neolithic, in some sense they were part of what allowed the Neolithic to happen; they even may have been recognised and appreciated as metaphors for that very process.

10.3 Phase 4 Late Neolithic to Early Bronze Age Ceremonial Activity

The Late Neolithic and Early Bronze Age periods witnessed a considerable decrease in the level of activity at Laurel Farm in comparison to the Early Neolithic period. The combined evidence suggests a significant change in the use of the area, which perhaps became a focus for funerary and ceremonial activity.

A low-level scattering of struck flint of this period was identified within the unstratified and residual material and a few pits within Area B did produce both Later Neolithic and Early Bronze Age pottery as well as some diagnostic flint artefacts, but the quantity of artefactual material recovered suggests that activity at the site was much less intense than during the Early Neolithic period. Less than twenty sherds of pottery from this period were recovered from the site, and of these only five were from contemporary features, the remainder representing material considered to be either residual or intrusive. The ceramic assemblage comprised mainly Beaker pottery, but significantly a single sherd of Grooved ware pottery was also recovered; this is relatively uncommon for the region (Longworth and Cleal 1999). Only a small quantity of flintwork could be confidently assigned a Late Neolithic to Early Bronze Age date; a few pits produced struck flint that was diagnostic of the Beaker period (see Chapter 4.2).

The most notable feature of this period, the ring-ditch located towards the central part of Area B, has been interpreted as representing the surviving remains of a round barrow probably dating from the Early Bronze Age period, the central mound having been ploughed flat in the later Post-Medieval period. It has been tentatively suggested that a broken flint axe (see Fig. 33.1) may have been as a significant or prestigious object and deliberately placed within the ring-ditch (see Chapter 4.2). An Early Bronze Age barbed and tanged arrowhead (Fig. 67) is a notable find. Such arrowheads are often found as stray finds and occasionally within settlement contexts, however, the quality of manufacture of the Laurel Farm example is remarkable and may tentatively suggest that it was associated with ceremonial or funerary activity.

Settlements of Late Neolithic/Early Bronze Age date are rare in Norfolk as elsewhere in the lowland zone (Brown and Murphy 1997, 14; see Chapter 1.2). The scarcity of pits and other sub-surface features on settlement sites of this period means that they are less visible archaeologically and a large number of artefacts are found in disturbed or unstratified contexts (Ashwin 1996a, 52). The few pits of this date at Laurel Farm contained very little in the way of artefactual or cultural material to indicate the presence of nearby settlement activity. It has been suggested that settlement sites from this period may be preserved on valley floors and thus East Anglia may have considerable potential for such evidence (Brown and Murphy 1997, 14).

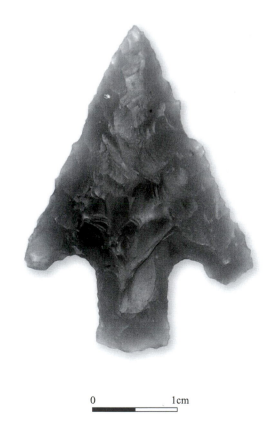

0   1cm

Fig. 67 Early Bronze Age barbed and tanged arrowhead

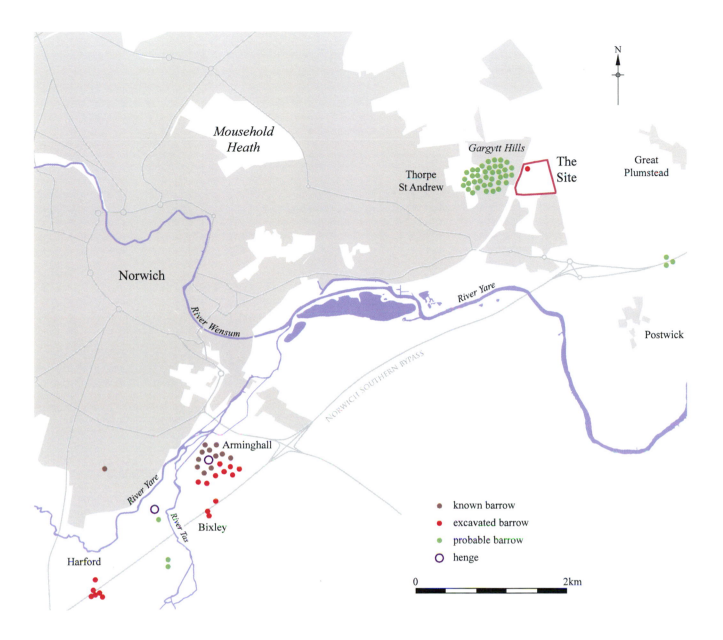

Fig. 68   Barrows in the Yare Valley (with information from Ashwin and Bates 2000, fig. 180) (scale 1:50 000)

Barrows in the Yare Valley

The area around the confluences of the Rivers Yare, Tas and Wensum to the south and east of Norwich appears to have been a focus for prehistoric activity and a large number of funerary and ceremonial monuments are known (Trimble 2006). The Arminghall Henge, which is located on the south of the river on the southern outskirts of Norwich, became the focus for an important group of round barrows. At least twenty barrows and ring-ditches have been identified in the Arminghall group (Ashwin and Bates 2000, 233), although most have been ploughed flat and only survive as crop marks visible on aerial photographs. Eight round barrows from this group were excavated in advance of the construction of the Norwich Southern by-pass, at Harford Farm and Bixley, on the southern side of the River Yare in the vicinity of the river

confluences (Ashwin and Bates 2000, see Fig. 68). Closer by three ring-ditches have been identified as cropmarks on aerial photographs at Postwick, *c*. 1km to the southeast of Laurel Farm. One of these was a large possible hengiform monument and the other two smaller ring ditches, interpreted as probable barrows (NHER 21766). The remains of a very similar feature to the Laurel Farm ring-ditch, also interpreted as a ploughed-out barrow, were excavated at Sweet Briar Road, north of Norwich in 1982 (Bown 1986). No original ground surface remained within this barrow and there were no traces of a central burial, although fragments of cremated bone recovered from the excavations were interpreted as representing disturbed cremations that would have been inserted into the mound.

Cartographic and documentary evidence suggests that a large barrow cemetery was located in the fields now

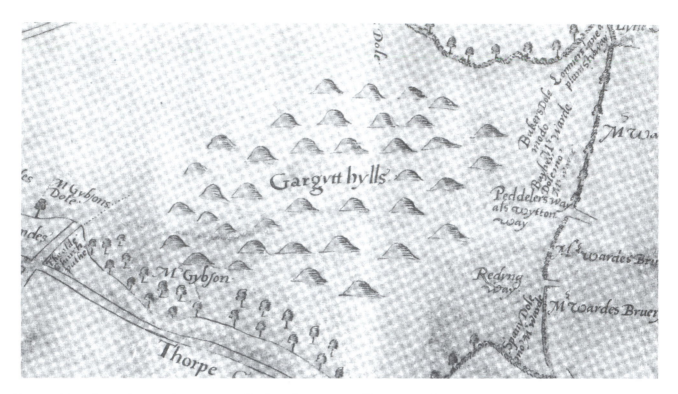

Fig. 69   Map of 1589 showing the 'Gargytt Hylls', thought to be round barrows, at Thorpe St Andrew

covered by the Dussindale Park housing estate, adjacent to the western limit of the Laurel Farm site. A 1589 map of Thorpe St Andrew (Fig. 69) depicts 38 mounds called the 'Gargytt Hylls', apparently barrows, which may be those referred to in 1847 thus: *'From the number of British barrows south of this place (Kett's Castle on Gas Hill), it is highly probable that this part of the Country was thickly populated'* (Woodward 1847, 2). No traces of these remained when the area was examined in 1933 and much of the area has now been developed for residential housing. It is therefore uncertain how far these extended towards the site although a number of ring-ditches, most probably ploughed-out barrows, are known from aerial photography across the immediate environs.

10.4 Phase 5 Middle to Late Bronze Age Ceremonial Activity

Middle to Late Bronze Age settlement and agriculture in the Yare Valley

A shaft, either purposely dug or a naturally formed solution hole, adjacent to a tree-throw hollow partially encircled by pits and postholes, provides the only evidence for Middle to Late Bronze Age presence at the site (Chapter 5). Material deposited within the shaft, such as struck flint, burnt quernstones, pottery, burnt clay and daub presumably represents domestic refuse and this seems most likely to have originated from a midden within an area of habitation located somewhere in the

near vicinity, though the focus of occupation was not identified during the excavations.

Vast areas of south-east Britain were converted into co-axial field systems during the later Bronze Age and although few traces of such systems had previously been found in Norfolk, recent research has identified large swathes of fields systems present to the east of Laurel Farm in the Norfolk Broads and coastal region (e.g. Albone *et al.* 2007; Gilmour and Mortimer 2011). There would be very little reason to suppose that such systems were not constructed upstream along the major river valleys from there. Recent pollen analysis work on deposits from the River Waveney and River Wensum, a tributary of the Yare in Norwich, has shown evidence for extensive tree clearance in the fourteenth century BC (Wiltshire forthcoming). Evidence in the pollen record for the presence of cultivated soils suggests that a mixed agricultural system had been established in this area during the Bronze Age, although there is scant settlement evidence (Wiltshire forthcoming). Traces of a Middle Bronze Age ditched enclosure system from which Deverel-Rimbury pottery was recovered were recorded at The Oaks (Trimble 2006). Also recorded at the site were a group of pits and postholes, possibly part of a rectangular structure, which also produced Deverel-Rimbury pottery. At Laurel Farm, Middle to Late Iron Age ditch systems were recorded within the north-western part of the development site, in Area B, and Iron Age field systems sometimes did have their antecedents in earlier, Bronze Age, systems. It is feasible then that the site and the immediate locality became incorporated into an agricultural landscape during the Middle Bronze Age period.

The infilling of the shaft in the Middle Bronze Age

The features recorded in the south-western corner of the Laurel Farm development site can be confidently dated to the Middle to Later Bronze Age by the presence of Deverel-Rimbury pottery. The Laurel Farm pottery is very similar to a large assemblage recovered from Grimes Graves where radiocarbon dating demonstrated that occupation spanned the period *c.* 1375–845 BC (Longworth *et al.* 1988).

A series of round shafts excavated beneath round barrows at Eaton Heath, just north of the River Yare on the southern outskirts of Norwich have been interpreted as natural solution holes (Healy 1986, 57; Ashwin 2000, 236; see Chapter 5.1). These contained quantities of Peterborough ware, Beaker and food vessels, some of which may have been deliberately deposited within the shafts when they were open (Ashwin 2000, 236). Similarly, a deposit of artefact-rich material was dumped within the upper part of the Laurel Farm shaft, after it had partially infilled with redeposited natural material. It is plausible that some of the burnt material may be either the residues from or the result of ceremonial activity. Similarly, considerable quantities of pottery, deriving from two vessels, were recovered from a posthole. Such quantities are unlikely to have been accidentally incorporated and, although the two broken pots may have been reused as post-packing, they may represent deliberate deposition, perhaps as a foundation offering. Some of the sherds originated from the same vessel as sherds from the shaft underlining the connection between these features and perhaps reinforcing the possibility that their deposition was ceremonially inspired.

Although the flint assemblage recovered from the Laurel Farm shaft was not particularly large, its relative size and the context of its deposition are reminiscent of other instances where larger quantities of struck flint were produced and deposited, sometimes in situations that suggest non-utilitarian disposal. The associated pottery is comparable to that from the midden deposits at Grime's Graves (see Percival, Chapter 5.3) and there extensive deposits of midden material that included vast quantities of struck flint had been periodically dumped into partially infilled Later Neolithic mineshafts (Saville 1981; Herne 1991). These deposits were essentially interpreted as representing the disposal of domestic debris generated from nearby settlements, although it is acknowledged that the material probably originated from a much larger and long established midden deposit that was likely to have been situated at some distance from the mineshaft (Longworth *et al.* 1991, 20, 62) and would appear to go beyond simple functional requirements of production and disposal. Many other occurrences of later Bronze Age flintwork being dumped within earlier monuments have been recorded in south-eastern Britain. These include deposits of cultural material containing flintwork that seal earlier Bronze Age barrows and ring-ditches (e.g. Trump 1956; Smith 1987; Evans and Knight 1996; Pollard 1998; 2002; Greatorex 2001; Ballin 2002), within Middle Bronze Age enclosure ditches (Brudenell 2004; Bishop 2008; Bishop and Mortimer in prep.), or earlier settlements sites (e.g. Fasham and Ross 1978; Drewett 1982; Seager Thomas 1999) and, appropriately here, used to fill or perhaps 'decommission' wells or shafts (Kemp 2005; Mortimer and Connor in prep.; Bishop forthcoming a).

The later Bronze Age struck flint from Laurel Farm seems typical of many of the deposits discussed here. It represents a number of episodes of flintworking, knapped elsewhere but dumped in the shaft after it had partially infilled, perhaps acting as a kind of closing deposit for the feature. The pattern that seems to be emerging is that, in certain circumstances, quantities of flintwork were deliberately deposited over or into earlier features within the landscape. This is not to suggest there were no practical reasons for working the flint; used tools are present and in most cases the flintwork is found alongside quantities of other material, such as pottery, burnt flint, animal bone and charcoal which may have accumulated as middens or possibly even from activities such as feasting episodes (e.g. Needham 1993; McOrmish 1996; Brück 1999). In nearly all cases the deposits seems to have accumulated elsewhere and to have been specifically dumped at the site, which may be located far from any known settlement where any practical use of flint would be expected to occur. Instead, these deposits are most closely associated with earlier features; they often constitute their final fills, physically cover or cut into them.

A concern with the past is a frequently noted feature of the later Bronze Age, an era when entire landscapes were rapidly becoming demarcated and perhaps barrows, like that at Laurel Farm, were important reference points in this process. There appears to have been a growing emphasis on concerns such as territoriality, land ownership and inheritance rights. In such circumstances, the marking of earlier centres of cultural significance with evidence of the community's presence may have become increasingly advantageous.

That elements of ceremonial activity may be discerned in the contents and acts of deposition occurring in the solution hole and one of the postholes does not necessarily designate the features recorded here as principally religious or esoteric in nature. During the later prehistoric period, from the Middle Bronze Age onwards, ceremonial activity was increasingly being expressed within the domestic sphere (cf. Brück 1999; Bradley 2003) with an emphasis being placed on marking important places such as nodal or liminal points within the agricultural systems. Significant items were deposited in such places, and the material designated for such treatment could consist of a wide variety of objects including 'everyday' pieces such as pottery or flintwork or refuse material. '*Rituals may employ mundane objects, potentially including refuse or the simultaneous destruction of objects*' (Needham and Spence 1997, 86). Brück (1999, 262) suggests that '*materials whose lives had ended or which were in a state of decay may have been seen as sources of fertility*'. Hill (1995, 98) has also highlighted the use of domestic refuse in ritual deposits. Close to the shaft was a large tree-throw hollow with a group of postholes to the north and east and it is postulated that further postholes, subsequently removed by truncation, may have been present and these could have encircled the uprooted or fallen tree. Circular structures, which may also have referenced natural features within the landscape, are known from other sites, mostly as small ditched circular enclosures, but the use of postholes here may reflect a local manifestation of similar concerns. A well-preserved example of a timber circle, dated by dendrochronology to 2049 BC, was excavated on the north Norfolk coast at Holme-next-the-Sea in 1999 (Brennand and Taylor 2003). This comprised a ring of split oak trucks enclosing an area *c.* 7m by 6m with a large inverted oak stump in the central area and it has been postulated that it may have functioned as a mortuary enclosure, perhaps for excarnation. It is possible that the features at Laurel Farm may have originally been part of a similar timber circle enclosing an uprooted tree.

10.5 Phase 6 Iron Age Farmstead

Iron Age date habitation at Laurel Farm was indicated by features concentrated towards the north-western part of the development site where two possible roundhouses were identified. A number of pits between the two contained large quantities of refuse material, probably of domestic origin, including charcoal derived most probably from sources such as hearths or ovens. Cattle and pig bones were identified amongst the material from the refuse pits, although as with earlier periods preservation of bone was very limited, and a single grain of emmer or spelt wheat was also recovered. The cumulative evidence evidence is suggestive of a small, relatively short-lived, later Iron Age open farmstead, possibly set within a system of cultivated fields. Enclosed settlements became common in the later Iron Age period elsewhere in south-east Britain, but unenclosed settlements seem to have persisted in Norfolk (Bryant 1997).

Roundhouses, surrounded by penannular or circular drip gullies, were the principal form of dwelling in the later Iron Age and such structures were most common during the third and second centuries BC (Bryant 1997). They could be used for a variety of functions; as well as for habitation, such buildings were often used for storage, manufacturing, industrial activities and ritual activities. The presence of a central hearth is generally a good indication that

a structure was for domestic habitation (Hingley 1989, 31) but on many sites such ephemeral features often do not survive plough truncation. Although no hearths survived within the Laurel Farm structure, the presence of hearth debris and other domestic refuse in nearby pits suggests domestic habitation. Roundhouses of comparable size to the two Laurel Farm examples, which measured *c.* 12m in diameter, are known in the region: at West Harling near Thetford a building of 11.5m diameter (Clark and Fell 1953) and along the line of the Norwich Southern Bypass numerous roundhouses have been recorded including a 12m-diameter structure defined by a ring of postholes at Harford Farm (Ashwin and Bates 2000, 95).

A calibrated radiocarbon date of AD 120–330 (Waikato-22913; see Appendix 1) obtained from charcoal recovered from a Structure 2 posthole may indicate that this building represents a long-lived tradition of roundhouse construction into the Roman period; however, the charcoal may equally have derived from intrusive material.

The Iron Age ditches within Area B appeared to form part of a field boundary system, although due to erosion, ploughing and truncation by later features it was fragmentary and difficult to reconstruct. The most convincing parts consisted of two parallel ditches on a north-east–south-west alignment with no compelling evidence for a co-axial system such as is commonly seen in later prehistoric and Roman field systems. The field system is far from closely dated; aside from a few struck flints, the latest pottery was Middle to Late Iron Age in date, contemporary with the Iron Age settlement evidence and, given the lack of later prehistoric settlement in the immediate vicinity, is the most plausible date for the setting out of the fields.

The ditches were spaced approximately 47m apart but as there was no real evidence for sub-divisions, it is not possible to suggest what the size of the fields may have been or the degree to which the system may have been formally laid out or the field size standardized. Across the site, ditches of similar size, form and infilling were recorded during the evaluation phase, although the lack of artefactual material in these areas means their chronology and form cannot be reconstructed. It is possible that some of these represent continuations of an agricultural field system throughout the site. In Area A, located in the south-western quadrant of the development site, a ditch of very similar form to the Iron Age field system within Area B and on an almost identical alignment may have been contemporary and formed part of the same boundary system. Similar extensive Iron Age field systems were also recorded at Valley Belt, Trowse (Ashwin and Bates 2000, 159).

An interesting feature, and one that has been noted at a number of other sites, is that the northern Iron Age boundary ditch within Area B appeared to focus upon a barrow mound. The Middle Iron Age site at Harford Farm was located amongst a group of round barrows, which would have been upstanding banks and mounds at the time, and the laying out of the settlement site seems to reference the earlier monuments (Ashwin and Bates 2000, 135–137). The use of earlier ceremonial and funereal monuments as marker points for setting out later prehistoric field systems has been noted from across south-eastern Britain (e.g. Bradley 1998; Yates 1999). In these cases, the development from a ceremonial to an agricultural landscape may not necessarily have been as abrupt as it would often appear in the archaeological record. As Bradley (1998, 147, 158) suggests, important themes do continue across this divide, and principles which governed the creation of the new landscape may have drawn heavily upon a symbolic code of considerable antiquity.

Iron Age settlement in the Norfolk region

A number of settlement sites were established in the western part of Norfolk in the Early Iron Age and by the Middle Iron Age, occupation had extended eastwards away from the fen-edge (Davies 1996, 68). Middle Iron Age activity was noted at Harford Farm and Valley Belt, Trowse (Ashwin and Bates 2000) as discussed above, but evidence for Late Iron Age activity was scarce on the Norwich Southern Bypass sites and it is possible that by this time these areas had become marginal and reverted to heathland (Ashwin and Bates 2000, 241). However, there is growing evidence to suggest that a major Late Iron Age settlement was established at Caistor St Edmund, situated *c*. 8km south-west of Laurel Farm (Davies 1996, 80; 1999, 35).

Extensive areas of large multi-period field systems have been identified by the National Mapping Programme (NMP), particularly in Norfolk and Suffolk. These have been broadly dated to the Iron Age and/or Roman period, most often on the basis of their morphology or their postulated relationship with other sites, rather than physical dating evidence. In Norfolk, while fragments of these field systems had been recorded prior to the NMP, the survey was the first time their true extent and overall coherence had been recognised, and their defining characteristics identified. The most striking, and most extensive, areas of field system were identified on the interfluves of the Norfolk Broads Zone (Albone *et al.* 2007). Here groups of rectilinear, coaxial fields, their primary alignment defined by parallel double-ditched boundaries or trackways, were identified running along the interfluves, presumably between the upland heath around Norwich to the grazing surrounding the low-lying wetlands to the east. These fields have parallels with the 'brickwork pattern' fields identified in North Nottinghamshire/South Yorkshire (Riley 1980); where for both, an Iron Age and/or Roman date has been established.

10. 6 Phase 7 Romano-British Activity

A substantial assemblage of pottery of probable late second to early third-century date was recovered from colluvial deposits in Area D (see Chapter 7.2). The absence of any associated settlement or features makes the substantial pottery assemblage recovered from the colluvial deposits within Area D all the more intriguing. Whilst this evidence is enigmatic, the findings are not isolated and fit into a broad pattern of Romano-British occupation of the area (see Chapter 1.2).

Some of the recovered pottery was probably manufactured at the Postwick kilns, a very short distance from Laurel Farm, whilst other material came from the Brampton kilns, *c*. 15km to the north (Green 1977). Excavations at Heath Farm in Postwick uncovered a well-preserved pottery kiln of the first century AD (Bates 1996). This kiln appears to have provided a range of non-specialist wares, but mostly jars, thought to have been intended to supply a local market, possibly at Caistor St Edmund. Further excavations revealed three pottery kilns dated to the second century AD, each of a different structural type. Two were thought to have produced grey wares, while the third contained oxidised mortaria and white coarse wares (Bates and Lyons 2003). A major pottery industry at Brampton (see below) reached its peak in the second century AD producing greyware dishes and jars, and buff-coloured flagons and mortaria that are distributed across central and eastern Norfolk (Green 1977).

The Laurel Farm assemblage included vessels with firing defects indicating products received direct from these kilns. However, the presence of vessels that were sooted, indicating use, demonstrates that this does not simply represent a deposit of pottery production waste. An unusually high proportion of jars was present and it may be that this material represents the discarded refuse from a specific activity that required large numbers of such vessels; although further speculation as to the nature of this is hampered by an absence of associated features. The composition of the Romano-British pottery assemblage as a whole recovered from the site and the small proportion of non-local imports indicates that whatever activity did take place at Laurel Farm was of relatively low status.

There was some rather ephemeral settlement evidence in both Areas B and D, in the form of occasional pits and postholes, but these were very sparse and it is possible that some contained residual material. Tree clearance, arable agriculture (residual abraded pot) and heavy colluviation are indicated. It is possible that the site may have been used for arable production, but devegetation may have caused considerable erosion as seen in earlier and later periods – perhaps even causing the site to revert to heathland.

There was slight evidence for later Romano-British activity (see Chapter 7.3); alongside four coins of first- or second-century AD date were a further four late third-century AD issues. An intact crossbow brooch with

SKETCH OF THE WEYBOURNE PITS.

Fig. 70   Antiquarian sketch showing the archaeological excavation of the Weybourne Pits in the 1850s

onion-shaped terminals is datable to the fourth century AD and is of a type probably worn by members of the Late Roman military and elite (for instance Swift 2001, 21–23).

10.7 Phase 8 Anglo-Saxon and Early Medieval Iron Processing

By the Late Anglo-Saxon period, there was a distinct change in the nature of activity at Laurel Farm. The investigations produced important evidence for widespread, intense and well-organised industrial activity associated with the initial stages of iron processing; a series of processes which are rarely recognised archaeologically (see Chapter 8.1). Radiocarbon dating indicated that this was established by c. 700 AD and appears to have continued into the early Medieval period with the latest date obtained being AD 1020–1210. A number of factors meant that Laurel Farm was an ideal location for this iron working and the considerable length of time over which iron processing was carried out at the site is testimony to the suitability of the area for such activity. The marginal nature of the land was combined with ready availabilty of raw materials and a plentiful water supply. The nearby

town of Norwich was an inland port of some importance by the Late Saxon period, and one which could have provided an easily accessible and large market for the smelted iron.

Plentiful evidence was recovered to indicate that ore was quarried, washed and subsequently roasted to remove impurities (see Chapter 8.2). The recovery of large quantities of slag from the smelting process, both during the fieldwalking survey and from a substantial refuse pit in Area B, demonstrates that this stage of iron production was also undertaken. No actual smelting furnaces were identified, but such features may have been relatively ephemeral and temporary and it is feasible that all traces could have been removed through ploughing and erosion.

It is not certain whether the ore roasting pits were fuelled with wood or charcoal; either may have been used, but numerous pits identified at the site demonstrate that charcoal was manufactured here in some quantity. Oak was the preferred fuel for smelting, and was found in the greatest quantities at Laurel Farm. Elm, beech and possibly hornbeam (cf. *Carpinus betulus*) were also identified and these hardwoods would also have been suitable for burning as wood and for charcoal production. Archaeobotanical evidence suggests that by the Anglo-Saxon and early Medieval period, oak

Fig. 71   Reconstruction of charcoal burning and extraction and roasting of ore, by Jake Lunt-Davies

woodland, with an under-storey that probably included hazel, holly and possibly hawthorn and cherry, was present locally and was seemingly sustained over centuries. Local woodland no doubt provided the fuel for the industrial activity undertaken at Laurel Farm and is strong evidence for the survival of Thorpe Wood into at least the twelfth to thirteenth century, although ultimately the use of the woodland as a source of fuel may have contributed significantly to its decline.

Vast numbers of quarry pits for the extraction of iron nodules have been noted across East Anglia, examples of these pits at Weybourne Wood on the North Norfolk coast are thought to be of the same date range as the Laurel Farm activity. Thousands of iron extraction pits have been recorded between Weybourne and West Runton (NHER 6280), examples of which were excavated by archaeologists in the 1850s (Fig. 70). Large quantities of slag have also been found in the Weybourne area and in the 1950s an iron smelting site was discovered (NHER 6280) indicating that smelting also occurred in this area in association with iron extraction pits.

Further afield a recent survey and excavation in advance of limestone extraction at Wittering near Peterborough has revealed a very rare example of an Early to Middle Saxon iron-working landscape with features such as slag scatters, furnace bases, tapping pits and charcoal burners identified (Abrams 2002; 2003; Abrams and Wilson 2003). Evidence of iron working on the fringes of the Rockingham Forest area near Peterborough has long been known, but until now these sites have been exclusively assigned a Roman date. Though not accompanied by artefacts, a series of radiocarbon dates has established that all the recently investigated examples are in fact Saxon in date.

An East Anglian context

Ian Riddler

The radiocarbon dates for the Anglo-Saxon features suggest that activity began on the site at some point in the late seventh to eighth century. This was a period of social and economic change both within the immediate environment and further afield in East Anglia. The origins and development of Middle Saxon Norwich remain obscure, notwithstanding a series of excavations in the city, culminating in the important work at Norwich Castle (Shepherd Popescu 2009). The earlier model for Norwich identified five small, discrete settlements, namely *Westwick, Coslany, Conesford, Needham* and *Northwic* (ibid., 48). The *Needham* settlement, whose place name suggests an impoverished farmstead or poor meadow, has been identified within the area of Norwich Castle and appears to have lived up to its name, displaying an impoverished material culture (Shepherd Popescu 2009,53–63). Little evidence has emerged, as yet, of the other settlements. Do these sites represent the destination for the iron smelted at Laurel Farm, or was it intended to go elsewhere?

One possibility lies to the east at Brundall, where early Anglo-Saxon cemeteries are recorded, but there is no evidence as yet for later settlement (Myres and Green 1973, 259). An alternative destination nearby to the south-west is the settlement at Caistor St Edmund, where a 'productive site' has been identified (Pestell 2003, 130–131; 2004, 57–58). The site lies close to a Roman walled town and administrative centre, with several cemeteries of Early Saxon date in its vicinity and the church of St Edmund located in the south-eastern corner of the Roman settlement (Myres and Green 1973; Penn 2000; Pestell 2003, 130). Middle Saxon artefacts have been found in three locations: to the west of the Roman town in the area extending towards the River Tas, to the north of the Roman town and nearby at Markshall. Penn identified this landscape as a location of trading or exchange, given the presence of Merovingian coinage there (Penn 2000, 101 and fig. 79). Equally, however, he noted that: *'If Caistor St Edmund remained a centre of activity into the 8th century, as the evidence suggests, then it is likely to have become an ecclesiastical centre too, and to have received a church relatively early'* (Penn 2000, 102–104).

Iron smelting at Laurel Farm begins just at the time when Anglo-Saxon minsters were being founded in East Anglia and this may be more than mere coincidence. Caistor St Edmund and Markshall are well positioned in close proximity to the Rivers Tas and Yare and they lie to either side of a boundary demarcating two proposed early land units. Markshall is situated in the north-eastern corner of a suggested *parochia* for Wymondham, whilst Caistor St Edmund lies at the western end of an adjacent land unit (Penn 2000, figs. 80–81; Pestell 2004, 194–196). Both Wymondham and Caistor St Edmund may have been early minsters, although this has yet to be demonstrated by excavation and the sparse historical documentation for both sites provides no conclusive evidence either way.

Blair (2005, 203 and 258-9) has understandably focused on the quality of artefacts found within early monasteries, noting that some may have been production centres, minting their own coins and producing their own ceramics. The requirement for iron within early minsters was also considerable and went beyond earlier practice. It extended beyond the provisioning of utilitarian artefacts like knives, agricultural or hunting implements, as well as the simpler forms of dress accessories (all of which continued in use) to a wider range of artefacts. These include styli for use on wax tablets, iron vessels and suspension chains for communal meals (the latter echoed perhaps in the finds from Burrows Hill, Butley) and coffin fittings, as seen at Dacre, Ripon, Wearmouth and Whithorn for example (Pestell 2003, 133; 2004, 40–48; Fenwick 1984, 41–44; Blair 2005, 259; Clogg 2006). The peculiar iron whips (*flagellorum ferreorum*) used on Saint Guthlac may also come into this category (Colgrave 1956, 105). Whilst high status implements like swords almost disappear from the archaeological record, because of the cessation of accompanied burial, there is no doubt that they remained in use and there is evidence from both Brandon and Wharram Percy for their repair and maintenance (Stamper and Croft 2000, 139).

Early monastic foundations included smithies, as at Brandon, Beverley and Wharram Percy, for example, whilst the smelting site at Ramsbury in Wiltshire may have been associated with a minster site (Tester *et al.* forthcoming; Armstrong *et al.* 1991, 13 and 239; Stamper and Croft 2000, 32–34; Blair 2005, 258). A recent study of the iron knives from Wharram Percy unexpectedly revealed that the raw material for the smithy may have come from as many as five separate sources (McDonnell *et al.* forthcoming). If this situation is more widely applicable – and it has yet to be tested elsewhere – it may suggest the extensive movement of batches of smelted iron to a range of settlements. The Middle Saxon landscape at Laurel Farm should perhaps be seen against this sort of background, supplying material to a wide range of sites within the local area, both secular and ecclesiastical, and catering for new demands, almost certainly by use of the river system that is so apparent (e.g. Fig. 3). That system leads via the River Yare to the sea, allowing for the possibility that more distant sites like Caistor-on-Sea and even Ipswich could have been provisioned with iron from Laurel Farm.

Anglo-Saxon settlement in Thorpe St Andrew

Small farmsteads, agricultural and industrial activity are likely to have been widely spread throughout the landscape in the vicinity of Laurel Farm by the Late Anglo-Saxon period and most villages in the area had been established by the time Domesday Book was compiled.

Place-name studies can give indications on the dates of the establishment of settlements, the ethnic origins of the founders and topographical and physiological features in the area. The following derivations follow those supplied by Mills (1998). It is thought that the Danes were in East Anglia as early as AD 870 and in AD 1004 Sweyn and his ships came up the River Yare to Norwich. Both Thorpe and Plumstead are mentioned in the Domesday Book of AD 1086, as *Torp* and *Plumestada* respectively, although both names are likely to considerably pre-date Domesday Book. Thorpe, which encompasses the settlements at Thorpe St Andrew, Thorpe End and Thorpe Hamlet, is a common Old Scandinavian name meaning 'outlying farmstead or hamlet'. Thorpe St Andrew takes its affix from the

Fig. 72   Mousehold Heath *c.* 1810 as depicted by John Sell Cotman (1782-1842). © Trustees of the British Museum

dedication of the parish church but only acquired this name after 1956. Prior to this it was known as Thorpe-next-Norwich, to distinguish it from other Thorpes in the county and, prior to 1536, as Thorpe Episcopi, due to the Bishop of Norwich owning the manor of Thorpe (Nuthall 2002). Also within the area is the settlement at New Rackheath, which evidently takes its name from the village of Rackheath, located a mile to the north. The original Rackheath is also in Domesday Book and its name derives from Old English, meaning 'landing-place near a gully or watercourse', the heath part deriving from hythe, which means inland port. This suggests that the stream that runs from Rackheath up to the River Bure may have been navigable during the late Anglo-Saxon period. The only other settlement within the vicinity is Postwick, which lies to the south-east of the site overlooking the marshes of the River Yare. Its name, also in Old English and recorded in Domesday Book, means 'dwelling or dairy farm of a man named 'Possa'', and possibly references the adjacent marshes which would have been ideally suitable for seasonal pasturage. The village of Salhouse probably meaning 'the sallow trees' lies to the north of Laurel Farm; to the east is Blofield, probably meaning 'exposed open country'; Brundall lies to the south-east, this name probably means 'broomy nook of land'. To the south of Laurel Farm is the River Yare, a pre-Roman ('Celtic') name

which probably means 'babbling stream' and to the west lies Norwich, which comes from the Old English, meaning 'the northern port or landing place'.

The evidence from place-names suggests that during the period of village formation in the latter parts of the first millennium AD, settlement patterns were complex with both English (Anglo-Saxon) and Scandinavian (Viking) names being found within the same area. Most of the names are mentioned in Domesday Book and the present settlement patterns and their nomenclature had been established by the late Anglo-Saxon period. The scattering of the root names, with both Thorpe and Plumstead being represented by three or four different locations, suggests a dispersed rather than nucleated settlement system was operating when the place names were being formed, with individual farms or small hamlets being scattered across the countryside. The name Blofield suggests exposed open country, Brundall indicates probable heathland, indicating that the wider countryside would be unlikely to have supported dense settlement, but would perhaps be more conducive to maintaining small, isolated farming units. Rackheath, with its hythe, may have had a trading role with goods being transported to and from its hinterland down to the River Bure and beyond, although Norwich was the main trading centre in the area from at least the late Saxon period.

10.8 Mousehold Heath in the Later Medieval and Post-Medieval Periods

Mousehold Heath was established by the later Medieval period as the sandy nature of the soil in this area, which was of generally low nutritional value, meant that it was highly susceptible to erosion and soil loss leading to early formation of heathland. By 1086 Thorpe Wood only retained woodland around Norwich and a reference to the murder of St William of Norwich in 1144 suggests that at this time woodland still extended over the present plateau of Mousehold Heath (Rackham 1986, 301). However, the replacement of the woodland with heathland continued apace and in 1156 pope Adrian IV referred to the 'Heath with all its wood' (Rackham 1986, 301). Another reference to the area in 1236 distinguishes 'the part of Thorpe Wood which is covered in oaks' from the heath part of the wood (Supple 1917). By the sixteenth century, maps and views of the area show that the heath extended all over the plateau with woodland only surviving on the steep slopes around the edges (Rackham 1986, 301).

Laurel Farm site lies on the eastern edge of Mousehold Heath and although considered marginal, would probably have been home to populations of smallholders and sheep farmers and would also have supplied a wide range of foodstuffs, building materials and other resources to both the inhabitants of the heath and for the burgeoning City of Norwich. The heath originally covered an extensive area of over 2,500 hectares from within the city boundaries towards the villages of Rackheath and Salhouse in the north (Rackham 1986, 299). No evidence for later Medieval settlement was encountered during the investigations, and the general dearth of cultural material from this period recovered during fieldwalking suggests that the immediate area was uninhabited during this period and would have comprised open heathland.

Mousehold Heath was the location of civil unrest on several occasions from the Medieval period right through into the nineteenth century. In 1381 during the Peasants' Revolt a rebel group led by Geoffrey Lister camped on the Heath before capturing Norwich, however they did not hold the city for long and retreated to North Walsham where they were defeated by forces led by the Bishop (Whittle 2007). During the Post-Medieval period, this marginal heathland area was subject to a similar pattern of landscape use as during the Medieval period. The area was quarried extensively for gravel, flint, lime and marl from the sixteenth century until the twentieth century leading to a characteristic landscape of hills and hollows. The land was mainly used for sheep folds with scattered smallholdings and industrial activity most likely continuing until the end of the eighteenth century. In 1549 Mousehold Heath again became the focus for civil unrest when it played a key role in Kett's Rebellion, an uprising in Norfolk led by Robert Kett against the enclosing of land. Rebel forces camped on the Heath and besieged Norwich before being finally defeated by government forces at the Battle of Dussindale. The forces

gathered at Mount Surrey, which seems to have been close to the area of the Laurel Farm excavations. The Reverend F. W. Russell, who wrote an account of the rebellion in 1859 described the location of Mount Surrey thus; '*The hill is separated from Norwich by the River Wensum, which flows by the foot of it: towards the south it was bounded by Thorpe Wood, and towards the east by Mousehold Heath, extending three or four miles in length and breadth*' (Russell 1859, 37). At the time when Russell wrote his account, he noted that Mousehold Heath was '*commonly called Mussel-hill, is a large heath now, but was most of it wood formerly*' (ibid.). Russell provides a lurid account of the behaviour of the rebels within the camp which gives an indication of the scale of destruction of the heathland: '*As they had spread devastation on all sides, so whatever was brought to the Camp was quickly consumed in surfeiting and revelling, to an extent that almost seems incredible: besides swans, geese, hens and ducks, and all kinds of fowls without number, about 3,000 bullocks and 20,000 sheep were riotously consumed in the Camp within a few days…the palings and hedges of parks…were pulled down… the spoiling of groves and woods, which were almost utterly uprooted and cut down to the ground*' (ibid., 69). The Norwich Roll records that Thorpe Wood was destroyed as the rebels cut down the trees to make huts and for use as fuel. An eyewitness account of the battle written by Sir John Smythe describes the volleys of arrows used at the battle while the Royal army had a high proportion of firearms (Champion 2001).

The Norfolk HER shows Laurel Farm within the northern area of the boundaries of the Battle of Dussindale, although the precise location of the battle has been the subject of some debate (NHER 21173). No artefactual remains that could be associated with the battle were recovered during the fieldwalking exercise, metal detecting survey or during the archaeological excavations. This would suggest that the battle site is not likely to have been located within the site boundaries.

In the seventeenth and eighteenth centuries, Mousehold Heath was a huge expanse of open land stretching from the edge of Norwich to the Broads. A Victorian copy of a map entitled 'Part of Mousehold Heath Lying in Thorpe, Surveyed by Thomas Waterush [probably Waterman], July 1624' and held by the Norfolk Records Office (Map 1624: MS 457/1) shows the heath pockmarked by numerous brick fields (quarries), kilns (clamps) and gravel pits (see Fig. 73).

During the later Post-Medieval period, new pressures on agricultural production resulted in the enclosure of the landscape. This had the effect of increasing the agriculture potential of the land and also resulted in the removal of many of the smallholders, to be replaced by fewer but larger and often gentrified farms. Faden's Map of 1797 (see Fig. 5) seems to indicate that at this time the stream in Dussindale Valley, a tributary of the River Yare which traversed the Laurel Farm site from north to south, was still flowing; though this could be partly artistic licence and, given the sandy nature of the soil, water may only have flowed through the valley seasonally, or in periods

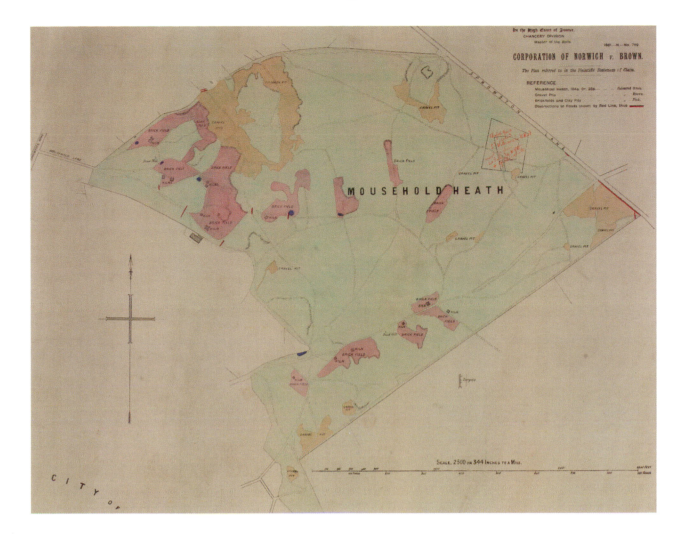

Fig. 73 Victorian copy of a map entitled 'Part of Mousehold Heath Lying in Thorpe, Surveyed by Thomas Waterush [probably Waterman], July 1624' and held by the Norfolk Records Office (Map 1624: MS 457/1)

of particularly heavy rain. Mousehold Heath was at this time largely deserted with the exception of a few structures marked 'Shepherds ho(uses)'. Shepherding would have been the principal agricultural activity that the heath could support, and this in turn would have maintained it as an open expanse, discouraging the growth of trees and shrubs. The enclosure acts meant that by 1800 the open land of Mousehold Heath had been reduced to a small area of common land immediately adjacent to the hamlet of Pockthorpe. The Thorpe St Andrew Enclosure Map of 1801 shows that the Laurel Farm site was enclosed by this date. Features associated with the agricultural use of the land were encountered within excavation Area B, with remnants of now defunct field boundaries demonstrating that this area was originally divided into smaller plots than those that existed immediately prior to the redevelopment of the site. Bryant's map of 1826 shows that the stream was still flowing through the Dussindale valley at this time and that by this date the road which bounds the eastern side of the development site had been constructed. The Norwich to Cromer railway line was constructed 1867–1874 along the western boundary of the site.

In 1857 Mousehold Heath again returned to public attention when resistance against Norwich Town

Council's proposal to turn the Heath into a public park became known as the 'Battle of Mousehold Heath' and an unusually rich archive describing these events survives. By 1800 the Heath had been reduced to a small tract of land situated on high land above the hamlet of Pockthorpe. *'It was this common land, an area of infertile glacial gravels, covered in a sparse growth of grass, heather, gorse and bushes, which became the object of conflict. During the sixteenth to eighteenth centuries the heath, the largest tract of land outside the walled city, had served as a location for hunting, wrestling, archery, shooting and military exercises. During the eighteenth and nineteenth centuries the common was associated with plebeian and rough sports, especially boxing and gambling'* (MacMaster 1990, 121). The common was a valuable resource to hamlets like Pockthorpe as industries such as quarrying and brickmaking were dependant on the exploitation of the Heath. The Heath was used as *'a source of wild foodstuffs, fuel, turf, building materials and pasturage... As late as 1821 the chapter had clamped down on "indiscriminate digging" of gravel, soil and flags'* (*ibid.*, 121). By the 1850s, mineral exploitation of the Heath increasingly played an important economic role for the inhabitants of Pockthorpe (*ibid.*, 125). Sand, gravel and stone had been quarried on a relatively small scale for centuries, but the expansion of the brickmaking industry in the mid nineteenth century saw the establishment of nearly 20 brickmaking operations on the Heath. Vast areas of the heath were destroyed by deep clay pits and quarries. The resistance against turning the Heath into a park continued for nearly 25 years and came to a head in 1881 when the City Council tried to control and regulate the brickmaking by granting licenses to brickmakers from rival hamlets. The Pockthorpe residents responded by occupying the Heath and held their ground and resisted the authorities for several months. The City authorities finally got their way and the park scheme was approved in 1883 and with the enclosure of the Heath in 1884 came a whole set of by-laws that aimed to control the use of this area and these give an insight into past exploitation: '*prohibitions on digging for minerals or cutting down trees and plants, they banned gamblers, card-sharps, gypsies, squatters and vagrants; quoits or any other game "destructive to the surface"; the throwing of any stone, stick or missile; any persons who shall "brawl or fight, or use violent or indecent or improper language; the selling of "any indecent or infamous book, print, photograph or pictures"; any assemblage of persons who might obstruct the public; and the drying of clothes or beating of carpets*' (MacMaster 1990, 127).

The tradition of public support to maintain and preserve the Heath has continued right into the twenty-first century. The War Office had to abandon their proposal to take over 150 acres of the Heath as a training ground due to public opposition to the scheme. In 1972 a new voluntary action group known as the Mousehold Heath Defenders was formed to 'protect Mousehold against encroachment on its area and its environment' (Mousehold Heath Defenders 2010). In 1984 a new Norwich Mousehold Heath Act setting out new byelaws for the Heath superseded the 1884 act.

The Laurel Farm site has been agricultural land from the time of enclosure until the early twenty-first century and prior to the recent large-scale developments which have resulted in extensive housing estates and the creation of a business park in the vicinity, remained relatively isolated. The first phase of the Broadlands Business Park which bounds Laurel Farm to the south was developed by the end of the twentieth century and plans for Phase 2 of the Broadlands Business Park to occupy the site led to the archaeological interventions and the important discoveries described in this publication.

Appendix 1: Radiocarbon dating

During the initial phase of post-excavation assessment a total of ten samples of charred plant material recovered from bulk soil samples were submitted to the Beta Analytic Radiocarbon Dating Laboratory in Florida for AMS radiocarbon dating (sample codes Beta-225540–225549). During the publication phase of work thirteen samples of charred plant material were submitted to the University of Waikato Radiocarbon Laboratory in New Zealand (sample codes Waikato-22902–22914). All of the results are listed in the following table.

Lab no	Fill/cut	Feature type	Material	Uncalibrated Radiocarbon date (years BP)	Calibrated 2 sigma range (95.4% probability)
Beta-225540	393/394	Charcoal burning pit	Charred material	970+/-40	AD 1020–1210
Beta-225541	366/367	Charcoal burning pit	Charred material	950+/-40	AD 1020–1200
Beta-225542	536/529	Charcoal burning pit	Charred material	1290+/-40	AD 660–780
Beta-225543	578/579	Charcoal burning pit	*Corylus avellana* twig	1320+/-40	AD 650–780
Beta-225544	596/597	Charcoal burning pit	*Corylus avellana* charcoal	1270+/-40	AD 670–880
Beat-225545	684/685	Charcoal burning pit	Indet. bark charcoal	1290+/-40	AD 660–810
Beta-225546	706/705	Charcoal burning pit	*Quercus* charcoal	1070+/-40	AD 890–1030
Beta-225547	832/827	Charcoal burning pit	cf. *Prunus* charcoal	1020+/-40	AD 900–920 and AD 950–1040
Beta-225548	849/850	Refuse pit	*Ilex aquifolium* charcoal	2130+/-40	BC 350-290 and BC 220–50
Beta-225549	918/919	Refuse pit	*Corylus avellana* charcoal	2090+/-40	BC 200–10
Waikato-22902	725/727	Charcoal burning pit	Indet charcoal	1278+/-30	660 to 810 AD (1290 to 1150 cal BP)
Waikato-22903	966/964	Charcoal burning pit	*Quercus* charcoal	1004+/-30	970 to 1160 AD (970 to 800 cal BP)
Waikato-22904	881/877	Charcoal burning pit	*Quercus* charcoal	1145+/-30	780 to 980 AD (1170 to 970 cal BP)
Waikato-22905	601/586	Charcoal burning pit	*Prunus* charcoal	985+/-30	980 to 1160 AD (960 to 800 cal BP)
Waikato-22906	584/585	Hearth	*Prunus* charcoal	965+/-30	1010 to 1160 AD (930 to 800 cal BP)
Waikato-22907	447/448	Quarry pit	*Corylus* charcoal	1837+/-30	80 to 250 AD (1865 to 1710 cal BP)
Waikato-22908	616/617	Ore roasting pit	Maloideae charcoal	1233+/-30	680 to 880 AD (1260 to 1070 cal BP
Waikato-22909	768/754	Refuse pit	Maloideae charcoal	2177+/-30	370 to 160 BC (2310 to 2070 cal BP)
Waikato-22910	571/744 and 787	Tree-throw	Maloideae charcoal	5098+/-33	397 to 3790 BC (5920 to 5750 cal BP)
Waikato-22911	1174/1173	Tree-throw	*Quercus* charcoal	17872+/-96	19550 to 18750 BC (21490 to 20720 cal BP)
Waikato-22912	636/744 and 787	Tree-throw	*Quercus* charcoal	5100+/-32	3970 to 3790 BC (5920 to 5750 cal BP)
Waikato-22913	580/581	Structure 2 posthole	*Quercus* charcoal	1801+/-30	120 to 330 AD (1820 to 1630 cal BP)
Waikato-22914	689/690	Hearth	*Prunus* charcoal	4571+/-30	3500 to 3100 BC (5440 to 5060 cal BP)

Table 28   Results of Radiocarbon dating

Appendix 2: Quantification of charred remains

Genus/species	Common name	number of samples: number of fragments by Phase							Comments
		2	3	5	6	7	8	10	
Acer campestre	Field Maple						1:4		
Aesculus sp.	Horse chestnut						1:2		Not native. Introduced early 17thC
cf. *Carpinus betulus*	Hornbeam						1:2		
Clematis vitalba	Traveller's Joy						2:16		
Corylus avellana	Hazel			1:3	4:11		9:38		
Euonymus europaeus	Spindle Tree						1:2		
Fagus sylvatica	Beech						1:2		
Frangula alnus	Alder Buckthorn						1:10		
Fraxinus excelsior	Ash		4:16				-		
Hedera helix	Ivy						2:3		
Ilex aquifolium	Holly				1:1		5:18	1:1	
Lonicera sp.	Honeysuckle						2:2		
Lonicera/Ligustrum	Honeysuckle/Privet				1:1		1:1		
Sub-Fam. Maloideae.(inc. *Crataegus, Malus, Pyrus, Sorbus*)	Hawthorn, Apple, Pear, Rowan, Whitebeams		2:5	1:1	1:4		3:15		Inc. *Crataegus* type
Prunus sp.	Blackthorn, Cherries		1:1		3:7	1:2	9:28		Inc. *P. Spinosa, P. avium*
Quercus sp.	Oak	1:3	7:160	1:13	4:76	2:6	30:1167	2:7	Native oaks cannot be differentiated
Quercus/Castanea	Oak/Sweet chestnut				1:2	2:8	14:24	1:1	*Castanea* = not native. Roman(?) introduction
Rosa sp	Rose						1:1		Twig - with thorn attached
Salix/Populus sp.	Willows/Poplars				1:1		-		
Ulmus sp.	Elm						1:1		

Table 29   Distribution of tree species by phase as identified from charred remains

Phase	Deposit/cut	Volume (L)	Feature description	Sample number	Taxon (qty)	Weight (g)	Comments
2	[1174]/ [1173]	20	Tree-throw	<84> [A2]	*Quercus* sp (3) Indet. (1)	0.015 0.005	Inc. x1 ?seed 100%
3	[435]/ [343]	20	Palaeochannel	<33>	*Quercus* sp. (44) Indet. (6)	3.235 0.05	inc. bark
				<33> [IP]	*Quercus* sp. (5)	NR	
3	[571]/ [744]	10	Tree-throw Spit 2	<74> [A2]	*Quercus* sp. (20) *Fraxinus excelsior* (1) Maloideae (1) Indet. (7)	0.261 0.003 0.015 0.027	100% id
3	[608]/ [745]	10	Tree-throw Spit 3	<75> [A2]	*Quercus* sp. (41) *Fraxinus excelsior* (6)	1.473 0.198	100% id
3	[636]/ [745]	10	Tree-throw Spit 4	<76> [A2]	*Quercus* sp. (25) *Fraxinus excelsior* (7) Indet. (1)	0.634 0.237 0.017	100% id
3	[608]/ [786]	10	Tree-throw Spit 3	<77> [A2]	*Quercus* sp. (18) *Fraxinus excelsior* (2) Maloideae (2) Indet. (4)	0.068 0.006 0.014 0.031	100% id
				<77> [A2]	*Quercus* sp. (3) Indet. (4)	0.035 0.007	100% id
				<77> [IP]	*Quercus* sp. (2) Maloideae (2) Indet. (1)	NR	
3	[636]/ [786]	10	Tree-throw Spit 4	<78> [A2]	*Quercus* sp. (4)	0.026	100% id
3	[689]/ [690]	10	Pit	<52> [A2]	*Quercus* sp. (3) *Prunus* sp. (1) Indet. (2)	0.017 0.007 0.018	100% id
5	[157]/ [1264]	10	Pit	<4>	cf *Corylus avellana* (3) *Quercus* sp. (13) cf Maloideae (1) Indet. (11)	0.089 0.317 0.024 0.442	100% id
6	[580]/ [581]	10	Posthole	<45> [A2]	*Quercus* sp. (43)	0.871	100% id
				<45> [IP]	*Quercus* sp. (3) *Quercus/Castanea* (2)	NR	
6	[768]/ [754]	30	Fill	<61> [A2]	*Quercus* sp (16) *Corylus avellana* (2) Maloideae (4) *Prunus* sp. (5) Indet. (12)	0.239 0.024 0.142 0.077 0.146	100% id
6	[766]/ [754]	10		<62>	*Quercus* sp (5) *Corylus avellana* (2) *Ligustrum/Lonicera* (1) Indet. (9)	0.048 0.042 0.057 0.182	100% id inc. bark
6	[849]/ [850]	30		<70> [A1]	*Ilex aquifolium* (1) *Salix/Populus* (1)	NR	
6	[918]/ [919]	30		<71> [A1]	*Corylus avellana* (1)	NR	
6	[1103]/ [1104]	10	Refuse pit	<82>	*Quercus* sp. (9) *Corylus avellana* (6) *Prunus* sp. (1) Indet. (18)	0.149 0.082 0.009 0.197	

Phase	Deposit/cut	Volume (L)	Feature description	Sample number	Taxon (qty)	Weight (g)	Comments
8	[536]/ [529]	30	Charcoal burning pit	<42>	*Quercus* sp. (88)	4.49	inc. twig-wood
					Corylus avellana (5)	0.133	inc. twig-wood
					Ilex aquifolium (6)	0.429	inc. twig-wood
					Prunus sp. (1)	0.049	
					Indet. (13)	0.362	inc. twig-wood
				<42> [A1]	*Quercus* sp. (2)	NR	
					Indet. twig (1)		
				<42> [IP]	*Quercus* sp. (3)	NR	
					Aesculus (2)		
8	[545]/ [546]	30	Charcoal burning pit	<43>	*Quercus* sp. (71)	7.086	
					Corylus avellana (1)	0.126	
					Bark (28)	1.440	
					Indet. (19)	1.322	Mostly ?bark
				<43> [IP]	*Quercus* sp. (4)		inc. twig-wood
					Corylus avellana (2)	NR	
					Indet. (4)		
					Fern rachis (1)		
8	[578]/ [579]	10	Charcoal burning pit	<44>	*Quercus* sp. (23)	0.788	
					Indet. (2)	0.038	inc. bark
				<44> [A1]	cf. *Corylus* (1)	NR	twig wood
				<44> [IP]	*Quercus* sp. (5)	NR	
					cf. *Quercus* sp. (1)		
					Quercus/Castanea (3)		
					Indet. (1)		
8	[584]/ [586]	10	Charcoal burning pit	<46> [A2]	*Quercus* sp. (6)	0.114	
					Maloideae (7)	0.119	
					Prunus sp. (7)	0.128	
					Indet. (7)	0.116	inc. cf *P.* avium
				<46> [IP]	Maloideae (1)	NR	100% ID
					Quercus/Castanea (1)		
8	[600]/ [586]	30	Charcoal burning pit	<49>	*Quercus* sp. (40)	2.714	
					Ilex aquifolium (1)	0.029	
					Indet. (9)	0.188	
8	[601]/ [586]	10	Charcoal burning pit	<48> [A2]	*Quercus* sp. (46)	1.683	
					Prunus sp. (2)	0.067	cf *P. spinosa*
					Indet. (4)	0.324	
				<48> [IP]	*Quercus* sp (5)	NR	
					Quercus/Castanea (5)		
8	[596]/ [597]	20	Charcoal burning pit	<47>	*Quercus* sp. (92)	7.172	
					Corylus avellana (3)	0.398	
					Maloideae (3)	0.309	*Crataegus* type
					Ilex aquifolium (1)	0.064	
					Rosa sp. (1)	0.027	Twig inc. thorn
					Indet. (3)	1.243	inc. Bark
				<47> [A1]	*Corylus avellana* (1)	NR	
				<47> [IP]	*Quercus* sp. (11)	NR	
					cf. *Quercus* sp (1)		
					Quercus/Castanea (1)		
					Indet. (2)		

Phase	Deposit/cut	Volume (L)	Feature description	Sample number	Taxon (qty)	Weight (g)	Comments
8	[616]/ [617]	10	Ore roasting pit	<50> [A2]	*Quercus* sp. (6)	0.025	100% id
					Maloideae (4)	0.039	
					Euonymus europaeus (2)	0.026	
					Prunus sp. (4)	0.038	
					Ulmus sp. (1)	0.002	
					Indet. ((9)	0.043	
8	[695]/ [696]	30	Charcoal burning pit	<53> [IP]	*Quercus* sp. (2)	NR	
					Quercus/Castanea (3)		
8	[699]/ [698]	10	Charcoal burning pit	<56>	*Quercus* sp. (12)	1.191	
					Corylus avellana (6)	1.398	
					Indet. (7)	0.261	inc. bark
8	[705]/ [706]	20	Charcoal burning pit	<58> [IP]	*Quercus* sp. (3)	NR	
					cf. *Quercus* sp. (1)		
					Quercus/Castanea (1)		
				<58> [A1]	*Quercus* (13)	NR	
8	[705]/ [706]	20	Charcoal burning pit	<59> [IP]	*Quercus* sp. (3)	NR	
					cf. *Quercus* sp. (1)		
					Quercus/Castanea (1)		
8	[716]/ [717]	30	Ore roasting pit	<55> [IP]	*Quercus* sp. (2)	NR	
					cf. *Quercus* sp. (2)		
					Quercus/Castanea (1)		
8	[725]/ [727]	30	Charcoal burning pit	<57> [A2]	*Quercus* sp. (25)	3.168	
8	[740]/ [741]	10	Ore roasting pit	<60> [IP]	*Quercus* sp. (2)	NR	
					Quercus/Castanea (2)		
					Indet. (1)		
8	[826]/ [827]	30	Charcoal burning pit	<65>	*Quercus* sp. (32)	2.377	
					Acer campestre (4)	0.12	
					Prunus sp. (2)	0.031	
					Indet. (12)	0.373	
8	[835]/ [836]	20	Refuse pit	<66>	*Quercus* sp. (82)	3.667	
					Prunus sp. (4)	0.049	
					Ilex aquifolium (4)	0.15	
					Frangula alnus (10)	0.201	
				<66> [A1]	*Quercus* sp. (5)	NR	
					cf. *Prunus* sp. (1)		
				<66> [IP]	*Quercus* sp. (5)	NR	
8	[837]/ [843]	10	Ore roasting pit	<64>	*Quercus* sp. (28)	1.854	inc. bark
					Indet. (2)	0.11	
				<64> [IP]	*Quercus* sp. (4)	NR	
					Quercus/Castanea (1)		
8	[856]/ [855]	30	Charcoal burning pit	<67>	*Quercus* sp. (83)	4.57	inc. twig-wood
					Clematis vitalba (10)	0.502	twig-wood
					Hedera helix (1)	0.049	
					Lonicera sp. (1)	0.046	twig-wood
					Indet. (5)	0.188	inc. twig & bark
				<67> [IP]	*Quercus* sp. (5)	NR	
8	[879]/ [877]	10	Charcoal burning pit	<79>	*Quercus* sp. (11)	0.828	100% id
					Corylus avellana (2)	0.047	
					cf. *Prunus* sp. (2)	0.164	
					Indet. (3)	0.167	

Phase	Deposit/cut	Volume (L)	Feature description	Sample number	Taxon (qty)	Weight (g)	Comments
8	[881/ [877]	10	Charcoal burning pit	<80> [A2]	*Quercus* sp. (23) *Corylus avellana* (5) *Prunus* sp. (4) Indet. (3)	3.430 0.780 0.918 0.324	100% id
				<80> [IP]	*Quercus* sp. (3) *Quercus/Castanea* (2) cf. *Carpinus betulus* (2) Indet. (3)	NR	
8	[966]/ [964]	10	Charcoal burning pit	<81> [A2]	*Quercus* sp. (23) *Corylus avellana* (2)	13.943 0.614	
10	[170]/ [171]	10	Fill of burnt out tree bole	<5> [IP]	*Quercus* sp. (5)	NR	
10	[742]	10	Layer	<73> [IP]	*Quercus* sp. (2) *Quercus/Castanea* (1) *Ilex aquifolium* (1) Indet. (1)	NR	
11	[491]/ [492]	20		<39>	*Quercus* sp. (31) Indet. (14)	0.632 0.05	100% id inc. bark

KEY: 2=Late glacial; 3=Early Neolithic; 5=Late Bronze Age; 6=Middle Iron Age; 7=Romano-British; 8=Saxon-Early Medieval; 10=Post-Medieval. NB: Table excludes all 'Indet.'/bark fragments.
(IP = Poole assessment data; A1 and A2 = Radiocarbon sample identifications)

Table 30   Quantification of charred remains by phase and context

Appendix 3: Quantification of ironworking slag

Context	Cut	Phase	Grid	Sample	Slag type	Weight (g)	Comment
1			050/100		undiagnostic	434	furnace slag?
1			050/150		undiagnostic	3	
1			075/050		undiagnostic	14	black, glassy areas
1			075/075		undiagnostic	18	
1			075/125		fired clay	31	
1			075/125		undiagnostic	234	
1			075/150		slagged stone	5	
1			075/175		cinder	3	tiny white silica inclusions
1			075/175		cinder	9	black & glassy
1			075/175		cinder	19	
1			075/175		undiagnostic	173	
1			100/100		furnace slag	568	run slag on surface
1			100/100		undiagnostic	302	
1			100/125		hearth lining	29	
1			100/125		run slag	5	
1			100/125		undiagnostic	56	
1			100/150		undiagnostic	114	
1			100/175		run slag	205	smelting
1			100/325		tap slag	27	
1			125/050		undiagnostic	7	
1			125/150		undiagnostic	72	
1			125/175		run slag	10	
1			125/175		undiagnostic	59	
1			125/275		ore	49	limonite
1			125/300		undiagnostic	148	
1			150/075		undiagnostic	18	
1			150/100		undiagnostic	52	
1			150/125		undiagnostic	133	areas of silica from burnt flint inclusions
1			150/175		cinder	2	
1			175/050		tap slag	76	
1			175/075		cinder	24	
1			175/125		undiagnostic	15	
1			175/125		undiagnostic	324	glassy areas in slag
1			175/175		cinder	9	
1			200/100		burnt coal	10	
1			200/100		undiagnostic	69	
1			200/125		cinder	3	
1			200/125		undiagnostic	114	
1			200/225		cinder	51	
1			225/100		undiagnostic	9	
1			225/150		cinder	83	
1			225/150		stone	54	
1			225/150		undiagnostic	112	
1			225/175		undiagnostic	101	smelting?

Context	Cut	Phase	Grid	Sample	Slag type	Weight (g)	Comment
1			225/200		cinder	11	
1			225/225		undiagnostic	78	
1			225/450		ore	43	limonite
1			225/450		tap slag	39	
1			250/125		undiagnostic	184	
1			250/150		undiagnostic	1249	incomplete; possibly furnace slag
1			250/275		undiagnostic	63	probably smelting
1			250/375		undiagnostic	193	possibly furnace slag
1			275/100		vitrified hearth lining	145	
1			275/150		cinder	25	
1			275/150		undiagnostic	273	
1			275/225		iron	21	
1			275/250		undiagnostic	22	
1			275/350		tap slag	49	
1			300/175		burnt flint	8	heat-reduced to silica
1			300/175		cinder	24	
1			300/175		undiagnostic	51	
1			300/250		burnt coal	35	
1			325/150		charcoal	3	
1			325/175		furnace slag	380	run slag on surface; very heavy; areas of glassy material
1			325/175		furnace slag	733	
1			350/150		run slag	64	smelting
1			350/175		undiagnostic	102	
1			350/175		undiagnostic	116	part of smithing hearth bottom or furnace slag?
1			375/175		furnace slag	119	black, glassy areas
1			375/175		ore	25	ore rind - limonite
1			375/175		undiagnostic	28	black, glassy areas
1			400/175		ore	29	limonite
1			400/325		undiagnostic	123	
1			Area B	553	burnt coal	17	
1			Tr. 15		smithing hearth bottom	1230	170mm long x 130mm breadth x 45mm deep
1				16	iron	156	
231	232	1	Tr. 65	18	ore	101	limonite
231	232	1	Tr. 65	18	sample residue	6	tiny slag fragments
253	234	1	Tr. 65	21	ore?	101	
271	251	1	Tr. 66	27	ore?	38	
636	787	3.1		78	ore		limonite
435	343	3.4		33	sample residue	200	one third charcoal & lots tiny flint inclusions
157	1264	5	70/125		stone	7	
157	1264	5	70/125		fired ore?	248	large
766	754	6	170/395	62	slag spheres	0.5	mis-shapen

Context	Cut	Phase	Grid	Sample	Slag type	Weight (g)	Comment
766	754	6	170/395	62	vitrified hearth lining	17	
766	754	6	170/395	62	sample residue	271	magnetic fines & some flake hammerscale & minute spheres
148	149	7	Tr.84	3	sample residue	1	tiny slag, fired clay, two tiny hammerscale spheres
319	320	7			burnt coal	1	
488	layer	7		37	sample residue	8	fines, iron slice, fired clay
273	274	8	240/345	28	fired stones	229	ore?
355	356	8		42	ore?	11	
364	367	8		29	ore	8	
393	394	8		31	sample residue	0.5	microslags
402	403	8		32	charcoal sample	67	
479	480	8		36	fines & ore	43	
509	510	8		40	ore?	13	and another stone
536	529	8		42	sample residue	1	tiny slag, fired clay, two tiny hammerscale spheres
536	529	8		42	sandstone	12	with inclusions
545	546	8		43	sample residue	56	mostly tiny charcoal frags., tiny pieces burnt flint & stone
545	546	8		43	sample residue	0.5	microslags
584	585	8		46	ore fines	15	and stone
596	597	8		47	charcoal sample	48	
596	597	8		47	sample residue	1	microslags from smelting
616	617	8		50	ore?	125	
706	705	8	175-180/380	58	charcoal sample	244	includes some large pieces
730	731	8		59	stone	20	ore?
740	741	8		60	sample residue	35	charcoal & tiny flint frags.
742	layer	10		73	ore?	27	
826	827	8		65	sample residue	67	fired clay, tiny slag frags & ore ?fines
826	827	8			stone	22	Carrstone
832	827	8	150-155/395-400	66	ore	302	fines with pieces of ore
832	827	8	150-155/395-400	66	ore fines	124	clean fines: no stones
832	827	8	150-155/395-400	66	roasted ore	33	
832	827	8	150-155/395-400	66	sample residue	894	ore fines & stones etc
832	827	8	150-155/395-400		burnt ore	248	
832	827	8	150-155/395-400		ore?	41	
832	827	8	150-155/395-400		stone	201	Carrstone quartz
832	827	8	150-155/395-400		tap slag	41	
833	834	8	120/365		tap slag	48	
878	871	8	115/355, 110-115/360		fired clay	17	
878	871	8	115/355, 110-115/360		poss. ore	42	
878	871	8	115/355, 110-115/360		stone	75	
878	871	8	115/355, 110-115/360		tap slag	258	

Context	Cut	Phase	Grid	Sample	Slag type	Weight (g)	Comment
878	871	8	115/355, 110-115/360		undiagnostic	156	probably smelting; high vesicularity
879	877	8	115/355, 110-115/360	79	sample residue	1967	ore fines, tiny flint frags., very occ. charcoal. All magnetic
879	877	8	115/355, 110-115/360	79	ore	144	limonite
880	877	8	115/355, 110-115/360	fired clay		30	
880	877	8	115/355, 110-115/360	stone		22	
880	877	8	115/355, 110-115/360	tap slag		409	
932	934	8	225-230/445; 225/450	72	dense slag	2525	
932	934	8	225-230/445; 225/450	72	fuel ash slag	5	
932	934	8	225-230/445; 225/450	72	furnace lining	402	
932	934	8	225-230/445; 225/450	72	furnace slag	170	high silica inclusion & more vitrified
932	934	8	225-230/445; 225/450	72	furnace slag	4678	
932	934	8	225-230/445; 225/450	72	stone	54	ochrous mineral & flint belemnite infilled with brown limonite iron
932	934	8	225-230/445; 225/450	72	run slag	2430	
932	934	8	225-230/445; 225/450	72	prills	1836	
932	934	8	225-230/445; 225/450	72	sample residue	32	sand, tiny elongated snail shells & charcoal
932	934	8	225-230/445; 225/450	72	sample residue	1092	furnace slag, tap slag & residual sand
932	934	8	225-230/445; 225/450	72	tap slag	7068	
932	934	8	225-230/445; 225/450	72	tap slag	8933	some concreted with sandy soil
932	934	8	225-230/445; 225/450	72	undiagnostic	6421	
932	934	8	225-230/445; 225/450	72	vitrified hearth lining	378	
73	layer	10	Tr.45	10	ore?	4	
226	227	10	Tr.177	23	ore?	48	ore?
671	layer	10	230/290		run slag	124	smelting
715	583	10			undiagnostic	35	smelting
9	10	11	Tr.55	1	charcoal sample	25	
9	10	11	Tr.55	1	sample residue	0.5	microslags - one or two broken hammerscale flakes & tiny spheres
297	layer	10			undiagnostic	21	probably smelting
122	123	11	Tr.30	14	sample residue	1	rounded microslags & clay
122	123	11	Tr.30	123	fired clay	1	
228	layer	11	Tr.185	15	burnt flint	136	
228	layer	11	Tr.185	15	burnt sandstone	219	
349	350	11			ore	55	limonite
491	492	11		39	sample residue	0	one small hammerscale sphere & occ. distorted microslags

Table 31   Quantification of ironworking slag by phase and context

Résumé

Agnès Shepherd

Pre-Construct Archaeology Limited a entrepris
un projet de fouilles archéologiques précédant des
constructions d'une extension de la zone commerciale
de Broadland Business Park sur un site à Laurel
Farm, Norfolk. Le site est situé à environ 1 km au
nord du village de Thorpe St Andrew et à 5km du
centre historique de la région Norfolk et couvrait une
superficie totale d'environ 19 hectares. A la suite de
levés géophysiques, de recherches sur le terrain et de
détection de métaux, une évaluation archéologique a
conclu l'ouverture d'environ 200 tranchées. Des fouilles
ultérieures ont été concentrées sur une zone mesurant
150m x 130m dans le nord-ouest du site, avec des
tranchées ciblées ailleurs.

Les fouilles ont révélé le passé extraordinairement
long et complexe de l'occupation et l'exploitation de cette
zone, qui est présenté ici sous la forme d'une série de
chapitres relatant chaque période importante de l'histoire
du site (chapitres 2 à 9), se terminant par une analyse de
l'occupation dans son ensemble (chapitre 10).

L'objet le plus ancien découvert était une hache du
Paléolithique inférieur, découverte par des hommes du
Néolithique quelques centaines de milliers d'années
plus tard, qui l'enterrèrent soigneusement dans une
fosse. Les premières preuves formelles de personnes
visitant vraiment le site survient pendant le Paléolithique
supérieur lorsque des communautés de chasseurs-
cueilleurs utilisaient l'abri fourni par les racines d'un
arbre renversé, possiblement comme campement
temporaire, et lors de leur séjour y fabriquèrent des
lames de silex. L'utilisation d'arbres renversés survint de
nouveau au Néolithique ancien quand les creux laissés
par deux arbres adjacents avaient été utilisés pour se
débarrasser de quantités d'os d'animaux, de poterie, et
d'environ 4.000 morceaux de silex frappés. L'analyse a
déterminé que ces matériaux avait été jetés en tas avant
d'être soigneusement recueillis et déversés dans les creux.

Un fossé circulaire et important de l'âge du Bronze
Ancien, interprété comme étant les vestiges d'un tumulus
circulaire érodé par le labourage, faisait probablement
partie de tumuli funéraires beaucoup plus grands qui
s'étendaient à l'ouest à travers les champs, de nos jours
couverts par le lotissement de Dussindale Park. On
peut voir ces tumuli représentés sur une carte datant de
1589 sous le nom de 'Gargytt Hylls'. La première preuve
d'habitation permanente à Laurel Farm date de l'Âge du
Fer moyen, montre une ferme composée d'une ou deux
maisons rondes comprenant plusieurs fosses à ordures,
placées parmi plusieurs champs.

Aucune évidence d'occupation Romano-Britannique
n'a été trouvée sur le site. Toutefois une quantité
importante de poterie jetée y a été trouvée, certaines
montrant des défauts de fabrication, ce qui pourrait être
les rejets de fabrication des fours avoisinants à Postwick
ou Brampton à une quinzaine de kilomètres du site.

A la période Saxonne tardive, la région était déjà
depuis longtemps à la lisière d'une vaste zone de landes.
Impropre à l'agriculture ou à l'habitation, le site est
devenu une zone d'activité industrielle intense incluant
les étapes préparatoires de la production de fer, précédant
la fonte. La datation au radiocarbone indique que cela
a commencé vers 700 après JC et semble avoir continué
jusqu'au début de la période Médiévale, vers 1200. Cette
activité industrielle est d'une importance considérable
puisse que très peu de sites ont produit de preuves des
premières étapes du processus de ferronnerie.

Les matières premières nécessaires pour la
transformation du fer étaient toutes disponibles à
proximité du site, et la ville voisine de Norwich, qui était
déjà bien établie en tant que port à l'intérieur des terres
d'importance dès l'époque Saxonne tardive, fournissait
un grand marché facilement accessible pour le fer forgé.
Nous avons trouvé d'immense fosses de carrière pour
l'extraction de minerai, des nodules de carrstone (grès) ou
de fer.

Le long des fosses de carrière, ont été trouvées des
preuves très inhabituelles de torréfaction du minerai,
sous la forme de trous montrant la présence de feu ardent
et contenant du charbon de bois et des fragments de
minerai de fer brûlé. On a aussi trouvé de nombreux trous
de fabrication de charbon de bois, ce charbon étant de
grande importance dans l'industrie de la transformation
du fer et il semblerait, était fabriqué à Laurel Farm en
grande quantité.

Suite à la disparition de l'industrie du fer, vers le XIII
siècle, le site est redevenu une zone reculée, regagnée par
la lande, probablement seulement régulièrement visité lors
du passage de bergers et peut-être occasionnellement par
des personnes venant cueillir des ressources naturelles.
Le besoin d'accroître la production agricole vers la fin
du XVIII siècle a entraîné le clôturage dans la région. La
carte de Thorpe St. Andrew Enclosure de 1801 montre
que les terres sur le site étaient déjà clôturées à cette date
et continuèrent à être utilisées à des fins agricoles jusqu'à
son aménagement récent. Une carte de 1818 montre que
la lande a continué à être utilisée pour ses ressources
naturelles, avec des carrières de gravier et des fours à
briques, exploitant les argiles naturelles.

Zusammenfassung

Sylvia Butler

Vor der Entwicklung des Baugeländes von Laurel Farm in Norfolk, welche den Broadland Business Park erweiterte, wurden von Pre-Construct Archaeology Limited eine Reihe von archäologischen Untersuchungen durchgeführt. Das Gelände befindet sich ca. 1km nördlich des Dorfes Thorpe St Andrew und 5km von dem historischen Kern von Norfolk entfernt und bedeckte eine Gesamtfläche von ca. 19 Hektar. Geophysischen, Feldbegehungs- und Metall Detektor Untersuchungen folgend wurden fast 200 Schnitte archäologisch ausgewertet. Eine darauffolgende Ausgrabung konzentrierte sich auf ein Gebiet von 150m x 130m im Nordwesten der Stätte, mit gezielt ausgerichteten Schnitten andernorts.

Die Untersuchungen offenbarten eine ungemein lange und komplexe Geschichte der Besiedlung und Erschließung des Gebietes, welche hier präsentiert wird als eine Reihe von Kapiteln bezogen auf jede bedeutende Periode der Geschichte der Stätte (Kapitel 2-9), bis hin zu einer Debatte über die Besiedlung in ihre Gesamtheit (Kapitel 10).

Das älteste Artefakt, das entdeckt wurde, war eine Handaxt aus dem Altpaläolithikum, welche von neolithischen Menschen hunderte von tausend Jahren später entdeckt wurde und sorgfällig in einer Grube vergraben wurde. Die frühesten definitiven Beweise von Menschen, die tatsächlich die Stätte besuchten, traten auf während des Jungpaläolithikums, als Jäger- und Sammler-Gemeinschaften möglicherweise als temporäres Camp den Schutz nutzten, der von den Wurzeln eines umgefallenen Baumes bereitgestellt wurde und während ihres Aufenthaltes Feuersteinklingen herstellten. Die Verwendung von Wurzellöchern tauchte im Frühneolithikum wieder auf, als ein Paar von nebeneinander liegenden Wurzellöchern verwendet wurden um eine Anzahl von Tonwaren, Tierknochen und nahezu 4,000 Stücke von gehauenem Feuerstein zu entsorgen. Eine Analyse ermittelte, dass dieses Material auf den Abfall geworfen worden war, bevor es sorgfältig wieder aufgesammelt wurde und in den Aushöhlungen abgeladen wurde.

Ein beachtlicher frühbronzezeitlicher Ringgraben, der als Überrest eines ausgepflügten Tumulus interpretiert wurde, war wahrscheinlich Teil eines viel größeren Hügelgräberfriedhofes, welcher sich westlich weiter über die Felder erstreckte, die jetzt von der Dussindale Park Wohnsiedlung bedeckt sind und auf einer Karte von 1589 als die "Gargytt Hylls" beschrieben wurde. Die ersten Anzeichen einer permanenten Besiedlung bei Laurel Farm datieren aus der Mittleren Eisenzeit, angezeigt von einem Bauerngehöft, welches aus ein oder zwei Rundhäusern und mehreren Abfallgruben bestand, die innerhalb eines Feldsystems positionierten waren.

Es gab keine Anzeichen einer Ansiedlung an der Stätte während der Romano-Britischen Zeit, es wurden hier jedoch eine beachtliche Menge von Tonwaren entsorgt, von denen manche Brenndefekte aufzeigten, was anzeigen könnte, dass es sich hier um Abfallprodukte aus benachbarten Brennereien bei Postwick oder Brampton etwa 15km entfernt handelte.

Bei der Späteren Sächsischen Periode grenzte das Gebiet seit langem an Heideland. Untauglich für die Landwirtschaft oder Bewohnung sah die Stätte stattdessen intensive, industrielle Aktivitäten in Form von Arbeitsgängen, die der Eisenproduktion vor der Schmelzung vorausgingen. C-14 Datierung zeigt an, dass diese Aktivitäten um 700 AD begannen und sich bis in die Früh-Mittelalterliche Periode um 1200 AD fortgesetzt zu haben scheinen. Diese industrielle Aktivitäten sind von erheblicher Bedeutung, da bisher nur sehr wenige Ausgrabungen Anzeichen der frühen Phasen der Eisenverarbeitungsarbeitsvorgänge vorwiesen. Die Rohmaterialien, die für die Eisenverarbeitung benötigt werden, waren alle in der Nähe der Stätte vorhanden und die nah gelegene Stadt Norwich, welche sich bei der Späten Sächsischen Periode als ein Inlandshafen von einiger Bedeutung etabliert hatte, lieferte einen leicht zugänglichen und großen Absatzmarkt für Schmiedeeisen. Es wurden ausgedehnte Grubenbrüche für die Gewinnung von eisenhaltigem Sandstein oder Eisenknollen gefunden.

Entlang der Grubenbrüche gab es höchst ungewöhnliche Hinweise für Erzröstung in Form von Gruben mit Anzeichen intensiver Verbrennung, Rückständen von Holzkohle und Fragmenten von verbranntem Eisenstein. Zahlreiche Holzkohlebrenngruben waren ebenfalls präsent; Holzkohle würde in der Eisenverarbeitungsindustrie von Wichtigkeit gewesen sein und wurde offensichtlich bei Laurel Farm in einiger Menge hergestellt.

Dem Untergang der Eisenindustrie folgend war die Stätte beim 13. Jahrhundert zu ihrem abgeschiedenen Heideland Charakter zurückgekehrt. Sie wurde wahrscheinlich regelmäßig nur von durchziehenden Schafhirten und möglicherweise gelegentlich von Bodenschatz sammelnden Menschen besucht. Druck auf die landwirtschaftliche Produktion zum Ende des 18. Jahrhunderts hin endete in der Einfriedung der Landschaft. Die Thorpe St Andrew Enclosure Karte aus dem Jahre 1801 zeigt an, dass Land an der Stätte bei diesem Datum eingezäunt war und es wurde fortlaufend für landwirtschaftliche Zwecke genutzt bis zu seiner kürzlichen Entwicklung. Eine Karte aus dem Jahre 1818 zeigt an, dass das Heideland weiter für seine Bodenschätze genutzt wurde, wobei Kiesgruben und Ziegelöfen die Ausbeutung der natürlichen Tonerde anzeigen.

Bibliography

Abrams, J. 2002. An Archaeological Watching Brief at Cross Leys Quarry, Wittering, Peterborough, Phase 3, Stages 3 and 4. Phoenix Consulting Archaeology Ltd, Unpublished Report

Abrams, J. 2003. An Archaeological Watching Brief at Cross Leys Quarry, Wittering, Peterborough, Phase 4, Stage 1. Phoenix Consulting Archaeology Ltd, Unpublished Report

Abrams, J. and Wilson, N. 2003, Archaeological Watching Brief: Cross Leys Quarry, Wittering, Peterborough, Phase 4, Stage2 & Phase 6, Stage 1. Phoenix Consulting Archaeology Ltd, unpublished, Unpublished Report

Adams, D. (in prep.). After the Younger Dryas: Carrow Road, Norwich: a dated Terminal Palaeolithic Long Blade industry with Bruised Blades

Albone, J., Massey, S. and Tremlett, S. 2007. The Archaeology of Norfolk's Coastal Zone. The Results of the National Mapping Programme. English Heritage Project Ref. 2913. Unpublished Norfolk Landscape Archaeology Report

Andrews, P. 2004. Mersham Archive Slag Report. Unpublished Report for CTRL, Oxford Wessex Archaeology Joint Venture, Salisbury

Armstrong, P., Tomlinson, D. and Evans, D.H. 1991. *Excavations at Lurk Lane, Beverley, 1979–82.* Sheffield: Sheffield Excavation Reports 1

Ashwin, T. 1996a. Neolithic and Bronze Age Norfolk. *Proceedings of the Prehistoric Society* 62, 41–62

Ashwin, T. 1996b. Excavation of an Iron Age site at Park Farm, Silfield, Wymondham, Norfolk. *Norfolk Archaeology* 42, (3), 241–282

Ashwin, T. 2001. Exploring Bronze Age Norfolk: Longham and Bittering. In: J. Brück (Ed.) *Bronze Age Landscapes: tradition and transformation*, 23–32. Oxbow Books. Oxford.

Ashwin, T. and Bates, S. 2000 *Excavations on the Norwich Southern Bypass, 1989–91.* Dereham: East Anglian Archaeology 91

Ashwin, T. and Tester, A. (eds) in press. Excavations at Scole 1993-4 East Anglian Archaeology

Asouti, E. and Austin, P. 2005. Reconstructing woodland vegetation and its exploitation by past societies, based on the analysis and interpretation of archaeological wood charcoal macro-remains. *Environmental Archaeology* 10, 1–18

Atkin S. 1987 *The clay pipe-making industry in Norfolk,* Norfolk Archaeol, vol 39 118-149

Atkin, M. 1993. The Norwich Survey 1971–1985: a Retrospective View. In J. Gardiner, *Flatlands and Wetlands: Current Themes in East Anglian Archaeology.* Dereham: East Anglian Archaeology 50, 127–143

Atkin, M., Ayers, B. and Jennings, S. 1983. Waterfront excavation and Thetford ware production, Norwich. East Anglian Archaeology Report 17

Atkin, M. and Evans, D.H. 2002. *Excavations in Norwich 1971-1978 Part III.* Dereham: East Anglian Archaeology 100

Atkinson, D. and Oswald. A., 1969. London clay tobacco pipes. *Journal of British Archaeology Association,* 3rd series, Vol. 32, 171–227.

Austin, L. 1997. Palaeolithic and Mesolithic. In J. Glazebrook (ed.) *Research and Archaeology: A Framework for the Eastern Counties, 1. Resource Assessment. Dereham:* East Anglian Archaeology Occasional Papers 3, 5–11

Avery, M. 1982. The Neolithic Causewayed Enclosure, Abingdon. In H.J. Case and A. Whittle (eds.) *Settlement Patterns in the Oxfordshire region, excavation at the Abingdon Causeway Enclosure and Other Sites,* 10–50. London: Council for British Archaeology Research Report 44

Ayres, B. 1993. The Urbanisation of East Anglia: the Norwich Perspective. In J. Gardiner, *Flatlands and Wetlands: Current Themes in East Anglian Archaeology.* Dereham: East Anglian Archaeology 50, 117–126

Bailey, G. 1992. *Detector Finds 1.* Essex: Greenlight Publishing

Bailey, G. 2004. *Buttons and Fasteners 500BC–AD1840.* Essex: Greenlight Publishing.

Ballin, T.B. 2002. Later Bronze Age Flint Technology: a presentation and discussion of post-barrow debitage from monuments in the Raunds Area, Northamptonshire. *Lithics* 23, 3–28

Bamford, H.M. 1982. *Beaker Domestic Sites in the Fen Edge and East Anglia.* Dereham: East Anglian Archaeology 16

Bamford, H. 2000. Cremation urn and accessory vessels. In T. Ashwin and S. Bates, *Excavations on the Norwich Southern Bypass, 1989–91.* Dereham: East Anglian Archaeology 91, 92–4

Barton, N. 1991. Technological Innovation and Continuity at the end of the Pleistocene in Britain. In R.N.E. Barton, A.J. Roberts and D.A. Roe (eds.) *Late Glacial Settlement in Northern Europe: human adaptation and environmental change at the end of the Pleistocene*, 234–245. Council for British Archaeology Research Report 77. London: Council for British Archaeology

Barton, N. 1998. Long Blade Technology and the Question of British Late Pleistocene/Early Holocene Lithic Assemblages. In N. Ashton, F. Healy and P. Pettitt (eds.) *Stone Age Archaeology: Essays in Honour of John Wymer*, 158–164. Oxford: Oxbow Monograph 102: Lithics Studies Society Occasional Paper 6

Barton, R.N.E. and Roberts, A. 1996. Reviewing the British late Upper Palaeolithic: new evidence for chronological patterning in the Late Glacial record. *Oxford Journal of Archaeology* 15 (3), 245–265

Batcock, N. 1991. *The Ruined and Disused Churches of Norfolk*. Dereham: East Anglian Archaeology 51

Bates, S. 1996. Heath Farm, Postwick. Norfolk Archaeological Unit Unpublished Report 162

Bates, S. 2006. Flint. In: G. Trimble, A Bronze Age and Early Romano-British Site at The Oaks, Thorpe St Andrew, Norwich: Excavations 1999–2000, 52–53. *Norfolk Archaeology* 45 (1), 41–59

Bates, S. and Lyons, A. 2003. *The Excavation of Romano-British Pottery Kilns at Ellingham, Postwick and Two Mile Bottom, Norfolk, 1995-7*. Dereham: East Anglian Archaeology Occasional Paper 13, 28–56

Beadsmoore, E. 2006. Earlier Neolithic Flint. In D. Garrow, S. Lucy and D. Gibson, *Excavations at Kilverstone, Norfolk: an episodic landscape history*, 53–70. Dereham: East Anglian Archaeology 113

Beijerinck, W. 1947. *Zadenatlas der Nederlandsche Flora*. Wageningen: Veenman and Zonen

Bergman, C.E., Barton, R.N.E., Collcut, S.N. and Morris, G. 1986. Intentional Breakage in a Late Upper Palaeolithic Assemblage from Southern England. In: G. De G. Sieveking and M.H. Newcomer (eds.) *The Human Uses of Flint and Chert*, 21–36. Cambridge: Cambridge University Press.

Birks, C. 2001. Report on an Archaeological Evaluation at Ellingham Hall Estate, Ellingham. Unpublished Norfolk Archaeological Unit Report 596

Bishop, B.J. 2008. *Lithic Assessment, Excavations at Linton Village College, Linton, Cambridgeshire. Site Code: LINVIC 08*. Oxford Archaeology East Unpublished Report

Bishop, B.J. (forthcoming a). The Lithic Material. In R. Mortimer and A. Connor, *Prehistoric and Romano-British occupation along Fordham Bypass, Fordham, Cambridgeshire*. Dereham: East Anglian Archaeology

Bishop, B.J. (forthcoming b). The Lithic Material. In G. Trimble, *Prehistoric activity in the Yare Valley, Norfolk: Harford Park and Ride*. Dereham: East Anglian Archaeology

Bishop, B.J. and Mortimer, R. (in prep.). Middle Bronze Age Enclosures and Depositional Activity at Sawston, South Cambridgeshire

Blair, J. 2005. *The Church in Anglo-Saxon Society*. Oxford: Oxford University Press

Bown, J.E. 1986. The Excavation of a Ring-Ditch on Sweet Briar Road, Norwich, 1982. In A.J. Lawson, *Barrow Excavations in Norfolk, 1950–82*, 59–64. Dereham: East Anglian Archaeology 29

Bradley, R. 1993. The Microwear Analysis. In R. Bradley, P. Chowne, R.M.J. Cleal, F. Healy and I. Kinnes, *Excavations On Redgate Hill, Hunstanton And Tattershall Thorpe, Lincolnshire*, 106–110. Dereham: East Anglian Archaeology 57

Bradley, R. 1998. *The Significance of Monuments: on the shaping of human experience in Neolithic and Bronze Age Europe*. Routledge. London

Bradley, R. 2003. A Life Less Ordinary: the ritualization of the domestic sphere in later prehistoric Europe. *Cambridge Archaeological Journal* 13 (1), 5–23

Brennand, M. and Taylor, M. 2003. The Survey and Excavation of a Bronze Age Timber Circle at Holme-next-the-Sea, Norfolk, 1998-9. *Proceedings of the Prehistoric Society* 69, 1–84

Brown, A. 1991. Structured Deposition and Technological Change among the Flaked Stone Artefacts from Cranbourne Chase. In J. Barrett, R. Bradley and M. Hall (eds.) *Papers on the Prehistoric Archaeology of Cranbourne Chase*, 101–133. Oxford: Oxbow Monograph 11

Brown, A.G. 2000. Floodplain Vegetation History: clearing as potential ritual spaces? In A.S. Fairbairn (ed.) *Plants in Neolithic Britain and Beyond*, 49–62. Neolithic Studies Group Seminar Papers 5. Oxford: Oxbow

Brown, N. and Murphy, P. 1997. Neolithic and Bronze Age. In J. Glazebrook (ed.) *Research and Archaeology: A Framework for the Eastern Counties, 1. Resource Assessment.* Dereham: East Anglian Archaeology Occasional Papers 3, 12–22

Brown, R. 2005. *Former Last Factory, Fishergate, Norwich. Archaeological Evaluation Report.* Unpublished Oxford Archaeology Unit Report, Job No. 2554

Brown, T. 1997. Clearances and clearings: deforestation in Mesolithic/Neolithic Britain. *Oxford Journal of Archaeology* 16 (2), 133–146

Brück, J. 1999. Ritual and Rationality: some problems of interpretation in European Archaeology. *European Journal of Archaeology* 2 (3), 313–344

Brudenell, M. 2004. Granta Park, Great Abington, Cambridgeshire: The Rickett Field Site. Unpublished Cambridge Archaeological Unit Report

Bryant, S. 1997. Iron Age. In J. Glazebrook, (ed.) *Research and Archaeology: A Framework for the Eastern Counties, 1. Resource Assessment, 23–34.* Dereham: East Anglian Archaeology Occasional Papers 3

Burchard, A. 1982. A Saxo-Norman Iron-Smelting Site at 'Co-op' in High Street. In C. Mahaney, A. Burchard and G. Simpson, *Excavations in Stamford, Lincolnshire 1963-1969, 105–144.* London: Society for Medieval Archaeology Monograph 9

Cappers, R.J.T., Bekker, R.M. and Jans, J.E.A. 2006. *Digital Zadenatlas Van Nederlands - Digital Seeds Atlas of the Netherlands.* Groningen Archaeological Studies Volume 4, Groningen: Barkhius Publishing

Carlin, N. 2008. Ironworking and Production. In N. Carlin, L. Clarke and F. Walsh, *The Archaeology of Life and Death in the Boyne Floodplain. The Linear Landscape of the M4.* Dublin: NRA Scheme Monographs 2, 87–112

Champion, M. 2001. Kett's Rebellion 1549: a Dussindale eyewitness? *Norfolk Archaeology* 43, Part 4, 642–645

Chapman, J.C. 2000. *Fragmentation in Archaeology: people, places and broken objects in the prehistory of South Eastern Europe.* London: Routledge

Charles, M.P. 1984. Introductory Remarks on Cereals. *Bulletin on Sumerian Agriculture*, 17–31

Clark, J. 1995. *The Medieval Horse and its Equipment, c. 1150-c. 1450.* Medieval Finds from Excavations in London 5. London: Museum of London

Clark, J.D.G. 1936a. The timber monument at Arminghall and its affinities. *Proceedings of the Prehistoric Society* 2, 1–51

Clark, J.G.D. 1936b. Report on a Late Bronze Age Site in Mildenhall Fen, West, Suffolk. *Antiquaries Journal* 16, 29–50

Clark, J.D.G. and Fell, C.I. 1953. The Early Iron Age site at West Harling, Norfolk, and its pottery. *Proceedings of the Prehistoric Society* 19, 1–40

Clark, J.D.G., Higgs, E.S. and Longworth, I.H. 1960. Excavations at the Neolithic Site at Hurst Fen, Mildenhall, Suffolk (1954, 1957 and 1958). *Proceedings of the Prehistoric Society* 26, 202–245

Cleal R. 1995. Pottery fabrics in Wessex in the fourth to second millennia BC. In I. Kinnes and G. Varndell, *'Unbaked Urns of Rudely Shape' Essays on British and Irish Pottery for Ian Longworth.* Oxford: Oxbow Monograph 55

Cleal, R. 2004. The Dating and Diversity of the Earliest Ceramics of Wessex and South–west England. In R. Cleal and J. Pollard (eds.), *Monuments and Material Culture, 164–192.* Salisbury: Hobnob Press

Clogg, P. 2006. Iron Coffin Fittings from Wearmouth. In R.J. Cramp, *Wearmouth and Jarrow Monastic Sites. Volume 2, 291–303.* Swindon: English Heritage

Colgrave, B. 1956. *Felix's Life of Saint Guthlac.* Cambridge: Cambridge University Press

Conneller, C. 2000. Fragmented Space? Hunter-Gather Landscapes of the Vale of Pickering. *Archaeological Review from Cambridge* 17 (1), 139–150

Conneller, C. 2007. Inhabiting New Landscapes: settlement and mobility in Britain after the last Glacial Maximum. *Oxford Journal of Archaeology* 26 (3), 215–237

Conneller, C. 2008. Lithic Technology and the Chaine Operatoire. In J. Pollard (ed.) *Prehistoric Britain,* 160–176. Oxford: Blackwell

Conneller, C. 2009. Investigation of a Final Palaeolithic Site at Rookery Farm, Great Willbraham, Cambridgeshire. *Proceedings of the Prehistoric Society* 75, 167–187

Cool, H. 2010. Objects of glass, shale, bone and metal (except nails). In P. Booth, A. Simmonds, A. Boyle, S. Clough, H. Cool and D. Poore ,*The Late Roman Cemetery at Lankhills, Winchester. Excavations 2000-2005.* Oxford: Oxford Archaeology Monograph 10, 267-308

Cooper, L.P. 2006. Launde, a Terminal Palaeolithic Camp-site in the English Midlands and its North European Context. *Proceedings of the Prehistoric Society* 72, 53–93

Darling, M. and Gurney, D. 1993. *Caister on Sea: Excavations by Charles Green 1951-55.* Dereham: East Anglia Archaeology Report 60

Davies, J.A. 1996. Where Eagles Dare: Iron Age of Norfolk. *Proceedings of the Prehistoric Society* 62, 63–92

Davies, J.A. 1999. Patterns, Power and Political Progress. In J. Davies and T. Williamson (eds.) *Land of the Iceni. The Iron Age in Northern East Anglia,* 14–43. Norwich: Centre of East Anglia Studies

Davison, A. 1990. *The evolution of settlement in three parishes in south-east Norfolk.* Dereham: East Anglian Archaeology 49

Devaney, R. 2005. Ceremonial and Domestic Flint Arrowheads. *Lithics* 26, 9–22

Donahue, R. 2002. Microwear Analysis. In J. Sidell, J. Cotton, L. Rayner and L. Wheeler, *The Prehistory of Southwark and Lambeth,* 81–88. London: Museum of London Archaeology Service Monograph 14.

Drewett, P. 1982. Later Bronze Age Downland Economy and Excavations at Black Patch, East Sussex. *Proceedings of the Prehistoric Society* 48, 321–400

Edmonds, M. 1995. *Stone Tools and Society: working stone In Neolithic and Bronze Age Britain.* London: Batsford.

Edmonds, M. 1997. Taskscape, Technology and Tradition. *Analecta Praehistorica Leidensia* 29, 99–110

Edmonds, M. 1999. *Ancestral Geographies of the Neolithic: landscape, monuments and memory.* London: Routeledge

Edmonds, M. 2006. The Lithics. In C. Evans, M. Edmonds and S. Boreham, 'Total Archaeology' and Model Landscapes: excavations of the Great Wilbraham Causewayed Enclosure, Cambridgeshire, 1975–76. *Proceedings of the Prehistoric Society* 72, 130–134

Edmonds, M., Evans, C. and Gibson, D. 1999. Assemblage and Collection – Lithic Complexes in the Cambridgeshire Fenlands. *Proceedings of the Prehistoric Society* 65, 47–82

Egan, G. 2005. *Material culture in London in an age of transition. Tudor and Stuart period finds c 1450–c 1700 from excavations at riverside sites in Southwark. London:* Museum of London Archaeology Service Monograph 19

Egan, G. 2007. Post-medieval non-ferrous metalwork and evidence for metalworking: AD 1500–50 to 1800-50'. In D. Griffiths, R.A. Philpott and G. Egan, *MEOLS. The Archaeology of the North Wirral Coast. Discoveries and observations in the 19th and 20th centuries, with a catalogue of collections.* Oxford and London: Oxford School of Archaeology Monograph 68, Institute of Archaeology, 213–128

Egan, G. and Forsyth, H. 1997. Wound Wire and Silver Gilt: changing fashions in dress accessories c.1400 – c.1600, 215-38. In D. Gaimster and P. Stamper (eds.), *The Age of Transition. The Archaeology of English Culture 1400-1600.* The Society for Medieval Archaeology Monograph 15, Oxbow Monograph 98

Eschenlohr, L. and Serneels, V. 1991. *Les bas fourneaux mérovingiens de Boécourt, Les Boulies (Jura suisse).* Cahiers d'archéologie française jurassienne 3, Porrentruy

Evans, J. 2001. Material approaches to the identification of different Romano-British site types. In S. James and M. Millett (eds.) Britons and Romans: advancing an archaeological agenda. London: Council for British Archaeology Research Report 125, 26–35

Evans. C. and Knight, M. 1996. *The Butcher's Rise Ring-ditches: excavations at Barley Croft Farm, Cambridge.* Unpublished Cambridge Archaeological Unit Report 283

Evans, C. and Knight, M. 2000. A Fenland delta: later prehistoric land-use in the lower Ouse reaches. In M. Dawson (ed.) *Prehistoric, Roman, and Post-Roman Landscapes of the Great Ouse Valley,* 89–106. London: Council for British Archaeology Research Report 119

Evans, C., Pollard, J. and Knight, M, 1999. Life in Woods: Tree-Throws, 'Settlement' and Forest Cognition. *Oxford Journal of Archaeology* 18 (3), 241–254

Fasham, P.J. and Ross, J.M. 1978. A Bronze Age Flint Industry from a Barrow in Micheldever Wood, Hampshire. *Proceedings of the Prehistoric Society* 44, 47–67

Fenwick, V. 1984. Insula de Burgh: Excavations at Burrow Hill, Butley, Suffolk, 1978–1981. *Anglo-Saxon Studies in Archaeology and History* 3, 35–54

Gaimster, M. and Gerrard, J. 2007. Metal and Small Finds Assessment. In J. Westmacott, Laurel Farm Phase II, Broadlands Business Park, Thorpe St. Andrew, Norwich, Norfolk. Post-Excavation Assessment Report. Unpublished Pre-Construct Archaeology Report

Gamble, C., Davies, W., Pettitt, P. and Richards, M. 2004. Climate Change and Evolving Human Diversity in Europe during the Last Glacial. *Philosophical Transactions of the Royal Society London. Series B* 359, 243–254

Gamble, C., Davies, W., Pettitt, P., Hazelwood, L. and Richards, M. 2005. The Archaelogical and Genetic Foundations of the European Population during the Last Glacial: implications for agricultural thinking. *Cambridge Archaeological Journal* 15 (2), 193–223

Garrow, D. 2006. *Pits, Settlement and Deposition during the Neolithic and Early Bronze Age in East Anglia.* Oxford: British Archaeological Report (British Series) 414

Garrow, D., Beadsmore, E. and Knight, M. 2005. Pit Clusters and the Temporality of Occupation: an earlier Neolithic Site at Kilverstone, Thetford, Norfolk. *Proceedings of the Prehistoric Society* 71, 139–157

Garwood, P. 1999. Grooved Ware in Southern Britain; Chronology and Interpretation. In R. Cleal and A. MacSween (eds.), *Grooved Ware in Britain and Ireland,* 145–176. Neolithic Studies Group Seminar Papers 3. Oxford: Oxbow.

Gibson, A.M. 1982. *Beaker Domestic Sites, a study of the Domestic Pottery of the Late Third and Early Second Millennium BC in the British Isles.* Oxford: British Archaeological Report (British Series) 107

Gibson, A. 2002. *Prehistoric Pottery in Britain and Ireland.* Stroud: Tempus

Gibson, A.M. and Woods, A. 1990. Prehistoric Pottery for the Archaeologist. Leicester: Leicester University Press

Gilmour, N. and Mortimer, R. 2011 Early Prehistoric settlement, Field systems and Enclosure, at Ormesby St Michael, Norfolk: post-excavation assessment and updated project design. Unpublished Oxford Archaeology East Report 1170

Going, C. 1997. Roman. In J. Glazebrook (ed.) *Research and Archaeology: A Framework for the Eastern Counties, 1. Resource Assessment,* 35–45. Dereham: East Anglian Archaeology Occasional Papers 3

Goodall, I. 1990. Horseshoes. In M. Biddle, *Object and Economy in Medieval Winchester,* 1053–1067. Oxford: Winchester Studies 7ii

Gosden, C. 1994. *Social Being and Time.* Oxford: Blackwell

Gosden, C. and Lock, G. 1998. Prehistoric Histories. *World Archaeology* 30 (1), 2–12

Grace, R. 1992. Use Wear Analysis. In F. Healey, M. Heaton and S.J. Lobb, Excavations of a Mesolithic Site at Thatcham, Berkshire, 53–63. *Proceedings of the Prehistoric Society* 58, 41–76

Greatorex, C. 2001. Evidence of Sussex Prehistoric Ritual Traditions. The Archaeological Investigation of a Bronze Age Funerary Monument Situated on Baily's Hill, near Crowlink, Eastbourne. *Sussex Archaeological Collections* 139, 27–73

Green, B. and Young, R.M.R. 1981. *Norwich, the Growth of a City, revised edition.* Norwich: Norfolk Museums Service

Green, C. 1977. *Excavations in the Roman Kiln Field at Brampton, 1973-4.* Dereham: East Anglian Archaeology 5, 31–95

Green, C.P. and Swindle, G.E. 2007. Geoarchaeological assessment. In J. Westmacott, Laurel Farm Phase II, Broadlands Business Park, Thorpe St. Andrew, Norwich, Norfolk. Post-Excavation Assessment Report. Unpublished Pre-Construct Archaeology Report

Green, H.S. 1980. *The Flint Arrowheads of the British Isles: a detailed study of material from England and Wales with comparanda from Scotland and Ireland: Part I.* Oxford: British Archaeological Report (British Series) 75

Green, S. 1984. Flint Arrowheads: Typology and Interpretation. *Lithics* 5, 19–39

Gregory, T. 1979. Early Romano-British Pottery Production at Thorpe St. Andrew, Norwich. *Norfolk Archaeology* 37, Part 2, 202–208

Greguss, P. 1954. *The identification of Central-European dicotyledonous trees and shrubs based on xylotomy.* Budapest: The Hungarian Museum of Natural History

Grew, F. and de Nergaard, M. 1988. *Shoes and Pattens, Medieval Finds from Excavations in London: 2.* London: HMSO

Haslam, J. 1980. A Middle Saxon Iron Smelting Site at Ramsbury, Wiltshire. *Medieval Archaeology* 24, 1–68

Hather, J. 2000. *The Identification of the Northern European Woods. A guide for archaeologists and conservators.* London: Archetype

Healy, F. 1984. Lithic Assemblage Variation in the Late Third and Early Second Millennia BC in Eastern England. *Lithics* 5, 10–18

Healy, F. 1986. The Excavation of Two Early Bronze Age Round Barrows on Eaton Heath, Norwich, 1969–1970. In A. Lawson, *Barrow Excavations in Norfolk, 1950-82*, 50–58. Dereham: East Anglian Archaeology 29

Healy, F. 1988. *The Anglo-Saxon Cemetery at Spong Hill, North Elmham, Part VI: occupation during the seventh to second millennia BC*. Dereham: East Anglian Archaeology 39.

Healy, F. 1995. Pots, Pits and Peat. In I. Kinnes and G. Varndell (eds.) *'Unbaked Urns of Rudely Shape' Essays on British and Irish Pottery for Ian Longworth*, 101–112. Oxford: Oxbow Monograph 55

Healy, F. 1996. *The Fenland Project, Number 11: The Wissey Embayment: Evidence for pre-Iron Age Occupation*. Dereham: East Anglian Archaeology 78

Herne, A. 1988. A time and place for the Grimston Bowl. In J.C. Barrett and I.A. Kinnes (eds.) *The Archaeology of Context in the Neolithic and Bronze Age: Recent Trends*, 2–29. Sheffield: Department of Archaeology and Prehistory

Herne, A. 1991. The Flint Assemblage. In: I. Longworth, A. Herne, G. Varndell and S. Needham, *Excavations at Grimes Graves Norfolk 1972 –1976. Fascicule 3. Shaft X: Bronze Age flint, chalk and metal working*, 21–93. Dorchester: British Museum Press

Hill, J.D. 1993. Can We Recognize a Different European Past? A Contrastive Archaeology of Later Prehistoric Settlement in Southern England. *Journal of European Archaeology* 1, 57–75

Hill, J.D. 1995. *Ritual and Rubbish in the Iron Age of Wessex: a study on the formation of a specific archaeological record*. Oxford: British Archaeological Reports (British Series) 242

Hillman, G.C., Mason S., de Moulins, D. and Nesbitt M. 1996. Identification of archaeological remains of wheat: the 1992 London workshop. *Circaea The Journal for Environmental Archaeology* 12 (2) (1996 for 1995), 195–209

Hingley, R. 1989. *Rural Settlement in Roman Britain*. London: Seaby

Hinton, D. A., 2011. Weland's Work: Metals and Metalsmiths, in M. Clegg Hyer and G. R. Owen-Crocker, *The Material Culture of Daily Living in the Anglo-Saxon World*, Exeter, 185-200

Hughes, R. 2006. Laurel Farm (Phase 2), Archaeological Desk Study. Unpublished IHCM Report

Humphrey, J. 2003. The Utilization and Technology of Flint in the British Iron Age. In J. Humphrey (ed.) *Re-searching the Iron Age: selected papers from the proceedings of the Iron Age research student seminars, 1999 and 2000*, 17–23. Leicester Archaeology Monograph 11.

Humphrey, J. 2007. Simple Tools for Tough Tasks or Tough Tools for Simple tasks? Analysis and Experiment in Iron Age Flint Utilisation. In C. Haselgrove and R. Pope (eds.) *The Earlier Iron Age in Britain and the near Continent*, 144–159. Oxford: Oxbow Books

Ingold, T. 1986. *The Appropriation of Nature: essays on human ecology and social relations*. Manchester: Manchester University Press

Ingold, T. 1993. The Temporality of the Landscape. *World Archaeology* 25 (2), 152–174

Ingold, T. 2000. *The Perception of the Environment: essays in livelihood, dwelling and skill*. London: Routeledge

Jacobi, R. 2004. The late Upper Palaeolithic Lithic Collection from Gough's Cave, Cheddar, Somerset and Human Use of the Cave. *Proceedings of the Prehistoric Society* 70, 1–92

Jacomet, S. 2006. *Identification of Cereal Remains from Archaeological Sites*. Second edition. Basel: IPAS Basel University

Janes, D. 1996. The golden clasp of the late Roman state. *Early Medieval Europe* 5(2), 127–153

Jennings, S. 1983. The pottery. In M. Atkin, B. Ayers and S. Jennings, *Waterfront excavation and Thetford ware production, Norwich*, East Anglian Archaeology Report 17, 74–92

Jones, G., Straker, V. and Davis, A. 1990. Early Medieval Plant Use and Ecology. In: A. Vince (ed.) Aspects of Saxo-Norman London, II: Finds and Environmental Evidence, London and Middlesex Archaeology Society Special Paper 12, 347–385

Keepax, C. 1988. *Charcoal analysis with particular reference to archaeological sites in Britain*. Unpublished PhD thesis submitted to the University of London

Kemp, S. 2005. *Assessment of Lithics from Burwell Newmarket Road 2005 (BUR NER 05)*. Unpublished Cambridgeshire County Council Field Archaeology Unit Manuscript

Kinnes, I., Gibson, A., Ambers, J., Bowman, S., Leese, M. and Boast, R. 1991. Radiocarbon dating and British Beakers: the British Museum programme. *Scottish Archaeological Review* 8, 35–78

Lamdin-Whymark, H. 2008. *The Residues of Ritualised Action: Neolithic depositional practices in the Middle Thames Valley.* Oxford: British Archaeological Reports (British Series) 466

Lawson, A. 1986. *Barrow Excavations in Norfolk, 1950-82.* Dereham: East Anglian Archaeology 29

Lawson, A.J., Martin, E.A. and Priddy, D. 1981. *The Barrows of East Anglia.* Dereham: East Anglian Archaeology 12

Levi-Sala, I. 1992. Functional Analysis and Post-Depositional Alterations of Microdenticulates. In R.N.E. Barton, *Hengistbury Head Dorset Volume 2: the Late Upper Palaeolithic and Early Mesolithic sites,* 238–246. Oxford: Oxford University Committee for Archaeology Monograph 34

Longworth, I. 1960. Pottery. In J.G.D Clark, Excavations at the Neolithic site at Hurst Fen, Mildenhall, Suffolk. *Proceedings of the Prehistoric Society* 26, 228–240

Longworth, I. 1971. The Neolithic Pottery. In G.J. Wainwright and I.H. Longworth, *Durrington Walls Excavations 1966 to 1968,* 48–155. London: Society of Antiquaries

Longworth, I. and Cleal, R. 1999. Grooved Ware Gazetteer. In R. Cleal and A. MacSween (eds.), *Grooved Ware in Britain and Ireland,* 177–206. Neolithic Studies groups Seminar Papers 3. Oxford: Oxbow

Longworth, I., Ellison, A. and Rigby, V. 1988. *Excavations at Grimes Graves, Norfolk 1972-1976. Fascicule 2. The Neolithic, Bronze Age and Later Pottery.* Dorchester: British Museum Press

Longworth, I., Herne, A., Varndell, G. and Needham, S. 1991 *Excavations At Grimes Graves Norfolk 1972 -1976. Fascicule 3. Shaft X: Bronze Age Flint, Chalk And Metal Working.* Dorchester: British Museum Press

Lyons, A. 2003. Roman Pottery. In S. Bates and A. Lyons, *The Excavation of Romano-British Pottery Kilns at Ellingham, Postwick and Two Mile Bottom, Norfolk, 1995-7.* Dereham: East Anglian Archaeology Occasional Papers 13

Lyons, A. 2004. *Romano-British Industrial Activity at Snettisham, Norfolk.* Dereham: East Anglia Archaeology Occasional Papers 18

Lyons, A. and Tester, C. (forthcoming). The Roman Pottery. In T. Ashwin and A Tester (eds.), *Excavations at Scole, 1993–4.* Dereham: East Anglian Archaeology

Macmaster, N. 1990. The Battle for Mousehold Heath 1857–1884: Popular Politics and the Victorian Public Park. *Past and Present* 127 (1), 117–154

Mangin, M. 2004. *Le Fer.* Paris: Collection "Archéologiques"

McDonnell, G., Blakelock, E. and Rubinson, S. (forthcoming). The Iron Economy of Wharram Percy. In S. Wrathmell, *Wharram. A Study of Settlement on the Yorkshire Wolds, XIII An Overall Synthesis.* York: York University Archaeological Publications

McOrmish, D. 1996. East Chisenbury: ritual and rubbish in the British Bronze Age – Iron Age transition. *Antiquity* 70 (267), 68–76

Millett, M. 1990. *The Romanization of Roman Britain.* Cambridge: Cambridge University Press

Mills, A.D. 1998. *A Dictionary of English Place-Names* (Second Edition). Oxford: Oxford University Press

Mitchiner, M. 1988. Jetons, medalets and tokens: the medieval period and Nuremberg. Vol I., London: Seaby.

Monaghan, J. 1987. *Upchurch and Thameside Roman Pottery.* Oxford: British Archaeological Reports (British Series) 173

Moore, P. 2006a. *Laurel Farm Aims and Objectives from Evaluation and Excavation WSI's.* Unpublished Pre-Construct Archaeology document

Moore, P. 2006b. *Written Scheme of Investigation for an Archaeological Field Evaluation at Laurel Farm (Phase II), Broadlands Business Park, Thorpe St Andrew, Norfolk.* Unpublished Pre-Construct Archaeology Limited document

Mortimer, R. and Connor, A. (forthcoming). *Prehistoric and Roman occupation from Fordham Bypass, Cambridgeshire.* Dereham: East Anglian Archaeology Occasional Papers

Mousehold Heath Defenders, 2010. Available online at: www.mouseholdheathdefenders.webeden.co.uk

Myres, J.N.L. and Green, B. 1973. *The Anglo-Saxon Cemeteries of Caister-by-Norwich and Markshall, Norfolk.* Report Research Committee Society Antiquaries London, 30

Needham, S. 1993. The Structure of Settlement and Ritual in the Late Bronze Age of South-East Britain. In C. Mordant and A. Richard (eds.) *L'habitat et l'occupation du Sol a` L'Age du Bronze en Europe,* 49 –69. Paris: Editions du Comite` des Travaux Historiques et Scientifiques

Needham, S. and Spence, T. 1996. *Refuse and Disposal at Area 16 East, Runnymede.* London: British Museum Press Needham, S. and Spence, T. 1997. Refuse and the formation of middens. *Antiquity* 71, 77–90

Nuthall, T. 2002. *Thorpe St Andrew: a history.* Norwich: Catton Print

Ottaway, P. and Rogers, N. 2002. *Craft, Industry and Everyday Life: Finds from Medieval York, The Archaeology of York, The Small Finds 17/15.* London: York Archaeological Trust

Parfitt, S.A., Ashton, N.M., Lewis, S.G., Abel, R.L., Coope, R., Field, M.H., Gale, R., Hoare, P.G., Larkin, N.R., Lewis, M.D., Karloukovski, V., Maher, B.A., Peglar, S.M., Preece, R.C., Whittaker, J.E. and Stringer, C.B. 2010a. Early Pleistocene Human Occupation at the Edge of the Boreal Zone in Northwest Europe. *Nature* 466, 229–233.

Parfitt, S., Ashton, N. and Lewis, S. 2010b. Happisburgh. *British Archaeology* 114, 15–23

Penn, K. 2000. *Norwich Southern Bypass, Part II: Anglo-Saxon cemetery at Harford Farm, Caistor St Edmund.* Dereham: East Anglian Archaeology 92

Penn, K. 2001. Report on an Archaeological Desk Top Survey for *Laurel Farm, Plumstead, Norwich.* Unpublished Norfolk Archaeological Unit Report No. 600

Percival, J.W. 2002. Neolithic and Bronze Age Occupation in the Yare Valley: Excavations at Three Score Road, Bowthorpe, 1999–2000. *Norfolk Archaeology* 44 (1), 59–88

Percival, S. 1996. The Pottery. In T Ashwin, Excavation of an Iron Age site at Silfield, Wymondham, Norfolk, 1992–93. *Norfolk Archaeology* 42 (3), 241–283

Percival, S. 2000. The Pottery (various sites) In T. Ashwin and S. Bates, *Excavations on the Norwich Southern Bypass, 1989–91.* Dereham: East Anglian Archaeology 91

Percival, S. 2004. The Prehistoric pottery. In D. Whitmore, Excavations at a Neolithic Site at the John Innes Centre, Colney 2000. *Norfolk Archaeology 44* (3), 422–426

Percival, S. 2006. The Pottery In G. Trimble, A Bronze Age and Early Romano-British Site at The Oaks, Thorpe St Andrew, Norwich: Excavations 1999–2000. Norfolk Archaeology 45, Part 1

Percival, S. with Trimble G.L. (in prep.). *Prehistoric Activity in the Yare Valley; Harford Park and Ride, Keswick, Norfolk, 2003.* Dereham: East Anglian Archaeology

Perrin, J. 1999. Roman pottery from excavations at or near to the Roman small town of *Durbobrivae*, Water Newton, Cambridgeshire, 1956–1958. *Journal of Roman Pottery Studies* 8, 1–141

Pestell, T. 2003. The Afterlife of 'Productive' Sites in East Anglia. In T. Pestell and K. Ulmschneider, *Markets in Early Medieval Europe. Trading and 'Productive' Sites, 650–850,* 122–137. Macclesfield: Windgather Press

Pestell, T. 2004. *Landscapes of Monastic Foundation. The Establishment of Religious Houses in East Anglia, c. 650–1200.* Anglo-Saxon Studies 5. Woodbridge: Boydell and Brewer

Pitts, M.W. 1978. Towards an Understanding of Flint Industries in Post-Glacial England. *Bulletin of the Institute of Archaeology* 15, 179–197 Pitts, M. 2005. Stone Plaque is First Neolithic Face in over a Century. *British Archaeology* 84, 9

Pitts, M.W. and Jacobi, R.M. 1979. Some Aspects of Change in Flakes Stone Industries of the Mesolithic and Neolithic in Southern Britain. *Journal of Archaeological Science* 6, 163–177

Pollard, J. 1998. Prehistoric Settlement and Non-Settlement in Two Southern Cambridgeshire River Valleys: the lithic dimension and interpretative dilemmas. *Lithics* 19, 61–71

Pollard, J. 1999. 'These Places Have Their Moments': Thoughts on Settlement Practices in the British Neolithic. In J. Brück and M. Goodman (eds.) *Making Places in the Prehistoric World: themes in settlement archaeology,* 76–93. London : University College of London Press

Pollard, J. 2002. The Ring-Ditch and the Hollow: excavation of a Bronze Age 'shrine' and associated features at Pampisford, Cambridgeshire. *Proceedings of the Cambridge Antiquarian Society* 91, 5–21

Poole, I., Branch, N.P. and McParland L. 2007. Laurel Farm, Norfolk (Site Code: TSA06): Preliminary Charcoal Assessment. Unpublished ArchaeoScape Report

Postma, G. and Hodgson, G.E. 1988. Caistor St Edmund pit. In P.L. Gibbard and J.A. Zalasiewicz, (eds.) *Pliocene-Middle Pleistocene of East Anglia.* Quaternary Research Association, Field Guide. Cambridge: Quaternary Research Association

Pre-Construct Archaeology Limited, 1999. Field Recording Manual. Unpublished Pre-Construct Archaeology Limited document

Prehistoric Ceramic Research Group, 1992. Guidelines for the Analysis and Publication, Prehistoric Ceramic Research Group, Occasional Paper 2

Prehistoric Ceramic Research Group, 1997. Guidelines for the Analysis and Publication, Prehistoric Ceramic Research Group, Occasional Paper 2 (revised)

Prehistoric Ceramic Research Group 2007. *The Study of Prehistoric Pottery: General Policies and Guidelines for Analysis and Publication.* Occasional Papers Nos 1 And 2. 3rd Edition Revised 2010

Preston, C.D., Pearman, D. A. and Dines, T. D. 2002. *New Atlas of the British and Irish Flora.* Oxford: Oxford University Press

Rackham, O. 1986. *The History of the Countryside.* London: Phoenix Press

Rackham, O. 2006. *Woodlands.* New Naturalist Library No.100. London: Collins

Rackham, O., 1994. Trees and Woodland in Anglo-Saxon England: the documentary evidence. In J. Rackham, *Environment and Economy in Anglo-Saxon England,* 7–11. London: Council for British Archaeology Research Report 89

Read, H.H. 1947. Rutley's Elements of Mineralogy. Thomas Murby and Co, London.

Richards, C. and Thomas, J. 1984. Ritual activity and structured deposition in Late Neolithic Wessex. In R. Bradley and J. Gardiner (eds.) *Neolithic Studies: a review of some current research,* 189–218. Oxford: British Archaeological Reports (British Series) 133

Riley, D.N. 1980. *Early Landscapes from the air.* Sheffield: Department of Archaeology and Prehistory, University of Sheffield

Robins, P. 2004. Flint. In M. Whitmore, Excavations at a Neolithic Site at the John Innes Centre, Colney, 2000, 416–422. *Norfolk Archaeology* 44 (3), 406–431

Robins, P. and Wymer, J. 2006. Late Upper Palaeolithic (Long Blade) Industries in Norfolk. *Norfolk Archaeology* 95, 86–104

Rose, E. and Davison, A. 1988. St Catherine's Thorpe: The birth and death of a myth. *Norfolk Archaeology* 40, 179

Russell, F.W. 1859. *Kett's Rebellion in Norfolk.* London: Longman

Saville, A. 1980. On the Measurement of Struck Flakes and Flake Tools. *Lithics* 1, 16–20

Saville, A. 1981. *Grimes Graves, Norfolk. Excavations 1971–2, Volume II: The Flint Assemblage.* London: Department of Environment Archaeological Reports 11

Schweingruber, F.H. 1990. *Mikroskopische Holzanatomie. Anatomie microscopique du bois. Microscopic wood anatomy.* Swiss Federal Institute of Forestry Research

Schweingruber, F.H., Börner, A. and Schulze, E.D. 2006. *Atlas of Woody Plant Stems. Evolution, structure, and Environmental Modifications.* Berlin: Heidelberg, Springer-Verlag

Scott, B.G. 1990. *Early Irish Ironworking.* Belfast: Ulster Museum Publication 266

Seager Thomas, M. 1999. Stone Finds in Context: a contribution to the study of later prehistoric artefact assemblages. *Sussex Archaeological Collections* 137, 39–48

Shepherd Popescu, E. 2009. *Norwich Castle: Excavations and Historical Survey, 1987–98.* Gressenhall: East Anglian Archaeology 132,

Simpson, D.D.A. 2004. Making an Impression: Beaker combs. In R Cleal and J. Pollard (eds.) *Monuments and Material Culture.* Salisbury, Hobnob Press, 207–214

Smith, G.H. 1987. A Beaker (?) Burial Monument and a Late Bronze Age Assemblage from East Northdown, Margate. *Archaeologia Cantiana* 104, 237–289

Smith, I.F. 1965. *Windmill Hill and Avebury.* Oxford: Clarendon Press

Stace, C. 1997. *New flora of the British Isles-* Second Edition. Cambridge: Cambridge University Press

Stamper, P. A. and Croft, R. A. 2000. *Wharram. A Study of Settlement on the Yorkshire Wolds, VIII. The South Manor Area.* York: York University Archaeological Publications 10

Supple, W.R. 1917. A history of Thorpe-by-Norwich. Norwich: Jarrolds

Swift, E. 2000. *Regionality in Dress Accessories in the late Roman West.* Motnagnac, Monographies Instrumentum 11

Taylor, G. 2001. Archaeological Evaluation at 11-13 Wensum Street, Norwich, Norfolk. Unpublished APS Report No. 117/01

Tebbutt, C.F. 1982. A Middle Saxon iron smelting site at Milbrook, Ashdown Forest, Sussex. *Sussex Archaeological Collections* 120, 19–36

Terberger T. and Street, M. 2002. Hiatus or Continuity? New Results for the Question of Periglacial Settlement in Central Europe. *Antiquity* 76 (292), 691-698

Tester, A., Anderson, S., Riddler, I. D. and Carr, R., forthcoming. *Staunch Meadow Brandon: a High Status Middle Saxon Settlement*, East Anglian Archaeology

Thomas, J. 1999. *Understanding the Neolithic: a revised second edition of rethinking the Neolithic.* London: Routledge

Tomber, R. and Dore, J. 1998. *The National Roman Fabric Collection.* London: MoLAS

Tomlinson, P. 1985. An aid to the identification of fossil buds, bud-scales and catkin-bracts of British trees and shrubs. *Circaea* 3, (2) 45–130

Trimble, G. 2006. A Bronze Age and Early Romano-British Site at The Oaks, Thorpe St Andrew, Norwich: Excavations 1999–2000. *Norfolk Archaeology* 45, Part 1, 41–59

Trimble, G.L. 2003. *An Archaeological Evaluation at Little Plumstead Hospital, Norfolk.* Unpublished Norfolk Archaeological Unit Report 887

Tringham, R., Cooper, G., Odell, G., Voytek, B. and Whitman, A. 1974. Experimentation in the Formation of Edge Damage: a new approach to lithic analysis. *Journal of Field Archaeology* 1, 171–196

Trump, D.H. 1956. The Bronze Age Barrow and Iron Age Settlement at Thriplow. *Proceedings of the Cambridge Antiquarian Society* 49, 1–12

Tylecote, R.F. 1967. The Bloomery Site at West Runton. *Norfolk Archaeology* 34, 187–214

Tylecote, R.F, Biek, L. and Haldane, J.W. 1982. Iron smelting residues. In C. Mahaney, A. Burchard and G. Simpson, *Excavations in Stamford, Lincolnshire 1963-1969*, 124–48. London: Society for Medieval Archaeology Monograph 9

Wade, K. 1997. Anglo-Saxon and Medieval (Rural). In J. Glazebrook (ed.) *Research and Archaeology: A Framework for the Eastern Counties, 1. Resource Assessment.* Dereham: East Anglian Archaeology Occasional Papers 3, 47–58

Wainwright, G.J. 1972. The excavation of a Neolithic settlement on Broome Heath, Ditchingham, Norfolk, England. *Proceedings of the Prehistoric Society* 38, 1–107

Wainwright, G.J. 1973. The excavation of Prehistoric and Romano-British Settlement at Eaton Heath, Norwich. *Archaeological Journal* 130, 1–43

Wall, W. (forthcoming). Middle Saxon Iron Smelting near Bonemills Farm, Wittering, Cambridgeshire. *Anglo-Saxon Studies in Archaeology and History*

Westmacott, J. 2007. Laurel Farm Phase II, Broadlands Business Park, Thorpe St. Andrew, Norwich, Norfolk. Post-Excavation Assessment Report. Unpublished Pre-Construct Archaeology Report

Whitbybird Limited, 2005a. *Factual Report on a Ground Investigation at Green Lane South, Broadland Business Park, Thorpe St. Andrew, Norwich.* Unpublished Xplor Ground Engineering Client Report

Whitbybird Limited, 2005b. *Interpretative Report on a Ground Investigation at Green Lane South, Broadland Business Park, Thorpe St. Andrew, Norwich.* Unpublished Xplor Ground Engineering Client Report

Whitmore, M. 2004. Excavations at a Neolithic Site at the John Innes Centre, Colney, 2000. *Norfolk Archaeology* 44 (3), 406–431

Whittle, A. 1999 The Neolithic Period, c. 4000–2500/2000 BC: changing the world. In J. Hunter and I. Rolston (eds.) *The Archaeology of Britain: an introduction from the Upper Palaeolithic to the Industrial Revolution.* London: Routeledge

Whittle, A.W.R. 1996. *Europe in the Neolithic: the creation of new worlds.* Cambridge: Cambridge University Press

Whittle, J. 2007. Peasant Politics and Class Consciousness: The Norfolk Rebellions of 1381 and 1549. *Past and Present* 195 (suppl 2), 233-247

Williams, D. 1996. Some recent finds from East Surrey, *Surrey Archaeological Collections* 83, 165–186

Williamson, T. 1987. Early co-axial field systems on the East Anglian boulder clays. *Proceedings of the Prehistoric Society*, 53, 419–431

Willson, J. 2001. Mersham. In P. Bennett, *Canterbury's Archaeology 1998–1999*, 30–2. Canterbury: Canterbury Archaeology Trust

Wiltshire, P.E.J. (forthcoming). Palynology. In T. Ashwin and A. Tester, *Excavations at Scole 1993–4.* Dereham: East Anglian Archaeology

Woodward, S. 1847. *History and Antiquities of Norwich Castle*

Wymer, J.J. 1976. *A Long Blade Industry from Sproughton, Suffolk*. Dereham: East Anglian Archaeology 3, 1–10

Wymer, J.J. 1984. East Anglian Palaeolithic Sites and their Settings. In C. Barringer (ed.) *Aspects of East Anglian Pre-History*, 31–42. Norwich: Geo Books

Yates, D.T.1999 Bronze Age Field Systems in the Thames Valley. *Oxford Journal of Archaeology* 18 (2), 157-170.

Young, R. and Humphrey, J. 1999. Flint Use in England after the Bronze Age: time for a re-evaluation? *Proceedings of the Prehistoric Society* 65, 231–242

Index

Illustrations are denoted by page numbers in *italics* or by *illus* where figures are scattered throughout the text. Places are in Norfolk unless indicated otherwise.